GW00854341

Cycling in London

Max Darkins

AA

Commissioning Editor: Paul Mitchell
Senior Editor: Donna Wood
Senior Designer: Phil Barfoot
Copy Editor: Helen Ridge
Proofreader: Jennifer Wood
Picture Researchers: Lesley Grayson (AA) and Jonathan Bewley (Sustrans)
Image retouching and internal repro: Sarah Montgomery and James Tims
Cartography provided by the Mapping Services Department of AA Publishing from data provided by Richard Sanders and Sustrans mapping team
Research and development by: Lindsey Ryle, Melissa Henry, Julian Hunt and Gill Harrison
Supplementary text: Nick Cotton
Production: Lorraine Taylor

Produced by AA Publishing

ISBN: 978-0-7495-6381-3 and
(SS) 978-0-7495-6530-5

Published by AA Publishing (a trading name of AA Media Limited, whose registered office is Fanum House, Basing View, Basingstoke RG21 4EA; registered number 06112600).

A04068

BRITISH WATERWAYS

Cyclists are no longer required to have a permit to cycle along towpaths in London, but you are encouraged to follow British Waterway's Towpath Code of Conduct; visit www.waterscape.com

The National Cycle Network has been made possible by the support and co-operation of hundreds of organisations and thousands of individuals, including: local authorities and councils, central governments and their agencies, the National Lottery, landowners, utility and statutory bodies, countryside and regeneration bodies, the Landfill Communities Fund, other voluntary organisations, Charitable Trusts and Foundations, the cycle trade and industry, corporate sponsors, community organisations and Sustrans' Supporters. Sustrans would also like to extend thanks to the thousands of volunteers who generously contribute their time to looking after their local sections of the Network.

Printed and bound in Dubai by Oriental Press
theAA.com/shop

Sustrans
2 Cathedral Square
College Green
Bristol BS1 5DD
www.sustrans.org.uk

Sustrans is a Registered Charity in the UK: Number 326550 (England and Wales) SC039263 (Scotland).

CONTENTS

THE RIDES

Riding a bike in Lo Terrifying? ...

Foreword by **Adam Hart-Davis,** writer and broadcaster

I have never lived in London, and when I first thought about riding a bike there I was terrified. The busy, crowded metropolis has never struck me as being one of the most welcoming places for cyclists. However, I found a map with good bike routes on it, and began following them, and soon I found that a bicycle was not only the most reliable means of transport but good fun too. In London's time-poor world cycling can often be your best way of getting around, a particular journey always has the same duration, and is often quicker than any other form of transport. What's more, on a bike you can hear the birds and smell the air – and you even get some healthy exercise.

Some years ago I was one of the presenters of the final series of *Tomorrow's World*, and once a week from February to April I cycled from

"What's more, on a bike you can hear the birds and smell the air ..."

Paddington to White City, watching as the cherry blossom appeared, then the leaves on the trees. The route goes from Praed Street up Craven Hill, round (or over) Notting Hill, and underneath the A40 (Westway). I was delighted to find, below a huge concrete roundabout, football pitches, tennis courts, and even a riding school, with small girls trotting around on fat ponies. The route is not entirely traffic-free, but I never had a nasty moment, and the only unpleasant section is the last half-mile down Wood Lane to TV Centre.

ndon ... definitely not!

I don't often ride from Buckingham Palace to Kensington Palace (see page 14), but I do often ride from Paddington down through the Park to Hyde Park Corner, down Constitution Hill, and down the Mall, and most of this is traffic-free. Then either up the Duke of York's steps to Carlton House Terrace, or across Whitehall (or Trafalgar Square) to The Strand. The direct route to these places is shorter, but

"... and you even get some healthy exercise"

heavy with traffic; by starting with a map I was easily able to find pleasant, quiet, and safe roads to ride. The only problem with this particular journey is that on the way back, it's uphill all the way!

I strongly commend the routes in this book. You don't have to follow them slavishly, but start with them and you can soon suss out your own variations, according to where you actually want to go.

Adam Hart-Davis

INTRODUCTION

There are so many reasons to get out on your bike and explore London – the fact that London is such an amazing city bursting with culture and history is just one. Cycling is not only a healthy, green and tranquil method of getting around but it is also fast and efficient.

Buckingham Palace and the Queen Victoria Memorial

The traffic-free trails using riverside cyclepaths, canal towpaths, greenways, parks and commons have made a surprisingly large part of London accessible to cyclists (and walkers), allowing them to get around quickly, safely and enjoyably. And there's so much greenery, you could easily forget that you are in one of Europe's largest cities. When there isn't an off-road option, you will probably find special road crossings, traffic-calming measures and even bridges to get you to your destination safely. Furthermore, you can also take your bicycle on many parts of the London Underground outside of rush hour, enabling you to cover even greater distances.

With the huge amount of investment being made to provide even more cycling routes and facilities for cyclists, there has never been a better time to get on your bike in London. More than half of the rides in this book are signed National Cycle Network routes. This massive network spans the country and is the result of hard work carried out by Sustrans, a charitable organization that campaigns tirelessly to improve the quality and quantity of cycle routes all over the UK. These well-signposted trails are either free from traffic or along traffic-calmed roads, usually linking communities to schools, stations, landmarks and attractions.

Alongside many on-road cycle lanes and routes developed over the last few years, there are literally thousands of miles of trails around the city. The London Cycling Campaign plays an important role in promoting cycling, and campaigns to improve facilities and cycleways in the capital (www.lcc.org.uk). Furthermore,

The Thames Barrier

Old plane trees in London Fields Park

Deer in Richmond Park

Transport for London (TfL) has invested heavily in the cause, and its excellent website (www.tfl.gov.uk) provides a wealth of information, from improving your cycling skills and maintaining your bicycle to route planning and security. TfL also provides brilliant, highly detailed, cycle-specific maps for the whole of London, free of charge, and is behind the London Cycle Hire Scheme. This provides 6,000 bicycles in the centre of London, enabling customers to simply collect a bicycle from one of the many docking stations (situated every 300 metres/330 yards), go for a ride, then return it to any of the docking stations.

This book provides a number of cycle routes for you to follow, and also some useful pointers as to where you can start to get out and about with friends and family on your bikes. There are routes to suit everyone, with short, traffic-free rides for families between major attractions, such as Buckingham Palace and Kensington Palace, to long rides taking you from the outskirts of London into the centre. Other adventures include riding around the 2,500 acres of Richmond Park, with its free-roaming deer; cycling alongside the River Thames, seeing the sights of Tower Bridge and the Thames Barrier; riding alongside the industrial canals of The Wandle Trail or through Hackney Marshes, home to 73 full-sized football fields; visiting city farms and zoos; or marvelling at historic and contemporary structures like Westminster Abbey and Canary Wharf Tower.

With such a variety of rides and attractions to visit, this book holds numerous memorable days out – for everyone – in London.

NATIONAL CYCLE NETWORK FACTS & FIGURES

More than half of the routes featured here are part of the National Cycle Network. The aim of this book is to enable you to sample some of the highlights of the region on two wheels, but the rides given here are really just a taster, as there are more than 12,000 miles of Network throughout the UK to explore. More than three-quarters of us live within two miles of one of the routes.

Over a million journeys a day are made on the Network; for special trips like days out and holiday rides, but also taking people to school, to work, to the shops, to visit each other and to seek out green spaces. Half of these journeys are made on foot and half by bike, with urban traffic-free sections of the Network seeing the most usage.

The National Cycle Network is host to one of the UK's biggest collections of public art. Sculptures, benches, water fountains, viewing points and award-winning bridges enhance its pathways, making Sustrans one of the most prolific commissioners of public art in the UK.

The Network came into being following the award of the first-ever grant from the lottery, through the Millennium Commission, in 1995. Funding for the Network also came from bike retailers and manufacturers through the Bike Hub, as well as local authorities and councils UK-wide, and Sustrans' many supporters. Over 2,500 volunteer Rangers give their time to Sustrans to assist in the maintenance of the National Cycle Network by adopting sections of route in communities throughout the UK. They remove glass and litter, cut back vegetation and try to ensure routes are well signed.

Developing and maintaining the National Cycle Network is just one of the ways in which Sustrans pursues its vision of a world in which people can choose to travel in ways that benefit their health and the environment.

We hope that you enjoy using this book to explore the paths and cycleways of the National Cycle Network and we would like to thank the many hundreds of organisations who have worked with Sustrans to develop the walking and cycling routes, including every local authority and council in the UK.

MAP LEGEND

Traffic Free Ride

On Road Ride

Ride Start or Finish Point

National Cycle Network (Traffic Free)

National Cycle Network (On Road)

AA recommended pub
Abbey, cathedral or priory
Aquarium
Arboretum
Campsite
Caravan site
Caravan & campsite
Castle
Cave
Country park
Farm or animal centre
Garden
Historic house
Industrial attraction
Marina
Monument
Museum or gallery
Local nature reserve
Picnic site
Roman remains
Theme park
Tourist Information Centre
Visitor or heritage centre
Zoo or wildlife collection
AA golf course
PO Post Office
LC Level Crossing
A&E Hospital A&E

Railway Station
London Underground Station
London Overground Station
Other light railway station
DLR Station
Minor Railway Station

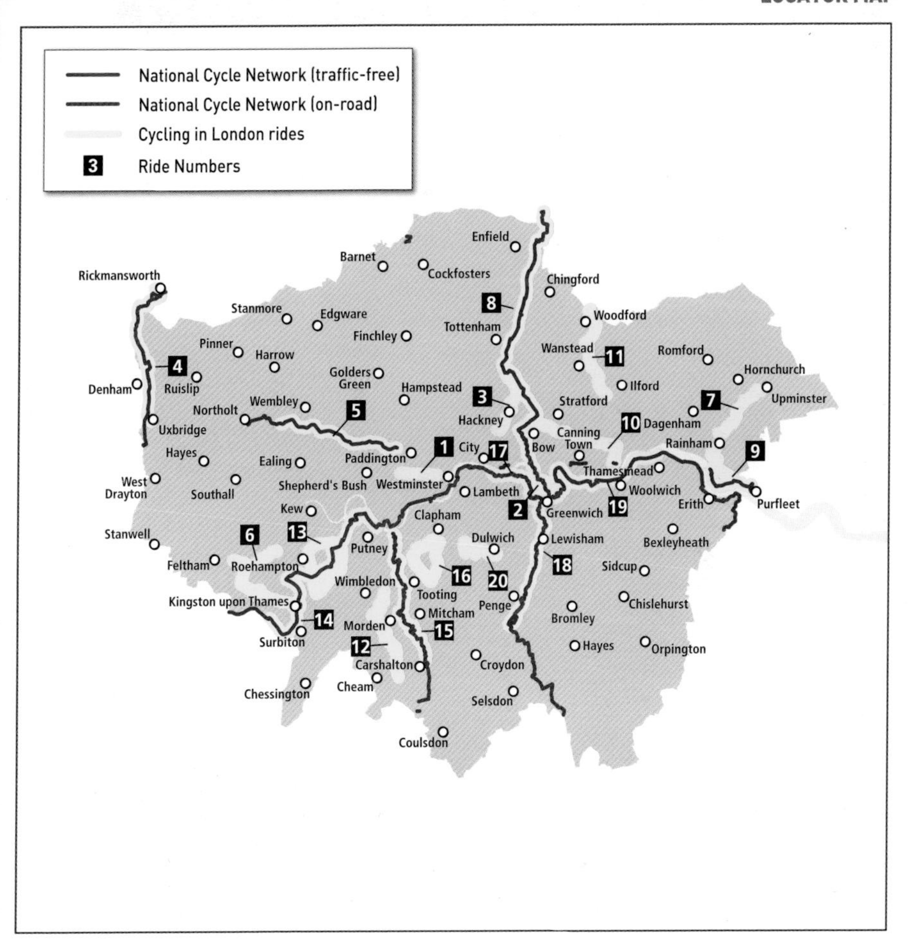

KEY TO LOCATOR MAP

1	Buckingham Palace to Kensington Palace	11	Roding Valley Way
2	Isle of Dogs	12	Wimbledon to Sutton
3	Hackney Parks	13	Tamsin Trail – Richmond Park
4	Uxbridge to Rickmansworth	14	Hampton Court to Putney Bridge
5	Little Venice to Horsenden Hill	15	The Wandle Trail
6	Twickenham to Hampton Wick	16	Commons Circular
7	Ingrebourne Valley	17	Tower Bridge to Greenwich
8	Lee Valley	18	Waterlink Way
9	Rainham Marshes	19	Thamesmead to Greenwich
10	Royal Albert Dock to Victoria Park	20	Brockwell Park & Dulwich Park

CYCLING WITH CHILDREN

Kids love bikes and love to ride. Cycling helps them to grow up fit, healthy and independent, and introduces them to the wider world and the adventure it holds.

TOP TIPS FOR FAMILY BIKE RIDES:

- Take along snacks, drinks and treats to keep their energy and spirit levels up.
- Don't be too ambitious. It's much better that everyone wants to go out again, than all coming home exhausted, tearful and permanently put off cycling.
- Plan your trip around interesting stops and sights along the way. Don't make journey times any longer than children are happy to sit and play at home.
- Even on a fine day, take extra clothes and waterproofs – just in case. Check that trousers and laces can't get caught in the chain when pedalling along.
- Wrap up toddlers. When a young child is on the back of a bike, they won't be generating heat like the person doing all the pedalling!
- Be careful not to pinch their skin when putting their helmet on. It's easily done and often ends in tears. Just place your forefinger between the clip and the chin.
- Ride in a line with the children in the middle of the adults. If there's only one of you, the adult should be at the rear, keeping an eye on all the children in front. Take special care at road junctions.
- Check that children's bikes are ready to ride. Do the brakes and gears work? Is the saddle the right height? Are the tyres pumped up?
- Carry some sticking plasters and antiseptic wipes – kids are far more likely to fall off and graze arms, hands or knees.
- Take a camera to record the trip – memories are made of this.

TRANSPORTING YOUNG CHILDREN ON TWO WHEELS

It's now easier than ever for you to ride your bike with young children.

- Child seats: *6 months to five years (one child).* Once a baby can support its own head (usually at 6-12 months) they can be carried in a child seat. Seats are fitted mainly to the rear of the bike.
- Trailers: *babies to five years (up to two children).* Young babies can be strapped into their car seat and carried in a trailer, and older children can be strapped in and protected from the wind and rain.
- Tag-along trailer bikes: *approx four to nine years.* Tag-alongs (the back half of a child's bike attached to the back of an adult one) allow a child to be towed while they either add some of their own pedal power or just freewheel and enjoy the ride.
- Tow bar: *approx four to eight years.* A tow bar converts a standard child's bike to a trailer bike by lifting their front wheel from the ground to prevent them from steering while enabling them to pedal independently. When you reach a safe place, the tow bar can be detached and the child's bike freed.

TEACHING YOUR CHILD TO RIDE

There are lots of ways for children to develop and gain cycling confidence before they head out on their own.

- Tricycles or trikes: available for children from ten months to five years old. They have pedals so kids have all the fun of getting around under their own steam.
- Balance bikes: are like normal bikes but without the pedals. This means children learn to balance, steer and gain confidence on two wheels while being able to place their feet firmly and safely on the ground.

- **Training wheels:** stabilisers give support to the rear of the bike and are the easiest way to learn to ride but potentially the slowest.

BUYING THE RIGHT BIKE FOR YOUR CHILD

Every child develops differently and they may be ready to learn to ride between the ages of three and seven. When children do progress to their own bike, emphasising the fun aspect will help them take the tumbles in their stride. Encouragement and praise are important to help them persevere.

Children's bikes generally fall into age categories based on the average size of a child of a specific age. There are no hard and fast rules, as long as your child isn't stretched and can reach the brakes safely and change gear easily. It's important to buy your child a bike that fits them rather than one they can grow into. Ask your local bike shop for advice and take your child along to try out different makes and sizes.

To find a specialist cycle retailer near you visit www.thecyclingexperts.co.uk

HOT TIPS & COOL TRICKS...

WHAT TO WEAR

For most of the rides featured in this book you do not need any special clothing or footwear. Shoes that are suitable for walking are also fine for cycling. Looser-fitting trousers allow your legs to move more freely, while tops with zips let you regulate your temperature. In cold weather, take gloves and a warm hat; it's also a good idea to pack a waterproof. If you are likely to be out at dusk, take a bright reflective top. If you start to cycle regularly, you may want to invest in some specialist equipment for longer rides, especially padded shorts and gloves.

WHAT TO TAKE

For a short ride, the minimum you will need is a pump and a small tool bag with a puncture repair kit, just in case. However, it is worth considering the following: water bottle, spare inner tube, 'multi-tool' (available from cycle shops), lock, money, sunglasses, lightweight waterproof (some pack down as small as a tennis ball), energy bars, map, camera and a spare top in case it cools down or to keep you warm when you stop for refreshments.

HOW TO TAKE IT

Rucksacks are fine for light loads but can make your back hot and sweaty. For heavier loads and for longer or more regular journeys, you are better off with panniers that attach to a bike rack.

BIKE ACCESSORIES

You may also want to invest in a helmet. A helmet will not prevent accidents from happening but can provide protection if you do fall off your bike. They are particularly recommended for young children. Ultimately, wearing a helmet is a question of individual choice and parents need to make that choice for their children.

A bell is a must for considerate cyclists. A friendly tinkle warns that you are approaching, but never assume others can hear you.

LOCKING YOUR BIKE

Unless you are sitting right next to your bike when you stop for refreshments, it is worth locking it, preferably to something immovable like a post, fence or railings (or a bike stand, of course). If nothing else, lock it to a companion's bike. Bike theft is more common in towns and cities, and if you regularly leave your bike on the streets, it is important to invest in a good-quality lock and to lock and leave your bike in a busy, well-lit location.

GETTING TO THE START OF A RIDE

The best rides are often those that you can do right from your doorstep, maximizing time on your bike and reducing travelling time. If you need to travel to the start of the ride, have you thought about catching a train?

FINDING OUT MORE – WWW.SUSTRANS.ORG.UK

Use the Sustrans website to find out where you can cycle to from home or while you are away on holiday, and browse through a whole host of other useful information.
Visit www.sustrans.org.uk

MAKING THE MOST OF YOUR BIKE

Making a few simple adjustments to your bike will make your ride more enjoyable and comfortable:

- Saddle height: raise or lower it so that you have good contact with your pedals (to make the most of your leg power) and so that you can always put a reassuring foot on the ground.
- Saddle position: getting the saddle in the right place will help you get the most from your pedal power without straining your body.
- Handlebars: well positioned handlebars are crucial for your comfort and important for control of your steering and brakes.

...BIKE MAINTENANCE

Like any machine, a bike will work better and last longer if you care for it properly. Get in the habit of checking your bike regularly – simple checks and maintenance can help you have hassle-free riding and avoid repairs.

- **Tools:** there are specialist tools for specific tasks, but all you need to get started are: a pump, an old toothbrush, lubricants and grease, cleaning rags, a puncture repair kit, tyre levers, allen keys, screwdrivers and spanners.

REGULAR CHECKS

- **Every week:** Check tyres, brakes, lights, handlebars and seat are in good order and tightly secured.
- **Every month:** Wipe clean and lubricate chain with chain oil.
  Wipe the dirt from wheels.
  Check tread on tyres.
  Check brake pads.
  Check gear and brake cables and make sure that gears are changing smoothly.
- **Every year:** Take your bike to an experienced mechanic for a thorough service.
- **Tip:** If in doubt, leave it to the professionals. Bike mechanics are much more affordable than car mechanics, and some will even collect the bike from your home and return it to you when all the work is done.

FIXING A PUNCTURE

Punctures don't happen often and are easy to fix yourself. If you don't fancy repairing a puncture on your journey, carry a spare inner tube and a pump so you can change the tube, then fix the puncture when you get home. If you don't mind repairing punctures when they happen, make sure you carry your repair kit and pump with you at all times. All puncture repair kits have full instructions with easy-to-follow pictures.

Alternatively, if you don't want to get your hands dirty, just visit your local bike shop and they will fix the puncture for you.

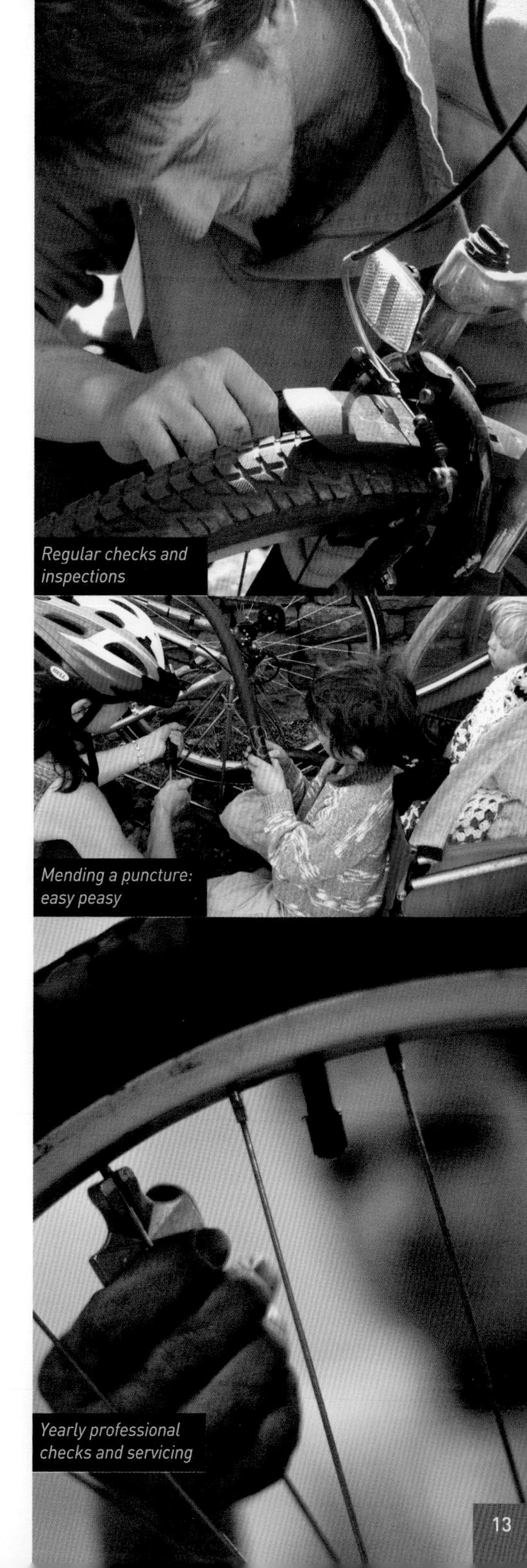

Regular checks and inspections

Mending a puncture: easy peasy

Yearly professional checks and servicing

BUCKINGHAM PALACE TO KENSINGTON PALACE

This is a great family-friendly ride in the heart of London. Starting by the forecourt of Buckingham Palace, it runs alongside Constitution Hill to Wellington Arch and, finally, across Hyde Park to finish at Kensington Palace.

Hyde Park was acquired by Henry VIII from the monks of Westminster Abbey in 1536. It was kept private and used for hunting deer until Charles I opened the park to the public a century later. In 1665, many Londoners set up camp in the park in a bid to escape the Great Plague. In the 1730s, Queen Caroline (wife of George II) had the Serpentine lake built. More recently, in 2004, the Diana, Princess of Wales Memorial Fountain was opened in Hyde Park to commemorate the princess, who died in a car crash in Paris in August 1997. As well as Buckingham Palace and Kensington Palace, there are a number of other places of interest along the route.

Changing of the Guards at Buckingham Palace

ROUTE INFORMATION

Start: Queen Victoria Memorial, in front of Buckingham Palace.
Finish: Kensington Palace.
Distance: 4 miles (6.5km).
Grade: Easy.
Surface: Good, flat, well-surfaced tarmac cycle tracks, shared with walkers.
Hills: Very slight uphill to Kensington Palace.

YOUNG & INEXPERIENCED CYCLISTS

Suitable for both.

REFRESHMENTS

- The Lido Cafe, Hyde Park, by the Diana, Princess of Wales Memorial Fountain.
- Serpentine Bar & Kitchen restaurant, Hyde Park, on the optional return around the north side of the Serpentine.

THINGS TO SEE & DO

- Buckingham Palace: official London residence of Britain's sovereigns since 1837 and the administrative headquarters of the monarch; around 600 rooms, of which the Queen has about 12 on the first floor of the north wing, overlooking Green Park; the 19

Kensington Palace gates

Relaxing in Hyde Park

state rooms are open to visitors in August and September, when the Queen makes her annual visit to Scotland; 020 7930 4832; www.royalcollection.org.uk; www.royal.gov.uk; www.changing-the-guard.com

- Kensington Palace: once the favoured home of some of Britain's most famous kings and queens, and also of Diana, Princess of Wales; parts of the palace are open daily to the public; 0844 482 7777; www.hrp.org.uk/kensingtonpalace
- Serpentine Gallery, Hyde Park: one of London's best-loved galleries for modern and contemporary art, set in the middle of the park; closed between exhibitions, but entry is free when open; 020 7402 6075; www.serpentinegallery.org
- Speakers' Corner, northeast end of Hyde Park: for over 150 years, one of London's most unique attractions; on Sundays, you can listen to speakers delivering their views on anything from politics and current affairs to religion and football; noted speakers have included Karl Marx, Vladimir Lenin and George Orwell.
- Diana, Princess of Wales Memorial Fountain: opened by the Queen in July 2004; built from Cornish granite and pieced together using traditional skills.
- Boat hire: This is available on the Serpentine; 020 7262 1330; www.royalparks.org.uk

Cycling through Hyde Park

TRAIN STATIONS

Victoria.

BIKE HIRE

- Transport for London (TfL): pay-as-you-go bicycles in central London (Zone 1), with docking stations every 300m (330 yards); www.tfl.gov.uk
- Go Pedal!: delivery to most areas of London; 07850 796320; www.gopedal.co.uk
- On Your Bike, London Bridge: 020 7378 6669; www.onyourbike.net
- Dutch Bike Hire, Hyde Park: delivers and collects bicycles; 07809 155577; www.dutchbikehire.com

Bench on the banks of the Serpentine

FURTHER INFORMATION

- To view or print National Cycle Network routes, visit www.sustrans.org.uk
- Maps for this area are available to buy from www.sustransshop.co.uk
- **Transport for London (TfL):** contact for free central London route map; 020 7222 1234; www.tfl.gov.uk
- **London Tourist Information:** 0870 156 6366; www.visitlondon.com

ROUTE DESCRIPTION

The ride starts by the Queen Victoria Memorial, in front of Buckingham Palace, but please note that cycling isn't allowed in the forecourt. Join the track along Constitution Hill, by Green Park, with its mature trees and open grassland. The road is closed to traffic on Sundays, which makes it quieter and more pleasant for cycling, especially with children. Follow this lovely road, leading to Wellington Arch and under Hyde Park Corner, into Hyde Park. Continue along the cycle track, along Rotten Row, passing various places of interest, such as the Holocaust Memorial Garden, the Diana, Princess of Wales Memorial Fountain, cafe and the Serpentine Gallery, all of which make great stopping points. Once you meet the junction with Broad Walk, turn right along this track (open to cyclists) to get to Kensington Palace, which is on the left, opposite Round Pond.

The return journey simply reverses your outward journey unless you opt to detour slightly, on the other side of the Serpentine. For this, you need to turn left just past the Serpentine Gallery, on a cyclepath alongside West Carriage Drive, with the Princess of Wales Memorial Fountain on your right. Take care crossing the Serpentine bridge, as you are now on the road. After following the road to the right, keep straight ahead, alongside the water. Keep straight ahead, past the restaurant at the end, and follow the trail back to Hyde Park Corner where you rejoin the outward route.

NEARBY CYCLE ROUTES

National Route 4 follows the Thames east to Greenwich and on to Kent, or west to Richmond Park and beyond.

The Little Venice to Horsenden Hill route (see page 36), starts close to Paddington train station and heads east along the canal. It can be followed as far as Windsor Great Park.

Cycling is permitted in Hyde Park alongside the road from the Serpentine Bridge to Victoria Gate, then east along North Carriage Drive and down the eastern side from Speakers' Corner, along Broad Walk to Hyde Park Corner.

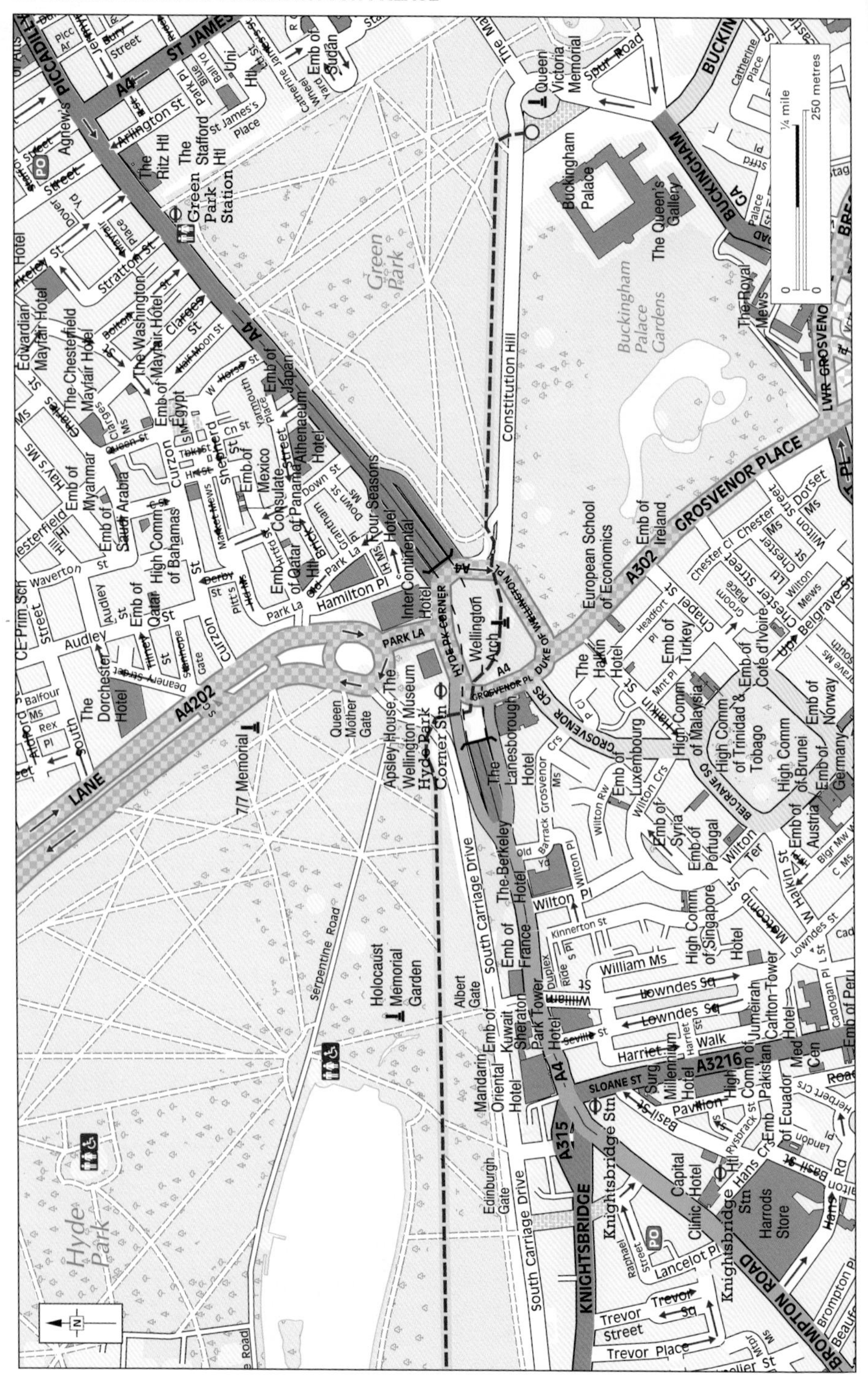
PICCADILLY
ST JAMES'S
Queen Victoria Memorial
Spur Road
BUCKINGHAM
Buckingham Palace
The Queen's Gallery
BUCKINGHAM GATE
Buckingham Palace Gardens
The Royal Mews
¼ mile
250 metres
Green Park
Constitution Hill
Green Park Station
The Ritz Htl
The Stafford Htl
Arlington St
St James's Place
Agnew's
Dover Street
Stratton St
Berkeley St
Edwardian Mayfair Hotel
The Chesterfield Mayfair Hotel
The Washington Mayfair Hotel
Clarges St
Half Moon St
Emb of Egypt
Emb of Japan
Athenaeum Hotel
Curzon St
Emb of Saudi Arabia
Emb of Myanmar
Hay's Ms
Chesterfield Hill
High Comm of Bahamas
Emb of Mexico
Emb of Panama
Emb of Qatar
Four Seasons Hotel
InterContinental Hotel
Hamilton Pl
Park La
PARK LA
HYDE PK CORNER
Wellington Arch
A4
DUKE OF WELLINGTON PL
GROSVENOR PL
GROSVENOR PLACE
A302
Emb of Ireland
European School of Economics
GROSVENOR CRS
The Halkin Hotel
Emb of Turkey
Chapel St
Chester Street
Wilton Street
Dorset Ms
Emb of Cote d'Ivoire
Upr Belgrave St
BELGRAVE SQ
High Comm of Malaysia
High Comm of Trinidad & Tobago
Emb of Norway
High Comm of Brunei
Emb of Germany
Emb of Austria
Emb of Luxembourg
Emb of Syria
Emb of Portugal
Wilton Crs
Wilton Ter
Emb of Singapore
Motcomb St
W Halkin St
Lowndes St
The Lanesborough Hotel
Hyde Park Corner Stn
Apsley House, The Wellington Museum
Queen Mother Gate
7/7 Memorial
The Dorchester Hotel
Audley St
Deanery Street
South Audley St
A4202
LANE
The Berkeley Hotel
Wilton Pl
Kinnerton St
William Ms
Lowndes Sq
Emb of France
Sheraton Park Tower Hotel
Emb of Kuwait
Mandarin Oriental Hotel
Albert Gate
South Carriage Drive
Holocaust Memorial Garden
Serpentine Road
Hyde Park
Edinburgh Gate
Harriet Walk
A3216
SLOANE ST
A4
A315
Knightsbridge Stn
KNIGHTSBRIDGE
Jumeirah Carlton Tower Hotel
Capital Hotel
Harrods Store
Hans Rd
Basil St
BROMPTON ROAD
Knightsbridge Stn
Raphael Street
Lancelot Pl
Trevor Street
Trevor Sq
Trevor Place

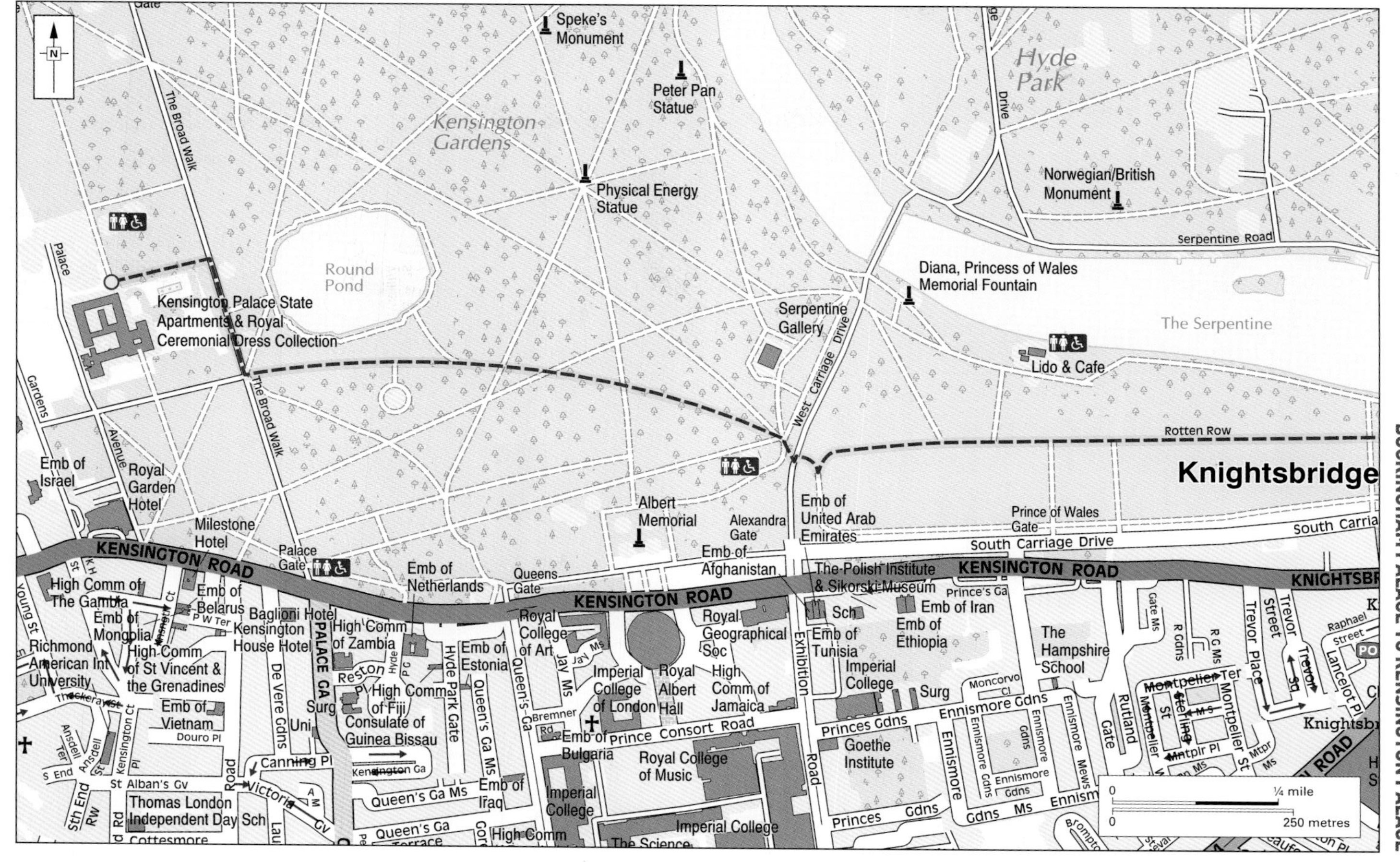
Knightsbridge
Hyde Park
The Serpentine
Serpentine Road
Norwegian/British Monument
Diana, Princess of Wales Memorial Fountain
Lido & Cafe
Rotten Row
South Carriage Drive
Prince of Wales Gate
KENSINGTON ROAD
West Carriage Drive
Serpentine Gallery
Peter Pan Statue
Physical Energy Statue
Speke's Monument
Kensington Gardens
Round Pond
Albert Memorial
Alexandra Gate
Emb of United Arab Emirates
The Polish Institute & Sikorski Museum
Emb of Afghanistan
Royal Geographical Soc
Royal Albert Hall
Royal College of Art
Queens Gate
Emb of Netherlands
Palace Gate
Milestone Hotel
Kensington Palace State Apartments & Royal Ceremonial Dress Collection
The Broad Walk
Royal Garden Hotel
Palace Gardens Avenue
Emb of Israel
Exhibition Road
Prince Consort Road
Royal College of Music
Imperial College
Goethe Institute
Princes Gdns
Ennismore Gdns
Ennismore Mews
The Hampshire School
Rutland Gate
Montpelier St
Trevor Place
Trevor Street
Trevor Sq
Lancelot Pl
Raphael Street
Emb of Iran
Emb of Ethiopia
Emb of Tunisia
High Comm of Jamaica
Emb of Bulgaria
Jay Ms
Queen's Ga
Queen's Ga Ms
Hyde Park Gate
Emb of Estonia
Emb of Iraq
High Comm of Zambia
High Comm of Fiji
Consulate of Guinea Bissau
PALACE GA
De Vere Gdns
Canning Pl
Victoria Road
Kensington House Hotel
Baglioni Hotel
Emb of Belarus
High Comm of The Gambia
Emb of Mongolia
High Comm of St Vincent & the Grenadines
Emb of Vietnam
Thomas London Independent Day Sch
Richmond American Int University
Kensington Ct
Young St
Thackeray St
Ansdell St
St Alban's Gv
¼ mile
250 metres

ISLE OF DOGS

The Isle of Dogs, to the east of the City of London, was originally marshland (known as Stepney Marsh) before it was drained in the 13th century. Not actually an island, the area is bounded on three sides by the River Thames. Millwall Docks, built in the 19th century, were best known in their heyday for the trading of grain but they also handled cargoes of timber, wine, liquor, fruit and vegetables. The docks were closed in 1980 and the waters around them are now used for water sports such as sailing and windsurfing. Today, the area is probably best known for the striking Canary Wharf Tower – currently the tallest building in Britain.

The start of this short figure of eight route goes through Island Gardens on the Southern-most point of the Isle of Dogs, which has plenty of seats alongside the river Thames, offering wonderful views of Greenwich on the far side. The route then goes through Millwall Park before doing a loop around the Millwall Docks and then back around the west side of the Millwall and Mudchute Park. Mudchute Park is home to Mudchute City Farm – well worth a visit if you have small children.

ROUTE INFORMATION

National Route: 1
Start and Finish: Island Gardens Park, Isle of Dogs.
Distance: Southeast loop: 2 miles (3km);
Northwest loop: 1.5 miles (2.5km).
Both loops: 3.5 miles (5.5km).
Grade: Easy.
Surface: Tarmac road and gravel/dirt tracks.
Hills: None.

Llama at Mudchute City Farm

YOUNG & INEXPERIENCED CYCLISTS

Road sections and crossings make this route unsuitable for young children. Novice cyclists should take extra care.

REFRESHMENTS

- Le Munch Bunch cafe, 11 Pepper Street (where the route crosses the docks).
- Pepper Saint Ontiod bar, 21 Pepper Street.
- Mudchute Kitchen, Mudchute City Farm.

THINGS TO SEE & DO

- Mudchute City Farm: the largest inner city farm in Europe, with a variety of animals, including many rare British breeds; 020 7515 5901; www.mudchute.org
- Mudchute Nature Trail, close to Mudchute Park and encircling Mudchute City Farm: a walk through unspoilt land on the otherwise heavily developed Isle of Dogs
- Docklands Sailing & Water Sports Centre: offers sailing, windsurfing, kayaking, dragon boat racing and rowing; 020 7537 2626; www.dswc.org
- The *Cutty Sark*, Greenwich: 85-m (279-ft)

Modern buildings at Docklands

long clipper ship, built in 1869, now dry-docked and used as a museum; closed for conservation until 2011; 020 8858 2698; www.cuttysark.org.uk

- **Island History Trust, 197 East Ferry Road:** community-led project on the history and heritage of the Isle of Dogs; 020 7987 6041; www.islandhistory.org.uk
- **Museum of London Docklands, Canary Wharf:** former sugar warehouse; exhibitions on London as a port, from Roman times to dockland regeneration, through trade, migration and commerce; www.museumindocklands.org.uk

TRAIN STATIONS

Greenwich (on the opposite side of the Thames, accessible via the Greenwich Foot Tunnel).

Note that the DLR (Docklands Light Railway) only allows folding bicycles in carrying cases.

BIKE HIRE

- **Greenwich Cycle Hire:** 020 8858 6677; www.flightcentregreenwich.co.uk
- **Go Pedal!:** delivery to most areas of London; 07850 796320; www.gopedal.co.uk

FURTHER INFORMATION

- To view or print National Cycle Network routes, visit www.sustrans.org.uk
- Maps for this area are available to buy from www.sustransshop.co.uk
- **Transport for London (TfL):** contact for free map (no. 7); 020 7222 1234; www.tfl.gov.uk
- **London Tourist Information:** 0870 156 6366; www.visitlondon.com

ISLE OF DOGS

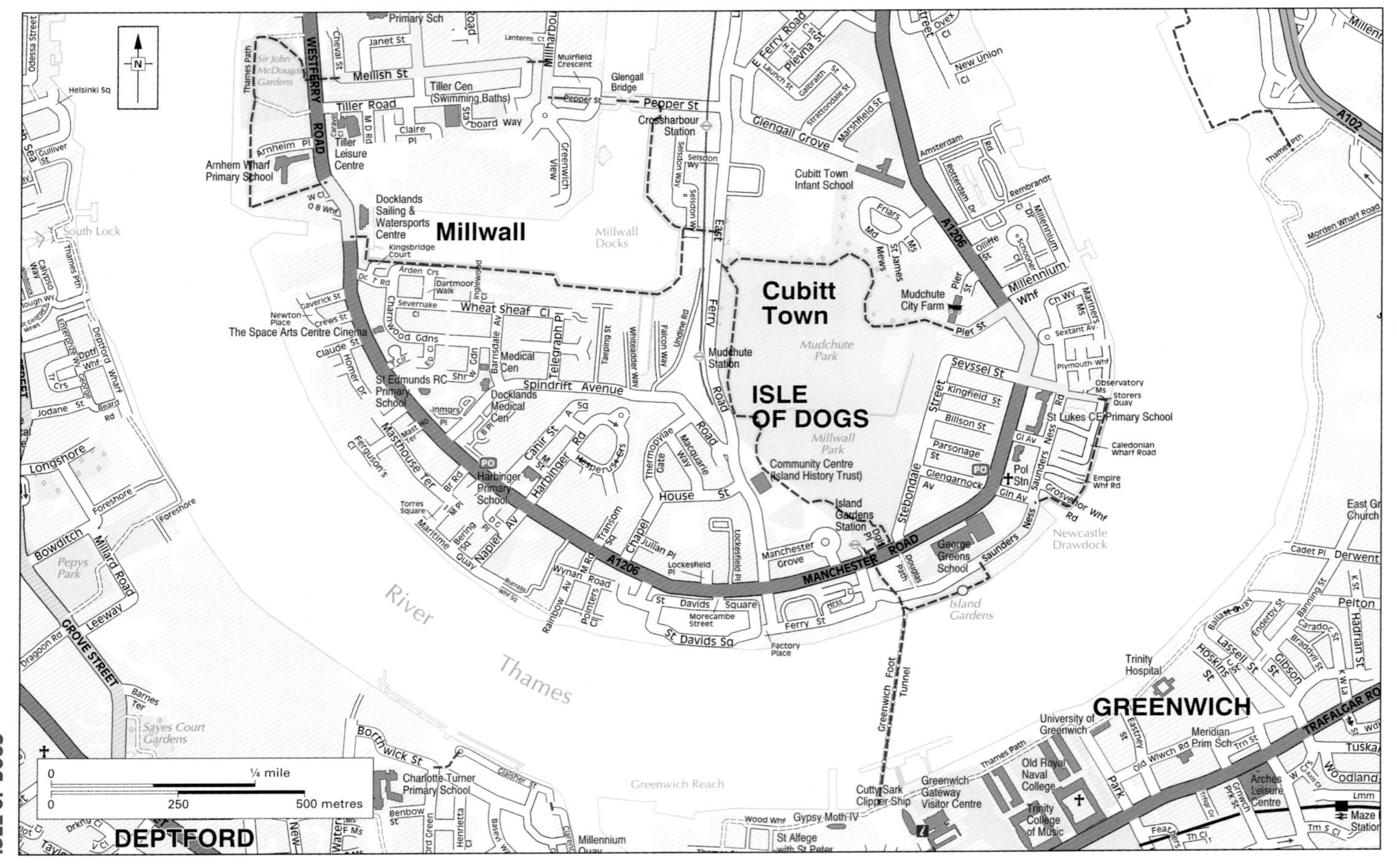

DEPTFORD
GREENWICH
ISLE OF DOGS
Cubitt Town
Millwall
River Thames
Greenwich Reach
Millwall Docks
Mudchute Park
Millwall Park
Island Gardens
Sir John McDougall Gardens
Sayes Court Gardens
Pepys Park
Newcastle Drawdock
South Lock
250
500 metres
¼ mile
WESTFERRY ROAD
MANCHESTER ROAD
A1206
GROVE STREET
TRAFALGAR RO
A102
East Ferry Road
Greenwich Foot Tunnel
Thames Path
Cutty Sark Clipper Ship
Greenwich Gateway Visitor Centre
Old Royal Naval College
Trinity College of Music
University of Greenwich
Trinity Hospital
Mudchute City Farm
Mudchute Station
Crossharbour Station
Island Gardens Station
Docklands Sailing & Watersports Centre
Arnhem Wharf Primary School
Tiller Leisure Centre
Tiller Cen (Swimming Baths)
Docklands Medical Cen
Barnsdale Av Medical Cen
Harbinger Primary School
St Edmunds RC Primary School
The Space Arts Centre Cinema
Community Centre (Island History Trust)
George Greens School
St Lukes CE Primary School
Cubitt Town Infant School
Charlotte Turner Primary School
Meridian Prim Sch
Arches Leisure Centre
East Greenwich Church
Odessa Street
Helsinki Sq
Stebondale Street
Saunders Ness Rd
Spindrift Avenue
Telegraph Pl
Harbinger Rd
Chapel House St
Glengall Grove
Pepper St
Millharbour
Greenwich View
Mellish St
Tiller Road
Ferry St
Manchester Grove
Pier St
Seyssel St
Amsterdam Rd
Rotterdam Dr
Millennium Dr
Millennium Whf
Mariners Ms
Saunders Ness
Morden Wharf Road
Thames Pth
Cadet Pl
Derwent
Pelton Rd
Hadrian St
Banning St
Enderby St
Ballast Quay
Lassell St
Hoskins St
Gibson St
Park Row
Eastney St
Old Woolwich Rd
Borthwick St
Bowditch
Longshore
Millard Road
Leeway
Foreshore
Dragoon Rd
Deptford Wharf
Barnes Ter
Henrietta Cl
Benbow St
Glaisher St
Gypsy Moth IV
St Alfege with St Peter
Wood Whf
Factory Place
St Davids Sq
Thermopylae Gate
Macquarie Way
Julian Pl
Lockesfield Pl
Transom Sq
Pointers Cl
Rainbow Av
Wyndham Rd
Napier Av
Bering Sq
Maritime Quay
Mast House Ter
Ferguson's Cl
Homer Dr
Claude St
Charnwood Gdns
Wheat Sheaf Cl
Dartmoor Walk
Inglewood Cl
Kingsbridge Court
Arden Crs
Taeping St
Whiteadder Way
Falcon Way
Undine Rd
Selsdon Way
Strattondale St
Marshfield St
Galbraith St
Plevna St
E Ferry Road
Friars Mews
St James Ms
Glengarnock Av
Parsonage St
Billson St
Kingfield St
Douglas Path
Glenaffric Av
Schooner Cl
Sextant Av
Storers Quay
Observatory Ms
Caledonian Wharf Road
Empire Wharf Rd
Grosvenor Whf Rd
Plymouth Wharf
Ovex Cl
New Union Cl
Muirfield Crescent
Glengall Bridge
Janet St
Cheval St
Claire Pl
Arnhem Pl
Newton Place
Caverick St
Crews St
Calypso Way
Jodane St
Sea
Gulliver St

The Royal Naval College, Greenwich

ROUTE DESCRIPTION

The route starts at Island Gardens Park, where you can sit and admire the view across the river. After a short stint on Saunders Ness Road, you rejoin the riverside path, until your way is blocked by Cubitt Town Wharf. This is your cue to head left, away from the Thames, in search of Mudchute Park. Past the allotments, follow the track to the right, where you can gain access to Mudchute City Farm – a great place to stop off. Carrying on into Mudchute Park, the route bears right off the main track, behind a crescent of trees. Then, bearing left, it cuts across the main path and across the park, to meet and join National Route 1. Here, you can either continue your ride on the second loop, around Millwall Docks, or head back down through the park back to the start.

The Millwall Docks loop follows Route 1 to the edge of the dock but then goes left around the edge of the water. At the far end of the docks is the Docklands Sailing & Watersports Centre – Sundays are particularly busy when sailboat races are held. After joining the River Thames for a short stretch, the route then heads inland, passing to the right of the tower blocks and crossing over the dock. Joining Route 1, the route now goes through Mudchute Park and Millwall Park, back to the start.

NEARBY CYCLE ROUTES

Part of this ride uses National Route 1, which you could use to cycle north along the Lee Valley. Alternatively, you could cross under the Thames to join Route 4 and head east alongside the Thames, past the O2 Arena and the Thames Barrier, and out of London. In the opposite direction, Route 4 heads west along the Thames to Central London.

Cycling through Docklands

HACKNEY PARKS

This central London ride starts in Springfield Park, which was officially opened as a public park in 1905. There are about 40 acres of both formalized garden and conservation areas, with extensive views across Walthamstow Marshes. The route then follows the towpath to Lea Bridge, where you can choose to keep the ride short and off-road if you want to by joining National Route 1 to return to the start, through Walthamstow Marshes.

Alternatively, if you continue, the route joins some quiet roads through Clapton and on to London Fields. Back in 1540, this was common land used for grazing livestock en route to market in London; nowadays, it provides residents with a green area for relaxing or playing sports. The route then continues down to Haggerston Park, where there are lots of attractions.

Cricket at London Fields, Hackney

ROUTE INFORMATION

National Route: Links to National Route 1
Start: Springfield Park, Hackney.
Finish: Haggerston Park, Hackney.
Distance: 3.5 miles (5.5km). Shorter option, over Lea Bridge and back, through Walthamstow Marshes 3 miles (5km).
Grade: Easy.
Surface: Tarmac roads, surfaced towpaths and park tracks.
Hills: Gradual.

YOUNG & INEXPERIENCED CYCLISTS

The first section to Lea Bridge is traffic-free and flat but, thereafter, sections of road may make it unsuitable for young children and novices. The parks along the route are good places to have a break and let non-riding children stretch their legs.

REFRESHMENTS

- Spark Cafe, Springfield Park.
- Frizzante restaurant, Hackney City Farm, Haggerston Park.
- Many more places on-road along the route.

THINGS TO SEE & DO

- Springfield Park: children's playground, fountains, pond and tennis courts; 020 8356 8428/9;

Walkers in London Fields Park

A game of football on Hackney Marshes

www.hackney.gov.uk/cp-parks-springfield

- **London Fields Park:** great range of facilities, including a lido, children's playground, paddling pool, cricket pitch, tennis courts, sports changing rooms and toilets.
- **Haggerston Park:** includes a children's play area, BMX track and a city farm, which is open all year (except Mondays) and has a cafe; 020 7729 6381; www.hackneycityfarm.co.uk

TRAIN STATIONS

Clapton; Hackney Downs; London Fields; Cambridge Heath.

BIKE HIRE

- **Transport for London (TfL):** pay-as-you-go bicycles in central London (Zone 1), with docking stations every 300m (330 yards); www.tfl.gov.uk
- **Go Pedal!:** delivery to most areas of London; 07850 796320; www.gopedal.co.uk
- **Dutch Bike Hire, Hyde Park:** delivers and collects bicycles; 07809 155577; www.dutchbikehire.com
- **City Bike Service, Shoreditch:** 020 7247 4151; www.citybikeservice.co.uk

FURTHER INFORMATION

- To view or print National Cycle Network routes, visit www.sustrans.org.uk
- Maps for this area are available to buy from www.sustransshop.co.uk
- **Transport for London (TfL):** contact for free maps (nos. 4 and 7); 020 7222 1234; www.tfl.gov.uk

- **London Tourist Information:** 0870 156 6366; www.visitlondon.com
- **England Tourist Information:** 020 7578 1400; www.visitengland.com

ROUTE DESCRIPTION

Starting at Springfield Park, the route heads south along the towpath on the River Lea all the way to Lea Bridge. Shortly past the weir, the route turns right to go through the park. (Riders wishing to stay off-road and keep the route shorter can use a bridge just a little further along, on the left, to join Route 1 and return to the start of the ride through Walthamstow Marshes.) Once through the park, the route joins Powerscroft Road, which you follow through Lower Clapton. After negotiating more roads, pedestrian crossings and back alleys, past Hackney Town Hall, you join Martello Street and pass along the edge of London Fields Park. On a fine day, the park is a great place to stop, especially if you have children with you – there is a playground, paddling pool and toilets. Back on the bike, you continue to the southernmost point of the park, where you rejoin the roads, keeping straight ahead (on Broadway Market), over the river, then on Goldsmith's Row. The cycle lane then crosses into Haggerston Park, where there is another children's playground, a BMX track and a city farm to visit.

NEARBY CYCLE ROUTES

Nearby, National Route 1 heads north up the Lee Valley and beyond into Essex, and south to the River Thames (see page 54).

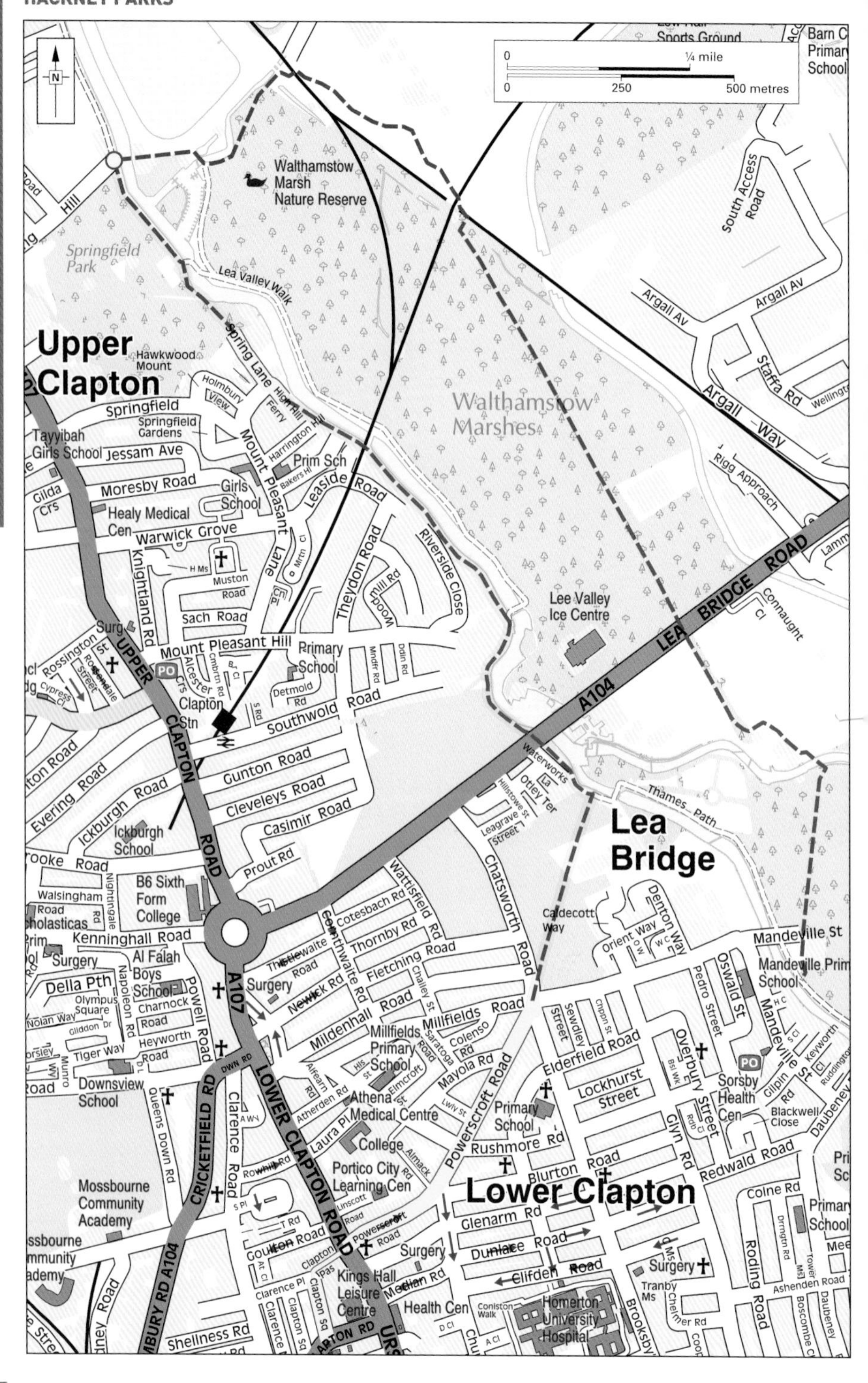
0 ¼ mile
0 250 500 metres
Walthamstow Marsh Nature Reserve
Springfield Park
Lea Valley Walk
Upper Clapton
Walthamstow Marshes
Lee Valley Ice Centre
Lea Bridge Road
A104
Thames Path
Lea Bridge
Upper Clapton Road
A107
Lower Clapton Road
Lower Clapton
Homerton University Hospital
Clapton Stn
Springfield
Mount Pleasant Hill
Southwold Road
Chatsworth Road
Powerscroft Road
Millfields Road
Argall Way
South Access Road
Mossbourne Community Academy
Kings Hall Leisure Centre
Cricketfield Rd

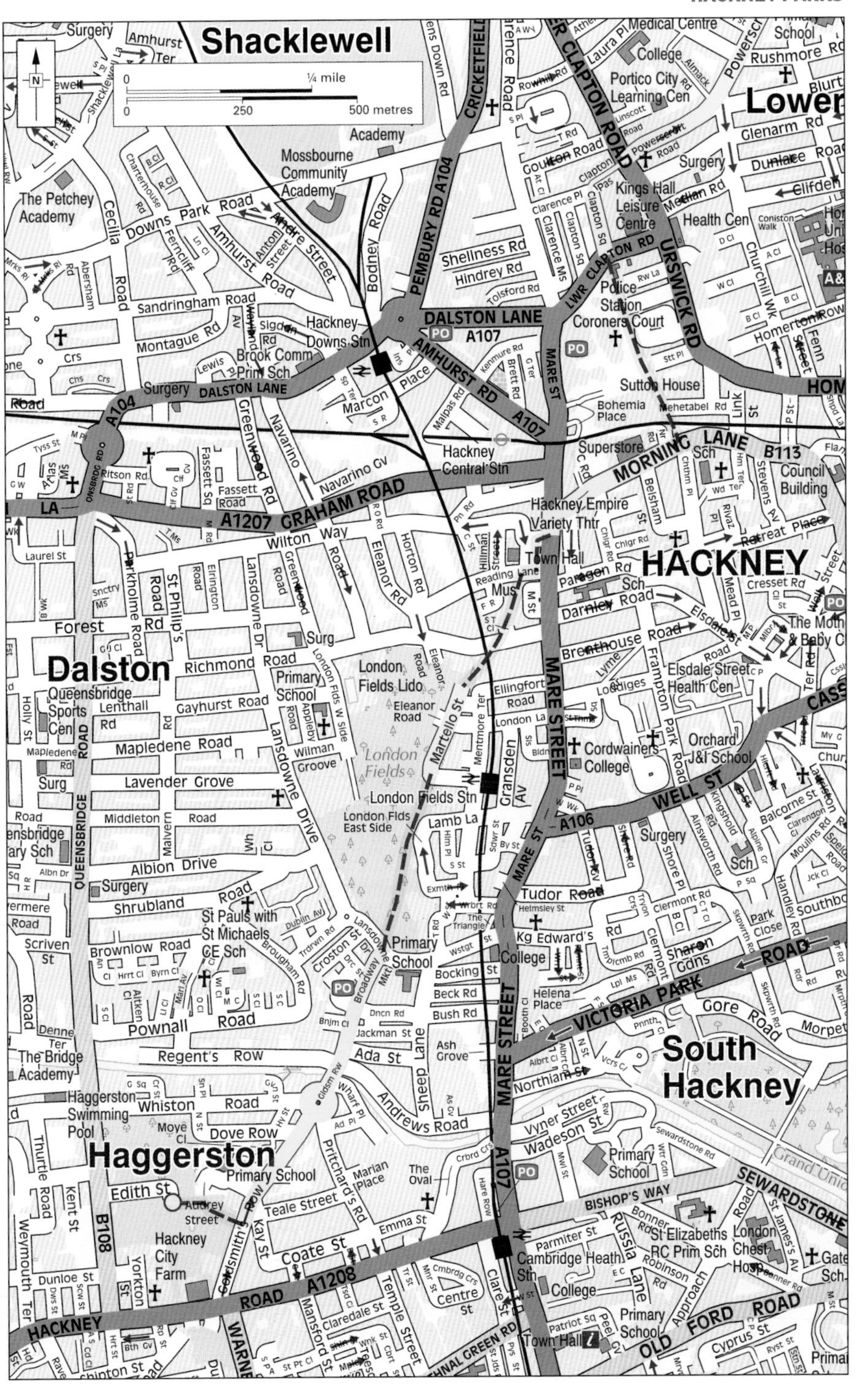
Shacklewell
¼ mile
0
250
500 metres
N
Surgery
Amhurst Ter
Academy
Mossbourne Community Academy
The Petchey Academy
Cecilia Road
Downs Park Road
Amhurst Road
Andre Street
Bodney Road
PEMBURY RD A104
CRICKETFIELD
Sandringham Road
Montague Rd
Hackney Downs Stn
Brook Comm Prim Sch
DALSTON LANE
A107
AMHURST RD
A107
Marcon Place
Surgery
A104
Navarino Gv
Hackney Central Stn
A1207 GRAHAM ROAD
Wilton Way
Forest Rd
Dalston
Richmond Road
Queensbridge Sports Cen
Mapledene Road
Lavender Grove
Middleton Road
Albion Drive
Surgery
Shrubland Road
St Pauls with St Michaels CE Sch
Brownlow Road
Pownall Road
Regent's Row
The Bridge Academy
Haggerston Swimming Pool
Whiston Road
Dove Row
Haggerston
Primary School
Edith St
Audrey Street
Hackney City Farm
HACKNEY ROAD A1208
B108
QUEENSBRIDGE ROAD
London Fields Lido
London Fields
London Fields Stn
London Flds East Side
Martello St
Primary School
Broadway Mkt
Andrews Road
Sheep Lane
The Oval
Teale Street
Coate St
Emma St
Pritchard's Rd
Temple Street
Hackney Empire Variety Thtr
Town Hall
Mus
MARE STREET
MARE ST
A107
HACKNEY
Paragon Rd
Darnley Road
Brenthouse Road
Elsdale Street Health Cen
Cordwainers College
Orchard J&I School
WELL ST
A106
Tudor Road
Surgery
Kg Edward's College
VICTORIA PARK ROAD
South Hackney
Gore Road
Vyner Street
Wadeson St
Primary School
BISHOP'S WAY
SEWARDSTONE
St Elizabeths RC Prim Sch
London Chest Hosp
Cambridge Heath Stn
College
Town Hall
Primary School
OLD FORD ROAD
Cyprus St
Morning Lane B113
Council Building
Superstore
Sutton House
Bohemia Place
Police Station
Coroners Court
URSWICK RD
LWR CLAPTON RD
CLAPTON ROAD
Kings Hall Leisure Centre
Health Cen
Medical Centre
College
Portico City Learning Cen
Lower
Glenarm Rd
Rushmore Rd
Homerton Row
Shellness Rd
Hindrey Rd
Clarence Pl
Retreat Place
Mead Pl
The Mother & Baby C
Sharon Gdns
Grand Union
PO

UXBRIDGE TO RICKMANSWORTH

This stretch of National Route 61 between Uxbridge and Rickmansworth runs alongside the Grand Union Canal on what is known as the Colne Valley Trail. It is an easy-to-follow 8-mile (13-km) route, with the option to extend if desired.

The Grand Union Canal used to be a very important way of transporting all kinds of goods between London and other UK cities. Nowadays, the towpaths once used by horses to pull the narrow boats provide lovely, peaceful, traffic-free cycling and walking routes. The ride passes close to Denham Country Park, where there are good picnic areas and facilities. While the canals are a good way of getting around London, they are also a means of leaving urban areas altogether. Although this route stays within the M25, you could continue well beyond London by following the canal further afield – check www.waterscape.com for details. Note that fishermen often use long rods (poles) to get their lines to the far side of the canal, so beware of obstructions on the track.

ROUTE INFORMATION

National Route: 61
Start: Uxbridge train station.
Finish: Rickmansworth train station.
Distance: 8 miles (13km).
Grade: Easy.
Surface: Mostly good canal paths, with some road sections and dirt tracks along the way.
Hills: None, apart from some slight inclines at the locks.

YOUNG & INEXPERIENCED CYCLISTS

The traffic-free sections alongside the canal are suitable for novices, but skills and confidence are needed to ride close to the canal. The road section from Uxbridge station is not suitable for young children.

REFRESHMENTS

- Lots of choice at each end of the route, and the Swan & Bottle on the Grand Union Canal.

Barge art on the Grand Union Canal

THINGS TO SEE & DO

- Colne Valley Regional Park: a mosaic of farmland, woodland and water, with 50 miles (80km) of river and canal and over 40 lakes.
- Denham Country Park: Situated in the centre of Colne Valley Regional Park, Denham is home to a variety of wildlife, including herons along the river and canal banks, and, if you are lucky, kingfishers; visitor centre and many visitor facilities, including car parking, refreshments, picnic areas and toilets; Frays Valley Nature Reserve uses a disused railway line to join the woodland between the Shire Ditch and Frays River; home to stoats and weasels, and birds such as siskins in the winter, and kestrels and sparrowhawks in the summer; Broadwater Lake is the biggest expanse of open water in the Colne Valley and home to a wide selection of waterbirds; Springwell Reedbed is popular with breeding reed warblers and sedge warblers, and in winter it's a roosting site for buntings and wagtails; 01895 833375; www.colnevalleypark.org.uk

TRAIN STATIONS

Uxbridge; Denham; Rickmansworth.

Church Street, Rickmansworth

BIKE HIRE

None locally.

FURTHER INFORMATION

- To view or print National Cycle Network routes, visit www.sustrans.org.uk
- Maps for this area are available to buy from www.sustransshop.co.uk
- **Transport for London (TfL):** contact for free map (no. 3); 020 7222 1234; www.tfl.gov.uk
- **London Tourist Information:** 0870 156 6366; www.visitlondon.com
- **Uxbridge Tourist Information:** 01895 250706; www.hillingdon.gov.uk

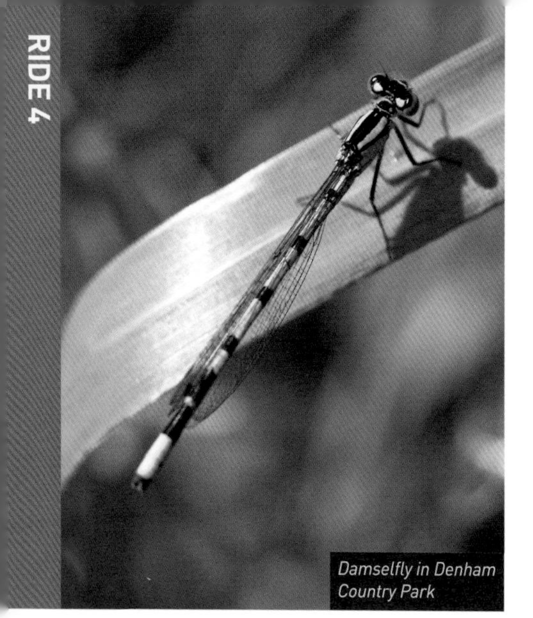
Damselfly in Denham Country Park

ROUTE DESCRIPTION

From Uxbridge station, the ride follows roads through Uxbridge, along High Street, to Oxford Road and over the water to join National Route 61 alongside the Grand Union Canal. Passing the Swan & Bottle (which serves good food), you follow the canal, entering a very different part of London, all still within the M25. The surface of the trail is generally very good, as well as flat and easy to navigate, so progress is steady. Along the way, there are boats, lock crossings and wildlife to hold your interest.

Be aware that about 0.6 miles (1km) past Denham Lock you need to cross the bridge on the right, leaving the Grand Union Canal (which is now on your left), so you are now in between a reservoir and the canal, still following the National Cycle Network route. Shortly past the marina, at South Harefield, a short section of road brings you back to the canal, which you stay beside to Black Jack's Lock. Here you leave the canal and follow a series of roads and paths to Springwell Lane. To get to Rickmansworth train station, follow the canal-side track to the other side of the A404, then bear left (north), leaving the canal, and follow Church Street to a crossroad with the high street. Go left on this, then first right on Station Road – the train station is to the left (one-way street) at the T-junction.

NEARBY CYCLE ROUTES

National Route 61 continues to Watford, St Albans and Hertford.

Batchworth Lock, Rickmansworth

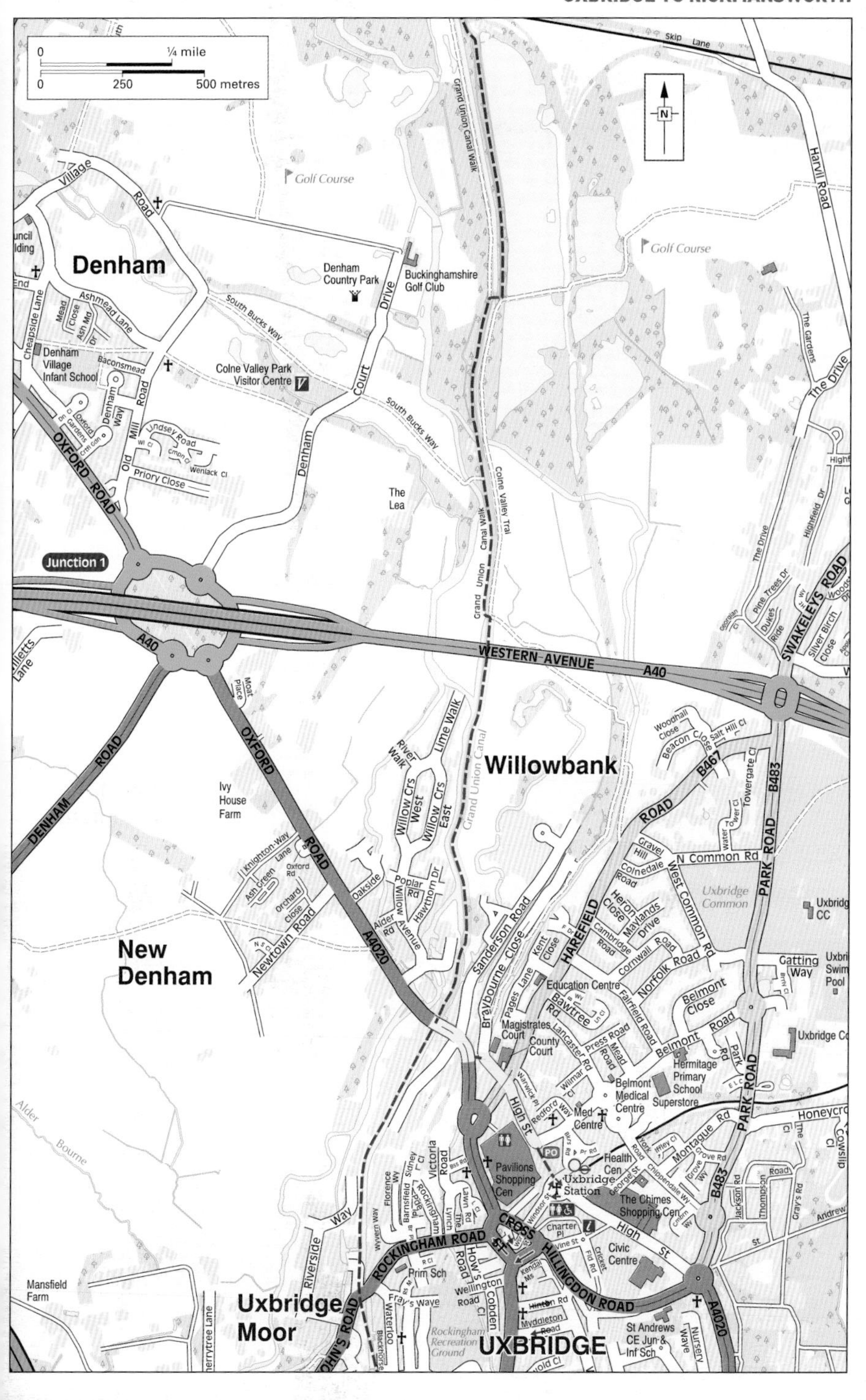
0 ¼ mile
0 250 500 metres
N
Denham
Denham Country Park
Buckinghamshire Golf Club
Golf Course
Golf Course
Colne Valley Park Visitor Centre
Denham Village Infant School
South Bucks Way
Grand Union Canal Walk
Colne Valley Trail
The Lea
Junction 1
OXFORD ROAD
A40
WESTERN AVENUE
Willowbank
Ivy House Farm
DENHAM ROAD
New Denham
Uxbridge Moor
UXBRIDGE
Grand Union Canal
Uxbridge Common
HAREFIELD ROAD
PARK ROAD
B483
B467
A4020
SWAKELEYS ROAD
Harvil Road
Skip Lane
Pavilions Shopping Cen
Uxbridge Station
The Chimes Shopping Cen
Civic Centre
Magistrates Court
County Court
Education Centre
Belmont Medical Centre
Hermitage Primary School
Superstore
Rockingham Recreation Ground
St Andrews CE Jun & Inf Sch
HILLINGDON ROAD
ROCKINGHAM ROAD
Mansfield Farm
Alder Bourne

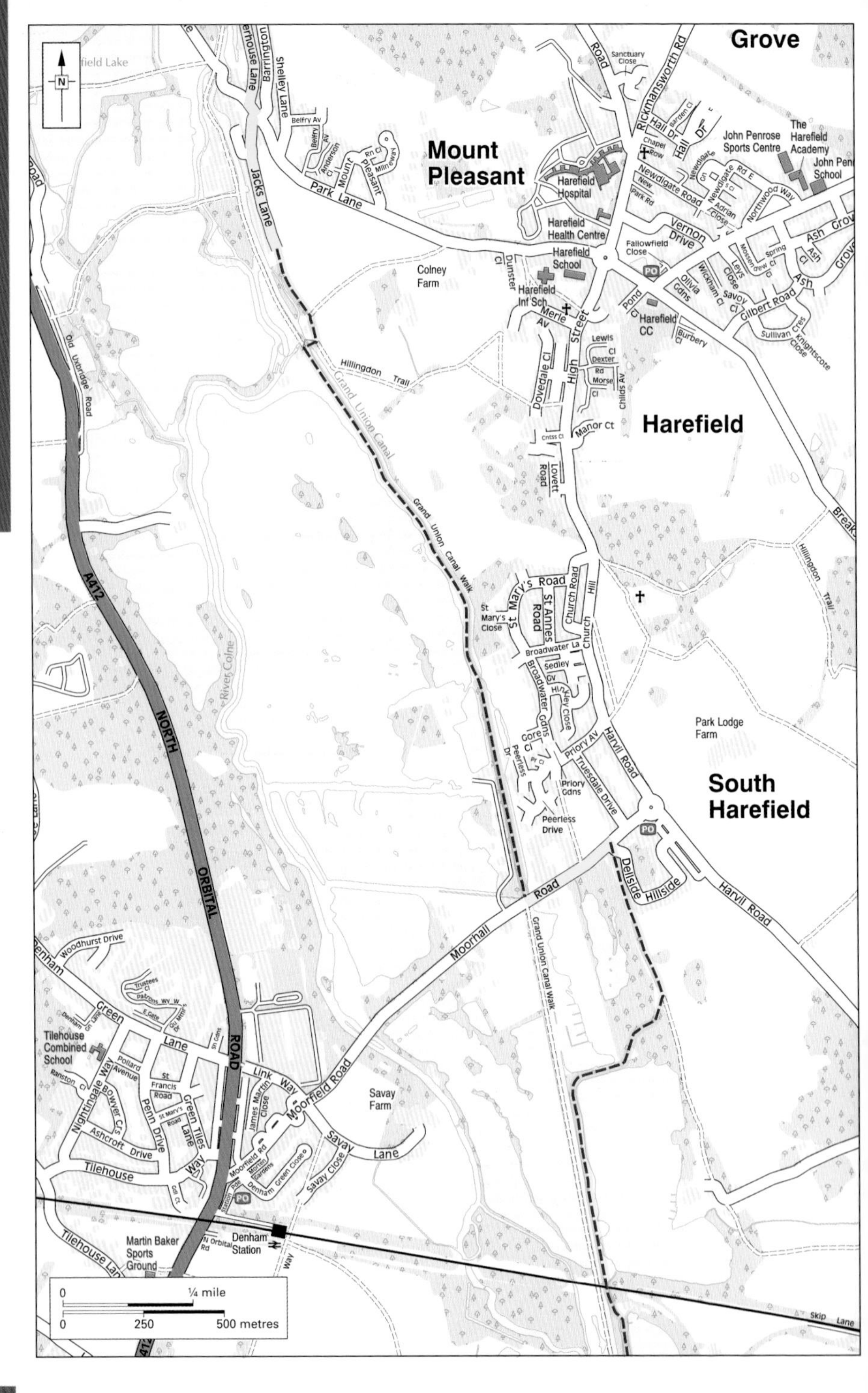
N
Grove
Mount
Pleasant
Harefield
South
Harefield
Rickmansworth Rd
Sanctuary
Close
Barrington
Shelley Lane
Belfry Av
Jacks Lane
Park Lane
Harefield
Hospital
Harefield
Health Centre
Harefield
School
Harefield
Inf Sch
Colney
Farm
John Penrose
Sports Centre
The
Harefield
Academy
Newdigate Road
Vernon
Drive
Fallowfield
Close
Northwood Way
Gilbert Road
Sullivan Cres
Knightscote
Close
Hillingdon Trail
Grand Union Canal
Grand Union Canal Walk
High Street
Dovedale Cl
Manor Ct
Lovett
Road
Harefield
CC
St Mary's Road
St Annes
Road
Church Road
Church Hill
St
Mary's
Close
Broadwater La
Broadwater Gdns
Priory Av
Truesdale Drive
Harvil Road
Park Lodge
Farm
Peerless
Drive
Priory
Gdns
Dellside
Hillside
Moorhall Road
River Colne
A412
NORTH
ORBITAL
ROAD
Old Uxbridge Road
Woodhurst Drive
Denham
Green
Lane
Tilehouse
Combined
School
Pollard
Avenue
St
Francis
Road
Penn Drive
Green Tiles
Lane
Way
Nightingale Way
Bowyer Crs
Ashcroft Drive
Tilehouse
Link Way
Moorfield Road
James Martin
Close
Savay
Farm
Savay
Lane
Savay Close
Denham Green Close
Denham
Station
Martin Baker
Sports
Ground
Tilehouse Lane
Skip Lane
0
¼ mile
0
250
500 metres

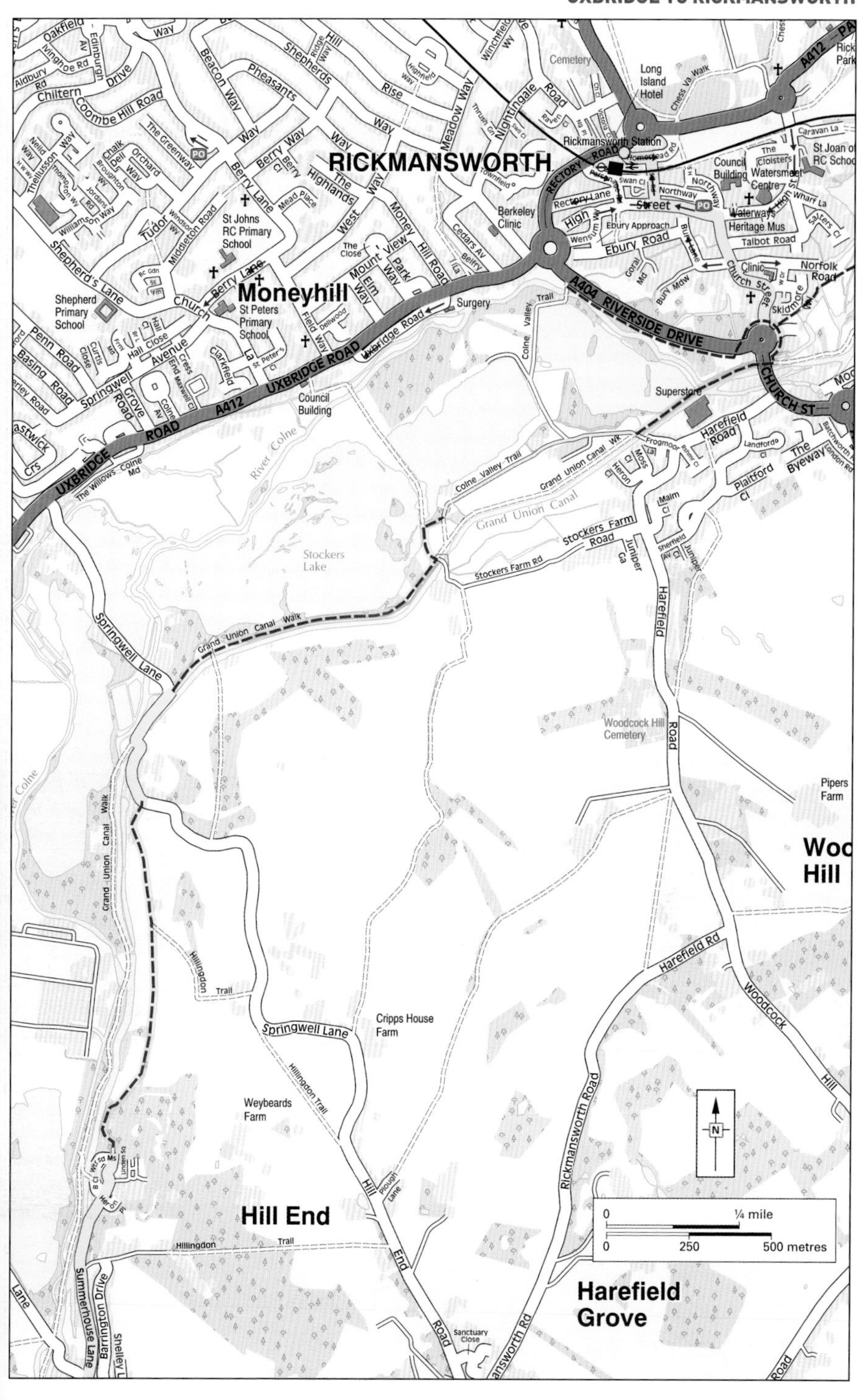
RICKMANSWORTH
Moneyhill
Hill End
Harefield Grove
Stockers Lake
Woodcock Hill Cemetery
Cripps House Farm
Weybeards Farm
Pipers Farm
Rickmansworth Station
Long Island Hotel
Cemetery
Council Building
Watersmeet Centre
Waterways Heritage Mus
Berkeley Clinic
Superstore
Surgery
St Johns RC Primary School
St Peters Primary School
Shepherd Primary School
A404 RIVERSIDE DRIVE
A412 UXBRIDGE ROAD
Grand Union Canal
Grand Union Canal Walk
Colne Valley Trail
Hillingdon Trail
Springwell Lane
Harefield Road
Rickmansworth Road
Woodcock Hill
Stockers Farm Road
Summerhouse Lane
Barrington Drive
CHURCH ST
Church Street
High Street
Ebury Road
Talbot Road
Norfolk Road
Money Hill Road
Shepherds Lane
Berry Lane
Chiltern Drive
Coombe Hill Road
Penn Road
Basing Road
0 ¼ mile
0 250 500 metres
N

LITTLE VENICE TO HORSENDEN HILL

Although very central and close to bustling Paddington station, this 7-mile (11-km) route offers a very quiet and beautiful ride along the traffic-free towpath of the Grand Union Canal. Along the way, you will find various places to eat and drink and let any children play. The ride starts from picturesque Little Venice, which lies at the junction of the Regent's Canal and the Grand Union Canal. Cycling is not actually permitted along this first section of the route, as there are so many pedestrians, but that is no great hardship since there is so much to look at, including 17th-century white stucco homes and colourful houseboats.

Little Venice is one of the more exclusive residential districts within London's Maida Vale district, but back in 1820, when the Grand Union Canal was opened, the area was home to artists, writers and prostitutes. This ride, like other canal rides, can be easily extended along the towpath if desired, or you can ride up Horsenden Hill, to a pub and good views of the city.

Colourful houseboats at Little Venice

Silverware for sale at Portobello Market

ROUTE INFORMATION

National Route: 6
Start: Bridge at Delamere Terrace, Little Venice.
Finish: Horsenden Hill.
Distance: 7 miles (11km).
Grade: Easy.
Surface: Tarmac and good canal towpath. Can get muddy in places when wet.
Hills: None.

YOUNG & INEXPERIENCED CYCLISTS

Care is needed with young children around the canal and at road crossings. The physical challenge of the ride isn't too great, apart from the distance.

REFRESHMENTS

Lots of choice in Little Venice, including:

- The Waterside Cafe, on a narrow boat by Warwick Crescent;
- Cafe La Ville, corner of Edgware Road and Aberdeen Place, perched above the mouth of Maida Vale Tunnel;
- Boat House Restaurant, close to Clifton Villas.
- The Bridge House Pub (also home to the Canal Cafe Theatre, performances nightly), 13 Westbourne Terrace Road.
- Ballot Box gastropub, by Horsenden Woods.

THINGS TO SEE & DO

- **Puppet Theatre Barge, Little Venice:** seating 55 people, this established venue has been open for over 25 years, hosting thousands of performances; every summer it tours the Thames; 020 7249 6876; www.puppetbarge.com
- **Paddington Basin, close to Little Venice:** currently being redeveloped on a scale to rival London's Docklands; www.paddingtonwaterside.co.uk
- **Cascade Floating Art Gallery, Blomfield Road, Regent's Canal:** former barge, now home to an art gallery with regularly changing exhibitions; 020 7289 7050
- **Portobello Market, Notting Hill:** popular shopping destination for Londoners as well as tourists, made famous by the film *Notting Hill* starring Julia Roberts and Hugh Grant; selling antiques and second-hand goods, fashion, and fruit and veg; www.portobellomarket.org
- **Horsenden Hill:** highest point in northwest

London, with wonderful views across the city; www.perivale.co.uk/horsenden-hill

- **London Zoo, Regent's Park:** opened in 1828 and almost closed in 1991 due to financial problems; the zoo was then transformed, with better living conditions provided for the animals; run by the Zoological Society of London (ZSL), a charity devoted to the worldwide conservation of animals and their habitats; 020 7722 3333; www.zsl.org

TRAIN STATIONS

Paddington; Sudbury Hill Harrow.

BIKE HIRE

- **Transport For London (TFL):** 'Pay as you go' bicycles in central London (Zone 1), with docking stations every 300m (330 yards); www.tfl.gov.uk
- **Go Pedal!:** delivery to most areas of London; 07850 796320; www.gopedal.co.uk
- **Dutch Bike Hire, Hyde Park:** delivers and collects bicycles; 07809 155577; www.dutchbikehire.com
- **Velorution, near Regents Park:** 020 7637 4004; www.velorution.biz

FURTHER INFORMATION:

- To view or print National Cycle Network routes, visit www.sustrans.org.uk
- Maps for this area are available to buy from www.sustransshop.co.uk
- **Transport for London (TfL):** contact for free maps (nos. 6 and 7); 020 7222 1234; www.tfl.gov.uk
- **London Tourist Information:** 0870 156 6366; www.visitlondon.com

Canal towpath at Little Venice

ROUTE DESCRIPTION

If you are starting from Paddington station, turn right onto Westbourne Terrace and follow the road under the A40. Bear right onto Westbourne Terrace Road, which will bring you to Little Venice.

From the southern side of the bridge on Delamere Terrace, head west along the Paddington branch of the Grand Union Canal. Cycling is not actually permitted along this first section, as there are lots of pedestrians, but there are plenty of interesting sights (and cafes) to occupy you while you walk. Once you mount your bicycle after the Warwick Community Centre on the A404, the pace picks up and, soon, residential building gives way to industrial. Along the route, there are some reminders of the canal's industrial origins, and also examples of new industry. After passing the gas works and an impressive tangle of railway tracks, the surroundings change, with Sudbury Golf Course providing refreshing views of open grassland.

Keep a look out for the towpath junction by the bridge with Horsenden Hill Lane – National Route 6 continues along the Grand Union Canal, but this route goes up to the road. Turn right on the cycle track alongside the road, to climb Horsenden Hill to the Ballot Box pub, with a garden and children's play area, and great views across London. For the return journey, you can either retrace your outward route or catch the train back to Paddington from Perivale tube station. (Bikes can be taken as far as White City on the Central Line.) Sudbury Hill Harrow is the closest mainline station, north of Horsenden Hill.

NEARBY CYCLE ROUTES

The Grand Union Canal towpath continues past Horsenden Hill, bearing south, past Greenford and Southall, to join another section of the towpath heading west to Uxbridge (see page 30), or east, back into London.

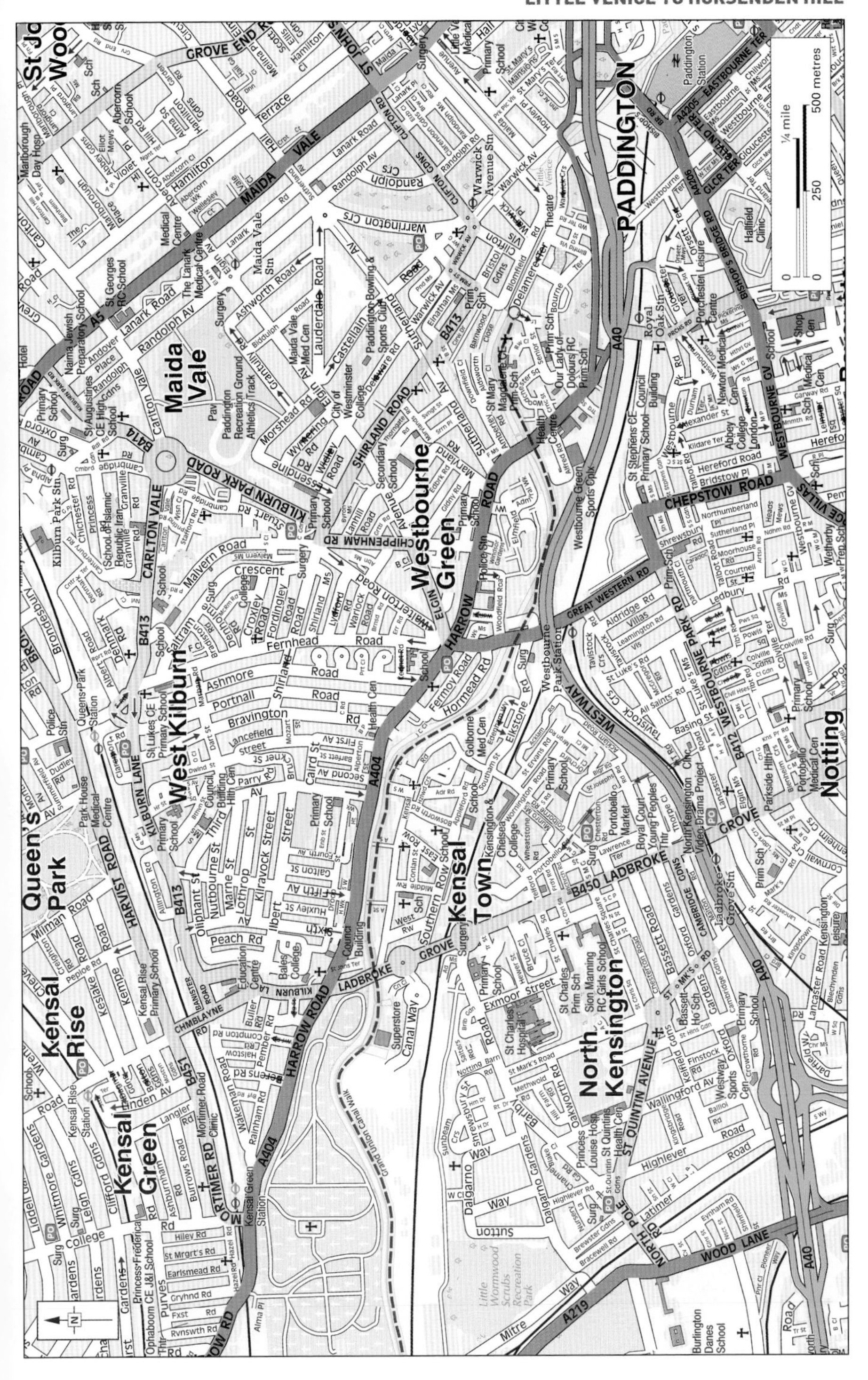

St John's Wood
Maida Vale
PADDINGTON
Paddington Station
West Kilburn
Westbourne Green
Queen's Park
Kensal Rise
Kensal Green
Kensal Town
North Kensington
Notting
MAIDA VALE
KILBURN PARK ROAD
HARROW ROAD
GREAT WESTERN RD
WESTWAY
LADBROKE GROVE
WOOD LANE
ST QUINTIN AVENUE
NORTH POLE RD
Grand Union Canal Walk
Little Wormwood Scrubs Recreation Park
Paddington Recreation Ground Athletics Track
Westbourne Park Station
Royal Oak Stn
Warwick Avenue Stn
Ladbroke Grove Stn
Kensal Green Station
Queens Park Station
Kilburn Park Stn
¼ mile
0
250
500 metres
N

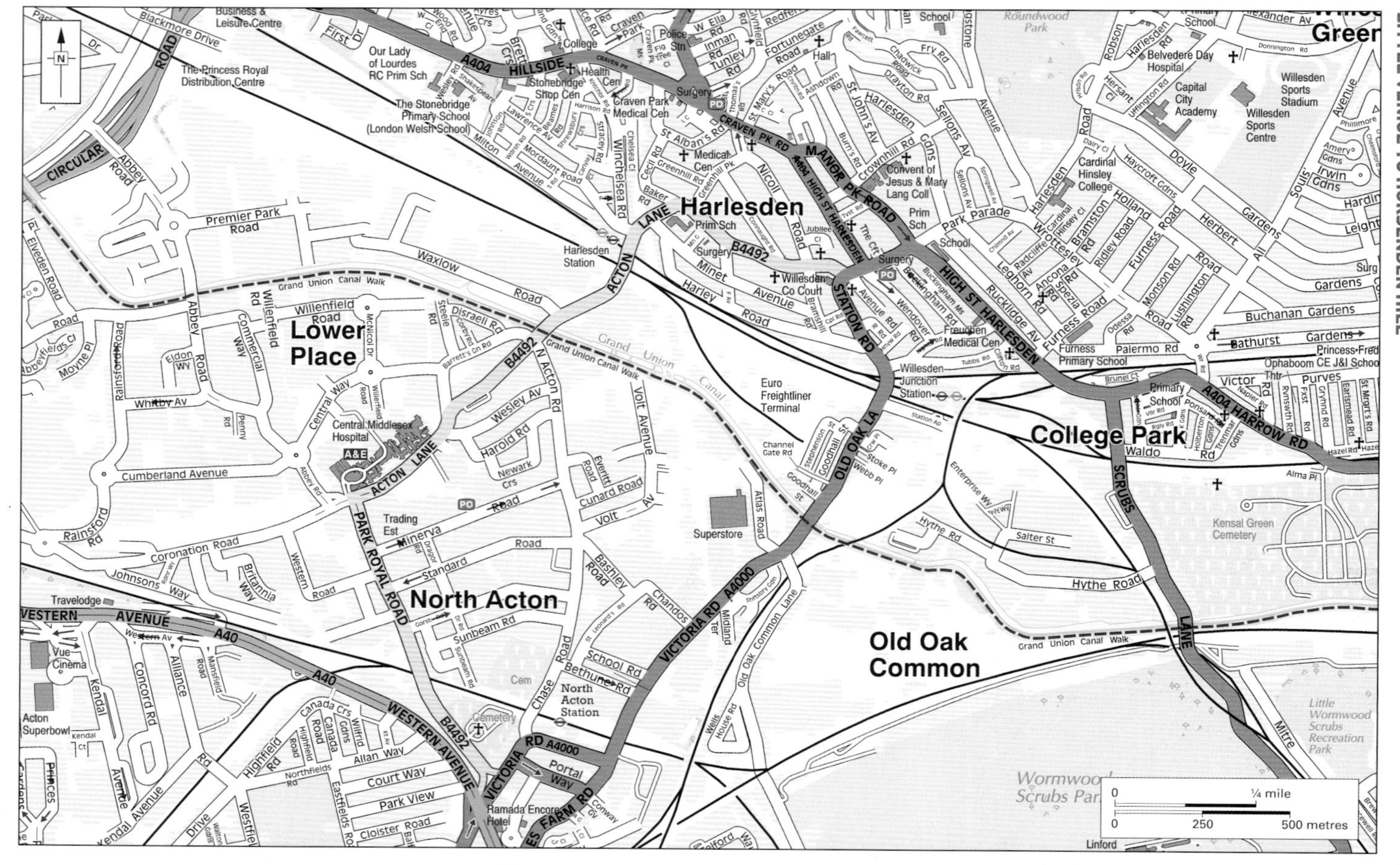
Harlesden
College Park
Old Oak Common
North Acton
Lower Place
Wormwood Scrubs Park
Little Wormwood Scrubs Recreation Park
Kensal Green Cemetery
Willesden Sports Stadium
Willesden Sports Centre
Capital City Academy
Willesden Junction Station
Harlesden Station
North Acton Station
Euro Freightliner Terminal
Superstore
Central Middlesex Hospital
Grand Union Canal Walk
A404 HARROW RD
SCRUBS LANE
HIGH ST HARLESDEN
MANOR PK ROAD
STATION RD
OLD OAK LA
VICTORIA RD A4000
ACTON LANE
PARK ROYAL ROAD
WESTERN AVENUE
A40
B4492
CIRCULAR ROAD
¼ mile
0
250
500 metres

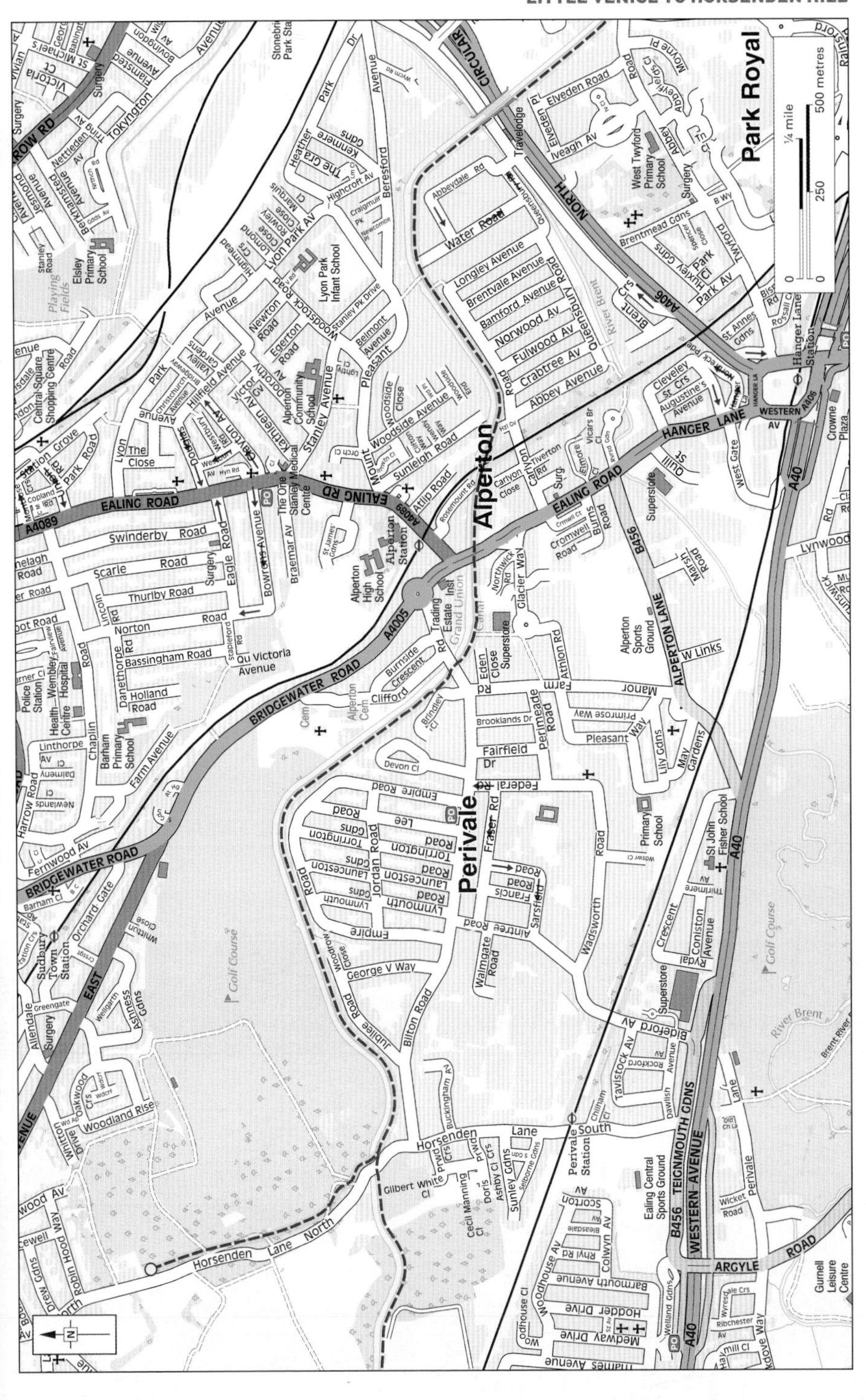
Park Royal
Alperton
Perivale
EALING ROAD
EALING RD
BRIDGEWATER ROAD
HANGER LANE
WESTERN AV
ALPERTON LANE
NORTH CIRCULAR
WESTERN AVENUE
TEIGNMOUTH GDNS
ARGYLE ROAD
Horsenden Lane North
Grand Union Canal
River Brent
Golf Course
A40
A406
A4005
A4089
B456
¼ mile
500 metres
250
0

TWICKENHAM TO HAMPTON WICK

This horseshoe-shaped route starts at Twickenham and follows the River Crane before cutting past Twickenham Golf Club and through Bushy Park to finish at Hampton Wick. Bushy Park is a large park where there is much to do and see – the free-roaming deer are reminiscent of a time when it was a favourite hunting place of Henry VIII.

Twickenham Stadium, once a humble cabbage patch, is now the home of English rugby. With seating for 82,000 spectators, it is the largest dedicated rugby union venue in the world. The first match to be played was between local rivals Harlequins and Richmond in 1909.

Where the route leaves the riverside, there is an optional extension that stays alongside the river, to the Crane Park Island Nature Reserve.

ROUTE INFORMATION

Start: Twickenham train station.
Finish: Hampton Wick train station.
Distance: 6.5 miles (10.5km).
Grade: Easy.
Surface: Cycle tracks and tarmac roads.
Hills: Slight, gentle hill in the middle of the ride – nothing too strenuous.

YOUNG & INEXPERIENCED CYCLISTS

There are some busy roads in places, so not best suited to young riders, but you could stay within Bushy Park or ride the traffic-free sections alongside the River Crane.

REFRESHMENTS

- Pheasantry Welcome Centre Cafe, Bushy Park, near the Diana Fountain.
- Lots of choice in towns along the way.

The Sunken Gardens at Hampton Court

Twickenham Rugby Stadium

THINGS TO SEE & DO

- Twickenham World Rugby Museum, east stand of Twickenham Stadium: learn about the history of the sport and see the rugby memorabilia; 020 8892 8877; www.rfu.com/microsites/museum
- Crane Park Island Nature Reserve: haven of nature among the hustle and bustle of Twickenham town; the 25-m (82-ft) tall Shot Tower, originally used for the production of lead shot, has been restored and is now a visitor and exhibition centre; 020 8755 2339; www.wildlondon.org.uk
- Bushy Park: offers a variety of activities and attractions, such as a water garden, woodland garden, free-roaming deer, children's playground and model boating pond, as well as the 17th-century Diana Fountain, the centrepiece of the park; www.royalparks.org.uk/parks/bushy_park
- Hampton Court Palace: Tudor palace, built by Cardinal Wolsey, alongside a baroque palace; favourite residence of Henry VIII; attractions include beautiful gardens, world-famous maze, medieval hall and Tudor kitchens; www.hrp.org.uk/hamptoncourtpalace

TRAIN STATIONS

Twickenham; Hampton Wick.

BIKE HIRE

- Go Pedal!: delivery to most areas of London; 07850 796320; www.gopedal.co.uk

FURTHER INFORMATION

- To view or print National Cycle Network routes, visit www.sustrans.org.uk
- Maps for this area are available to buy from www.sustransshop.co.uk
- Transport for London (TfL): contact for free map (no. 9); 020 7222 1234; www.tfl.gov.uk
- London Tourist Information: 0870 156 6366; www.visitlondon.com

ROUTE DESCRIPTION

Exit Twickenham train station and use the cycle lane on London Road (A310) to join March Road. At the end of this road, turn left (west) along the back roads to the start of the traffic-free track by an industrial estate. Passing close to Harlequins rugby stadium, the route starts its journey alongside the River Crane, where your immediate surroundings become greener and the trail traffic-free and easy to navigate. Pass through Kneller Gardens and continue along the waterside to a sports ground, where you keep left, crossing the water and the A316.

The route now starts to head south along Glebe Way, past a sports club and a golf course before an on-road section, which may not be suitable for children.

Statuary at Hampton Court Palace

After crossing Pantile Bridge, the route turns into Bushy Park, where you are allowed to cycle on all the roads. Pass by the Water Gardens (pools and cascades created in 1710 by the Earl of Halifax), then bear right through the middle of the park to meet Chestnut Avenue. To the right (south), along Chestnut Avenue, is the Diana Fountain and Pheasantry Welcome Centre. (Note that you can continue south on Chestnut Avenue for Hampton Court.) The route continues straight ahead through the park, along Cobbler's Walk, to Hampton Wick Gate. For Hampton Wick train station, follow Park Road and turn left on the High Street, the A310.

NEARBY CYCLE ROUTES

National Route 4 runs past Hampton Wick, heading southwest through Hampton Court and continuing alongside the River Thames, past Sunbury Lock to Weybridge. It also heads northeast through Kingston-upon-Thames to Teddington Lock, then up through Richmond Park (see the Tamsin Trail, page 82), rejoining the Thames by The Wetland Centre in Barnes, and on to Putney Bridge (see page 88).

Deer at Bushy Park

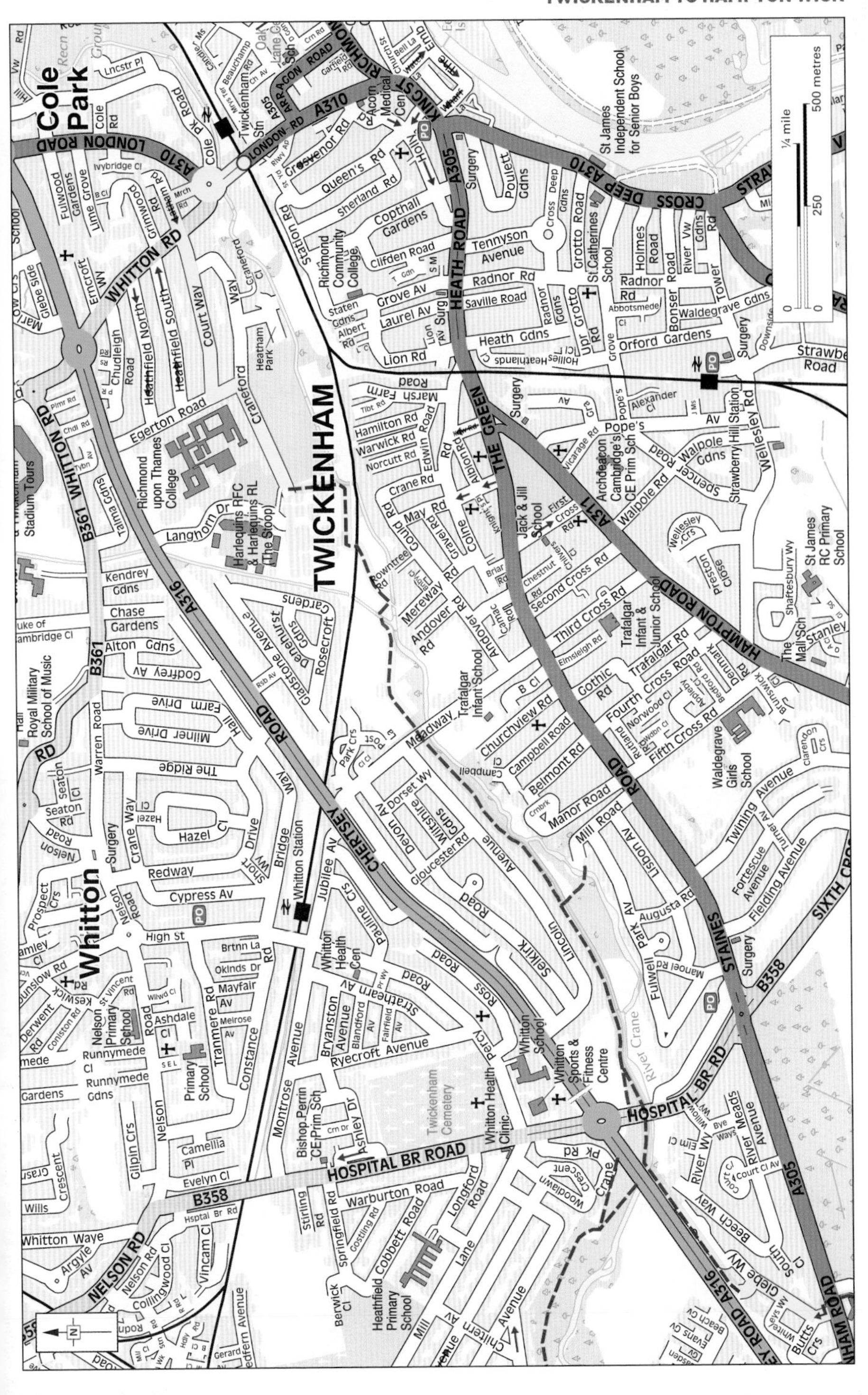
Cole Park
LONDON ROAD
A310
Cole Pk Road
Twickenham Stn
LONDON RD
ARRAGON ROAD
A305
RICHMOND
KING ST
Grosvenor Rd
Queen's Rd
Sherland Rd
Copthall Gardens
Station Rd
Richmond Community College
Clifden Road
HEATH ROAD
Poulett Gdns
Cross Deep Gdns
CROSS DEEP A310
St James Independent School for Senior Boys
Grotto Road
St Catherines School
Holmes Road
River Vw Gdns
Tower Rd
Tennyson Avenue
Radnor Rd
Saville Road
Radnor Gdns
Upr Grotto Rd
Bonser Road
Waldegrave Gdns
Orford Gardens
Heath Gdns
Lion Rd
Grove Av
Laurel Av
Staten Gdns
Albert Rd
Strawberry Road
Surgery
1/4 mile
500 metres
250
0
WHITTON RD
Whitton Rd
Fulwood Gardens
Lime Grove
Ivybridge Cl
Grimwood Rd
Court Way
Craneford Way
Heathfield North
Heathfield South
Heatham Park
Chudleigh Road
Egerton Road
Craneford
Richmond upon Thames College
Harlequins RFC & Harlequins RL (The Stoop)
Langhorn Dr
TWICKENHAM
Marsh Farm Road
Hamilton Rd
Warwick Rd
Norcutt Rd
Edwin Road
Crane Rd
May Rd
Gould Rd
Colne Rd
Gravel Rd
Albion Rd
THE GREEN
Pope's Gro
Alexander Cl
Vicarage Rd
Pope's Av
Walpole Gdns
Spencer Road
Strawberry Hill Station
Wellesley Rd
Archdeacon Cambridge's CE Prim Sch
Walpole Rd
A311
HAMPTON ROAD
Jack & Jill School
First Cross Rd
Second Cross Rd
Third Cross Rd
Wellesley Crs
Preston Close
Shaftesbury Wy
St James RC Primary School
Stanley Rd
The Mall Sch
Trafalgar Infant & Junior School
Trafalgar Rd
Fourth Cross Road
Fifth Cross Rd
Denmark Rd
Waldegrave Girls School
Stadium Tours
B361 WHITTON RD
Talma Gdns
Kendrey Gdns
Chase Gardens
Alton Gdns
Godfrey Av
Hall Farm Drive
Milner Drive
The Ridge
Warren Road
Royal Military School of Music
A316
ROAD
CHERTSEY
Gladstone Avenue
Denehurst Gdns
Rosecroft Gardens
Rowntree Rd
Mereway Rd
Andover Rd
Trafalgar Infant School
Meadway
Churchview Rd
Campbell Road
Belmont Rd
Manor Road
Mill Road
Lisbon Av
Twining Avenue
Fortescue Avenue
Fielding Avenue
SIXTH CROSS
Seaton Cl
Seaton Rd
Nelson Road
Hazel Cl
Crane Way
Short Drive
Redway
Cypress Av
Bridge Way
Whitton Station
Park Crs
Dorset Wy
Wiltshire Gdns
Gloucester Rd
Devon Av
Jubilee Av
Pauline Crs
Selkirk Road
Lincoln Avenue
Park Av
Augusta Rd
Fulwell
Manoel Rd
STAINES ROAD
B358
Whitton
Prospect Crs
High St
Brtnn La
Oklnds Dr
Mayfair Av
Nelson Rd
Whitton Health Cen
Strathearn Av
Ross Road
Percy Road
Whitton School
Whitton Sports & Fitness Centre
River Crane
Keswick Rd
Nelson Primary School
St Vincent Rd
Ashdale Cl
Tranmere Rd
Melrose Av
Constance Rd
Runnymede Cl
Runnymede Gdns
Primary School
Bryanston Avenue
Blandford Av
Ryecroft Avenue
Montrose Avenue
Twickenham Cemetery
Whitton Health Clinic
HOSPITAL BR RD
Bishop Perrin CE Prim Sch
Ashley Dr
HOSPITAL BR ROAD
Pk Rd
Crescent
Crane
River Wy
River Meads Avenue
Court Cl Av
A305
Nelson
Gilpin Crs
Camellia Pl
Evelyn Cl
B358
Wills Crescent
Stirling Rd
Springfield Rd
Warburton Road
Cobbett Road
Longford Road
Woodlawn Crescent
Beech Way
South Cl
Glebe Wy
Whitton Waye
Argyle Av
NELSON RD
Nelson Rd
Collingwood Cl
Vincam Cl
Gerard
Redfern Avenue
Berwick Cl
Heathfield Primary School
Mill
Lane
Chiltern
Avenue
Evans Gv
Beach Gv
Butts Crs
HAMPTON ROAD
A316
N

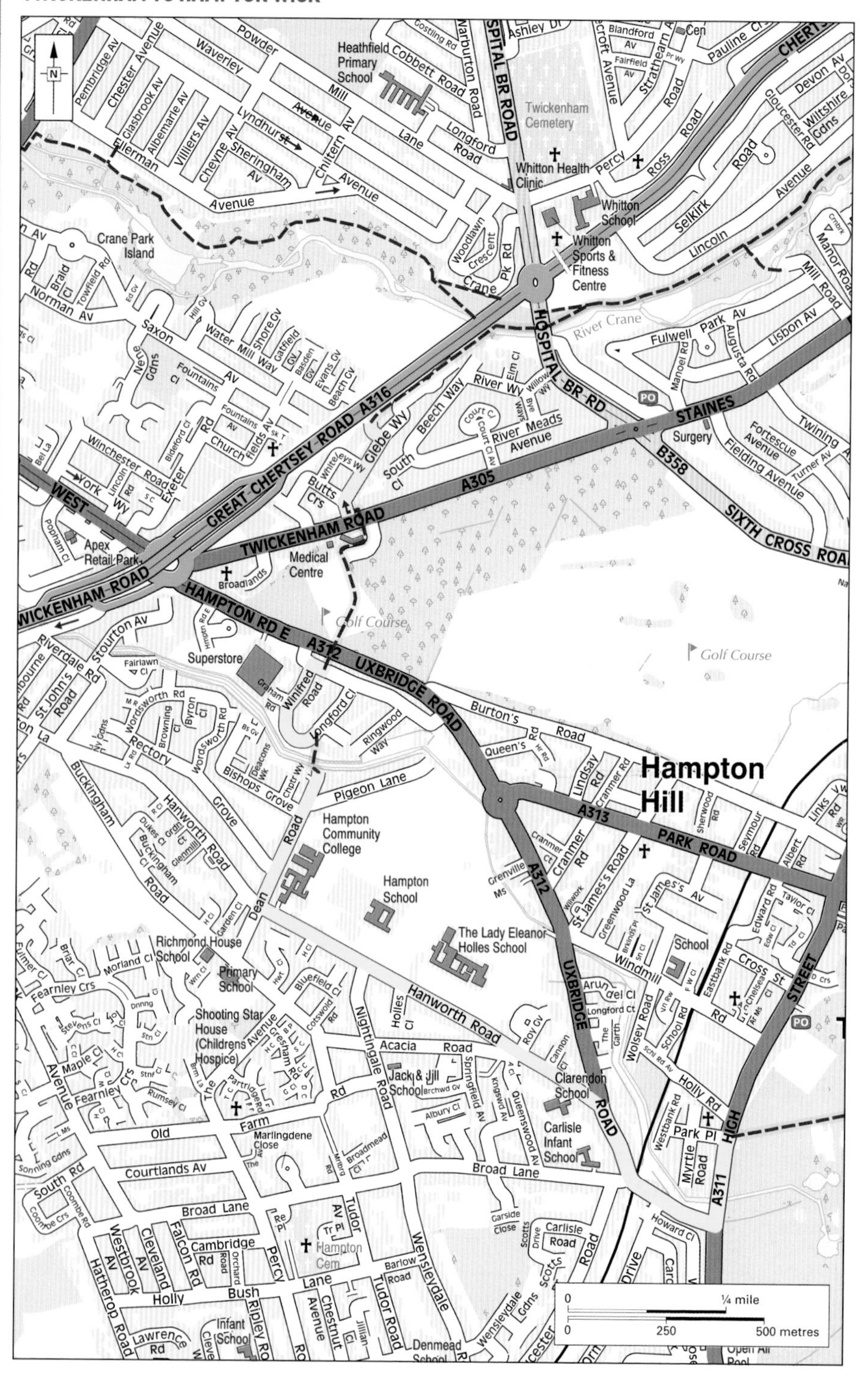
N
Pembridge Av
Chester Avenue
Glasbrook Av
Albemarle Av
Villiers Av
Cheyne Av
Sheringham Av
Powder Mill Lane
Waverley Avenue
Lyndhurst Avenue
Chiltern Av
Ellerman Avenue
Heathfield Primary School
Cobbett Road
Warburton Road
Longford Road
HOSPITAL BR ROAD
Ashley Dr
Blandford Av
Fairfield Av
Strathearn Road
Pauline Cr
Twickenham Cemetery
Whitton Health Clinic
Percy
Ross Road
Gloucester Rd
Devon Av
Wiltshire Gdns
Whitton School
Whitton Sports & Fitness Centre
Selkirk Road
Lincoln Avenue
Manor Road
Mill Road
Crane Park Island
Woodlawn Crescent
Crane
Pk Rd
River Crane
Norman Av
Towfield Rd
Braid Cl
Saxon
Water Mill Way
Shore Gv
Gatfield Gv
Basden Gv
Evans Gv
Beach Gv
Nene Gdns
Fountains Av
Fountains Cl
Church
Fields Av
Bideford Cl
Winchester Road
Exeter
York Wy
Lincoln Wy
Bel La
GREAT CHERTSEY ROAD A316
Glebe Wy
Whiteleys Wy
Butts Crs
South Cl
Beech Way
Court Cl
River Wy
River Meads Avenue
Elm Cl
Willow Wy
Bye Ways
HOSPITAL BR RD
Fulwell Park Av
Manoel Rd
Augusta Rd
Lisbon Av
PO
STAINES
Surgery
B358
Twining
Fortescue Avenue
Fielding Avenue
Turner Av
SIXTH CROSS ROAD
A305
TWICKENHAM ROAD
WEST TWICKENHAM ROAD
Popham Cl
Apex Retail Park
Broadlands
Medical Centre
HAMPTON RD E
A312
UXBRIDGE ROAD
Golf Course
Stourton Av
Riverdale Rd
Fairlawn Cl
Superstore
St John's Road
Wordsworth Rd
Byron Cl
Browning Cl
Graham Rd
Winifred Road
Longford Cl
Ringwood Way
Burton's Road
Queen's Rd
Rectory Grove
Deacons Wk
Chptr Wy
Bishops Grove
Pigeon Lane
Lindsay Rd
Cranmer Rd
Hampton Hill
A313
PARK ROAD
Sherwood Rd
Seymour Rd
Albert Rd
Links Vw
Buckingham
Hanworth Road
Dukes Cl
Buckingham Cl Road
Glenmill
Dean Road
Hampton Community College
Hampton School
Grenville Ms
Cranmer Ct
St James's Road
Greenwood La
St James's Av
Edward Rd
Taylor Cl
The Lady Eleanor Holles School
School
Windmill
Eastbank Rd
Cross St
STREET
Garden Cl
Richmond House School
Morland Cl
Briar
Fulmer Cl
Fearnley Crs
Primary School
Bluefield Cl
Cotswold
Holles Cl
Hanworth Road
Arundel Cl
Longford Ct
Wolsey Road
School Rd
Chelsea
Shooting Star House (Childrens Hospice)
Stevens Cl
Maple Cl
Avenue
Gresham Rd
Nightingale Road
Acacia Road
Roy Gv
Cannon Cl
UXBRIDGE ROAD
The Garth
Holly Rd
Westbank Rd
Park Pl
HIGH
Jack & Jill School
Springfield Av
Queenswood Av
Clarendon School
Rumsey Cl
Partridge Rd
Old Farm Rd
Marlingdene Close
Broadmead Cl
Albury Cl
Carlisle Infant School
Myrtle Road
A311
Sonning Gdns
South Rd
Coombe Rd
Coombe Crs
Courtlands Av
Broad Lane
Broad Lane
Tudor Av
Tr Pl
Garside Close
Carlisle Road
Howard Cl
Westbrook Av
Cleveland Av
Falcon Rd
Cambridge Rd
Orchard Road
Percy
Hampton Cem
Barlow Road
Wensleydale
Scotts Drive
Hatherop Road
Holly Bush Lane
Ripley Road
Chestnut Avenue
Tudor Road
Jillian Cl
Wensleydale Gdns
Infant School
Lawrence Rd
Denmead School
Open Air Pool
Drive
0
¼ mile
0
250
500 metres

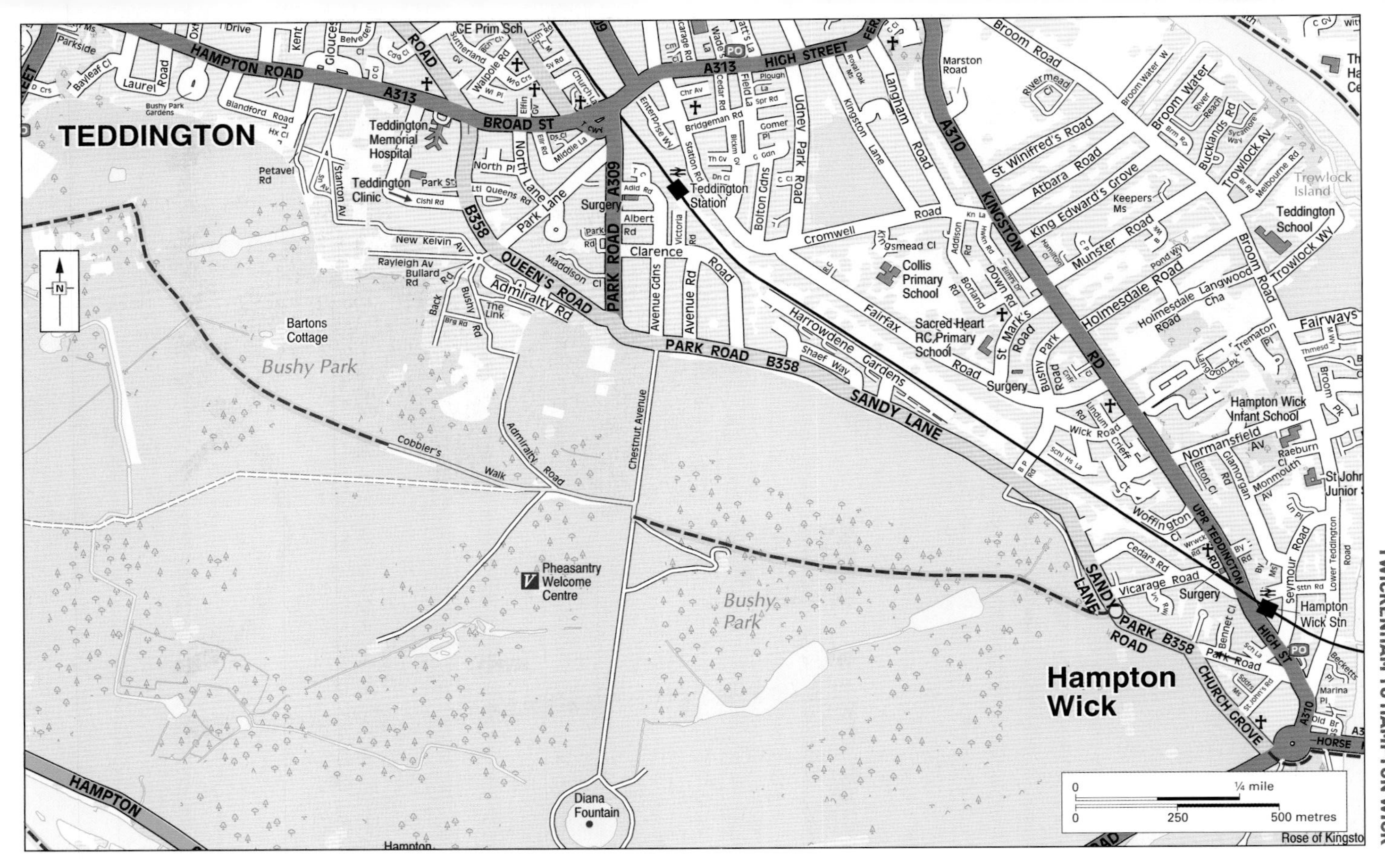
TEDDINGTON
Hampton Wick
Bushy Park
Bushy Park
HAMPTON ROAD
A313
BROAD ST
HIGH STREET
A310
KINGSTON RD
UPR TEDDINGTON RD
HIGH ST
PARK ROAD
A309
QUEEN'S ROAD
B358
PARK ROAD B358
SANDY LANE
SANDY LANE
PARK B358 ROAD
CHURCH GROVE
HAMPTON
Chestnut Avenue
Diana Fountain
Pheasantry Welcome Centre
Bartons Cottage
Cobbler's Walk
Admiralty Road
Admiralty Rd
Teddington Station
Hampton Wick Stn
Teddington Memorial Hospital
Teddington Clinic
Teddington School
Collis Primary School
Sacred Heart RC Primary School
Hampton Wick Infant School
CE Prim Sch
Trowlock Island
Broom Road
Broom Water
Marston Road
Langham Road
Kingston Lane
Udney Park Road
Cromwell Road
Fairfax Road
Harrowdene Gardens
Shaef Way
Avenue Rd
Avenue Gdns
Clarence Road
Victoria Rd
St Winifred's Road
Atbara Road
King Edward's Grove
Keepers Ms
Munster Road
Holmesdale Road
Trowlock Wy
Trowlock Av
Bucklands Rd
Fairways
Normansfield Av
Glamorgan Rd
Monmouth Av
Woffington Cl
Cedars Rd
Vicarage Road
Seymour Road
Lower Teddington Road
Park Road
Bennet Cl
Wick Road
St Mark's Road
Bushy Park Road
Down Rd
North Lane
Park Lane
Stanton Av
Petavel Rd
Blandford Road
Laurel Road
Parkside
Bayleaf Cl
New Kelvin Av
Rayleigh Av
Bullard Rd
Back Rd
Bushy Rd
The Link
Maddison Cl
Station Rd
Bridgeman Rd
Bolton Gdns
Surgery
¼ mile
0
250
500 metres
Rose of Kingston

INGREBOURNE VALLEY

This short ride starts at Ingrebourne Hill, heads up Ingrebourne Valley through Hornchurch Country Park and finishes at Upminster Park. It's a lovely easy ride, suitable for all the family, with plenty of picnic spots along the way.

Ingrebourne Hill used to be just a flat field for grazing cattle. During World War II, its close proximity to RAF Hornchurch, the Spitfire fighter station, meant that it was badly bombed. After the war, it went to pasture, was quarried for gravel and then was used for landfill in the 1980s. Nowadays, it offers a wonderful space for sports and exercise. Recent developments have created 1.8 miles (3km) of cycling trails, a 0.8-mile (1.3-km) mountain bike trail, 1.3 miles (2.1km) of horse-riding trails, two play areas and numerous picnic spots.

Carefree cycling with a friend!

ROUTE INFORMATION

Start: Ingrebourne Hill car park.
Finish: Upminster Park.
Distance: 3.5 miles (5.5km).
Grade: Easy.
Surface: Well-surfaced cyclepaths and the choice of an off-road mountain bike trail.
Hills: Just a small one at the end of the ride.

YOUNG & INEXPERIENCED CYCLISTS

A great place for children and novices, as there is the option of staying within Ingrebourne Hill and riding the cycle trails.

REFRESHMENTS

- Lots of choice in both Rainham and Upminster.

THINGS TO SEE & DO

- Ingrebourne Hill: offers a variety of cycle routes, with fun trails for all abilities and a pump track for riders to practise their cycling rhythm and flow; also a horse-riding trail, picnic spot, two play areas and ponds; at the highest point, there are good views of the surrounding area, including the Thames, Epping Forest and City of London; www.forestry.gov.uk/ingrebourne

Ingrebourne Hill has a horse-riding trail

- **Rainham Hall:** Georgian house in Dutch domestic-style architecture, with red brick, decorative stonework and impressive wrought iron entrance gate; 020 7799 4552; www.nationaltrust.org.uk

TRAIN STATIONS

Rainham; Upminster.

Ducks on the River Ingrebourne

BIKE HIRE

None locally.

FURTHER INFORMATION

- To view or print National Cycle Network routes, visit www.sustrans.org.uk
- Maps for this area are available to buy from www.sustransshop.co.uk
- **Transport for London (TfL):** contact for free maps (nos. 5 and 8); 020 7222 1234; www.tfl.gov.uk
- **London Tourist Information:** 0870 156 6366; www.visitlondon.com

Bullrushes flourish in marshland

ROUTE DESCRIPTION

This ride starts at the free car park at Ingrebourne Hill, just off the A125, north of Rainham, but it also explores further afield, heading northeast up the Ingrebourne Valley along the 'London Loop' trail. You pass through the pleasant Hornchurch Country Park, staying close to the River Ingrebourne, which makes navigation along the ride fairly straightforward. As you approach the towns of Hornchurch and Upminster, stay with the riverside until you get to the foot of Hornchurch Stadium. Here, you turn right. At the junction with Bridge Avenue, keep straight ahead on Brookdale Avenue, which leads you to Upminster Park.

NEARBY CYCLE ROUTES

The Rainham RSPB route (see page 60), part of National Route 13, also starts at Rainham and provides a pleasant, traffic-free ride, passing through Rainham Marshes.

The Redbridge Cycling Centre in Hainault has 1.2 miles (2km) of road and 1.8 miles (3km) of off-road cycle tracks, ideal for adults and children wanting to develop their skills.

There's also a good pump track. Visit www.vision-rcl.org.uk/redbridge_cycle_centre for more information.

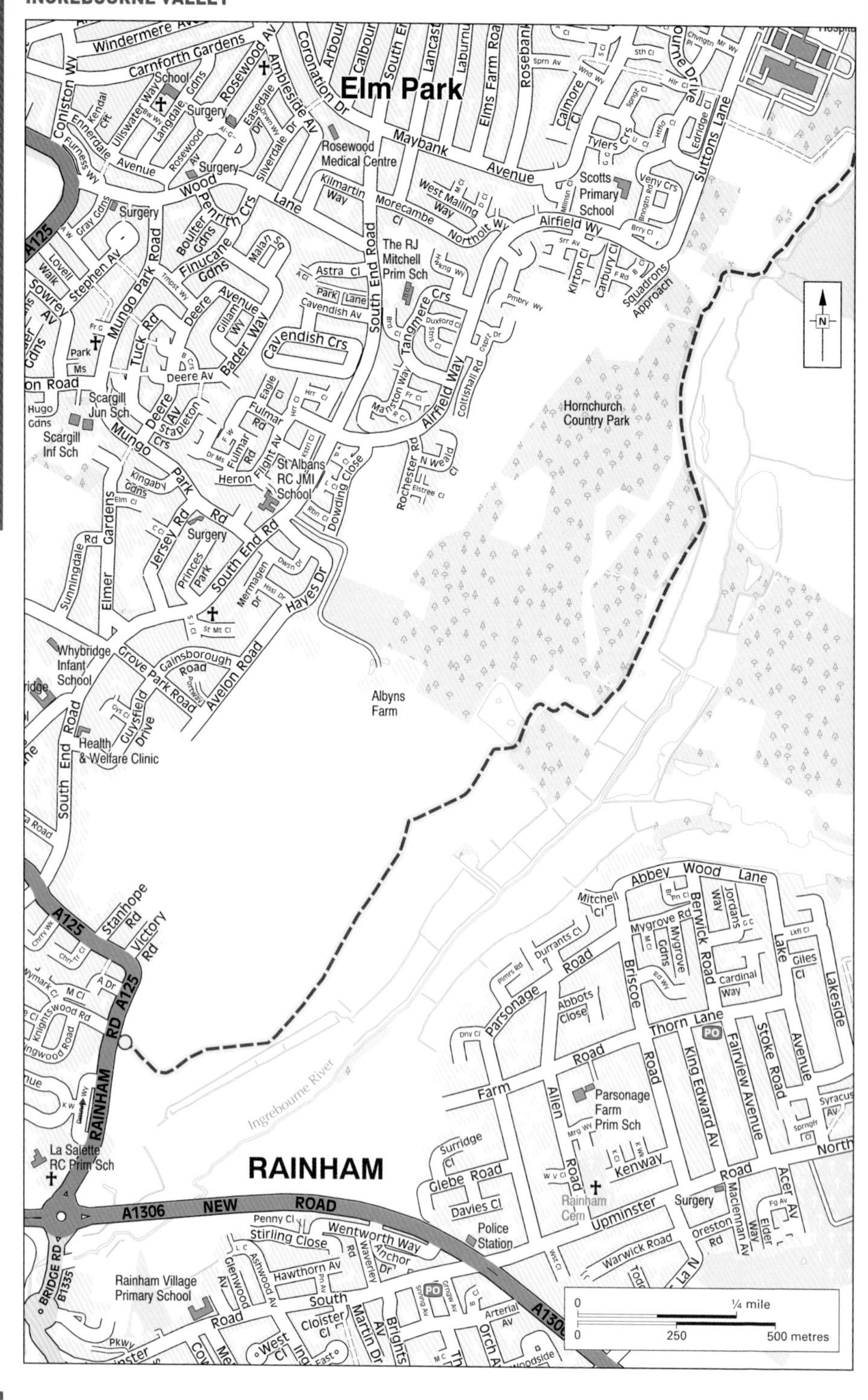
Elm Park
RAINHAM
Windermere Av
Carnforth Gardens
Coniston Wy
Rosewood Av
Ambleside Av
Coronation Dr
Calbourne
Lancaster
Laburnum
Elms Farm Road
Rosebank
Calmore Cl
Tylers Crs
Suttons Lane
Maybank Avenue
Rosewood Medical Centre
Scotts Primary School
Kilmartin Way
Morecambe Cl
West Malling Way
Northolt Wy
Airfield Wy
Surgery
School
Ullswater Way
Langdale Gdns
Ennerdale Avenue
Furness Wy
Wood Lane
Penrith Crs
Silverdale Dr
Easedale Dr
Boulter Gdns
Finucane Gdns
Malan Sq
Mungo Park Road
Stephen Av
Gray Gdns
Lovell Walk
Sowrey Av
A125
Astra Cl
Park Lane
Cavendish Av
Cavendish Crs
South End Road
The RJ Mitchell Prim Sch
Tangmere Crs
Duxford Cl
Squadrons Approach
Kirton Cl
Carbury Cl
Pmbry Wy
Deere Avenue
Gillam Wy
Bader Way
Tuck Rd
Deere Av
Stapleton Crs
Scargill Jun Sch
Scargill Inf Sch
Hugo Gdns
Eagle Cl
Fulmar Rd
Flight Av
Heron
St Albans RC JMI School
Dowding Close
Manston Way
Airfield Way
Coltishall Rd
Rochester Rd
N Weald Cl
Elstree Cl
Hornchurch Country Park
Kingaby Gdns
Elmer Gardens
Sunningdale Rd
Jersey Rd
Princes Park
South End Rd
Mermagen Dr
Hayes Dr
St Mt Cl
Whybridge Infant School
Grove Park Road
Gainsborough Road
Avelon Road
Guysfield Drive
Health & Welfare Clinic
Albyns Farm
Stanhope Rd
Victory Rd
Wood Rd
M Cl
A Dr
RAINHAM RD A125
La Salette RC Prim Sch
Ingrebourne River
A1306 NEW ROAD
Penny Cl
Stirling Close
Wentworth Way
Anchor Dr
Waverley
Hawthorn Av
Glenwood Av
Ashwood Av
South Road
Cloister Cl
Martin Dr
West Cl
Rainham Village Primary School
BRIDGE RD B1335
Pkwy
Arterial Av
Orch Av
Woodside
A1306
Abbey Wood Lane
Mitchell Cl
Jordans Way
Berwick Road
Mygrove Rd
Mygrove Gdns
Durrants Cl
Briscoe Road
Parsonage Road
Abbots Close
Lake Avenue
Giles Cl
Lakeside
Cardinal Way
Thorn Lane
PO
Stoke Road
Fairview Avenue
King Edward Av
Farm Road
Allen Road
Parsonage Farm Prim Sch
Kenway
Surridge Cl
Glebe Road
Davies Cl
Police Station
Rainham Cem
Upminster Road
Surgery
Warwick Road
Oreston Rd
Maclennan Av
Elder Way
Acer Av
Syracuse Av
North
N
0
¼ mile
250
500 metres

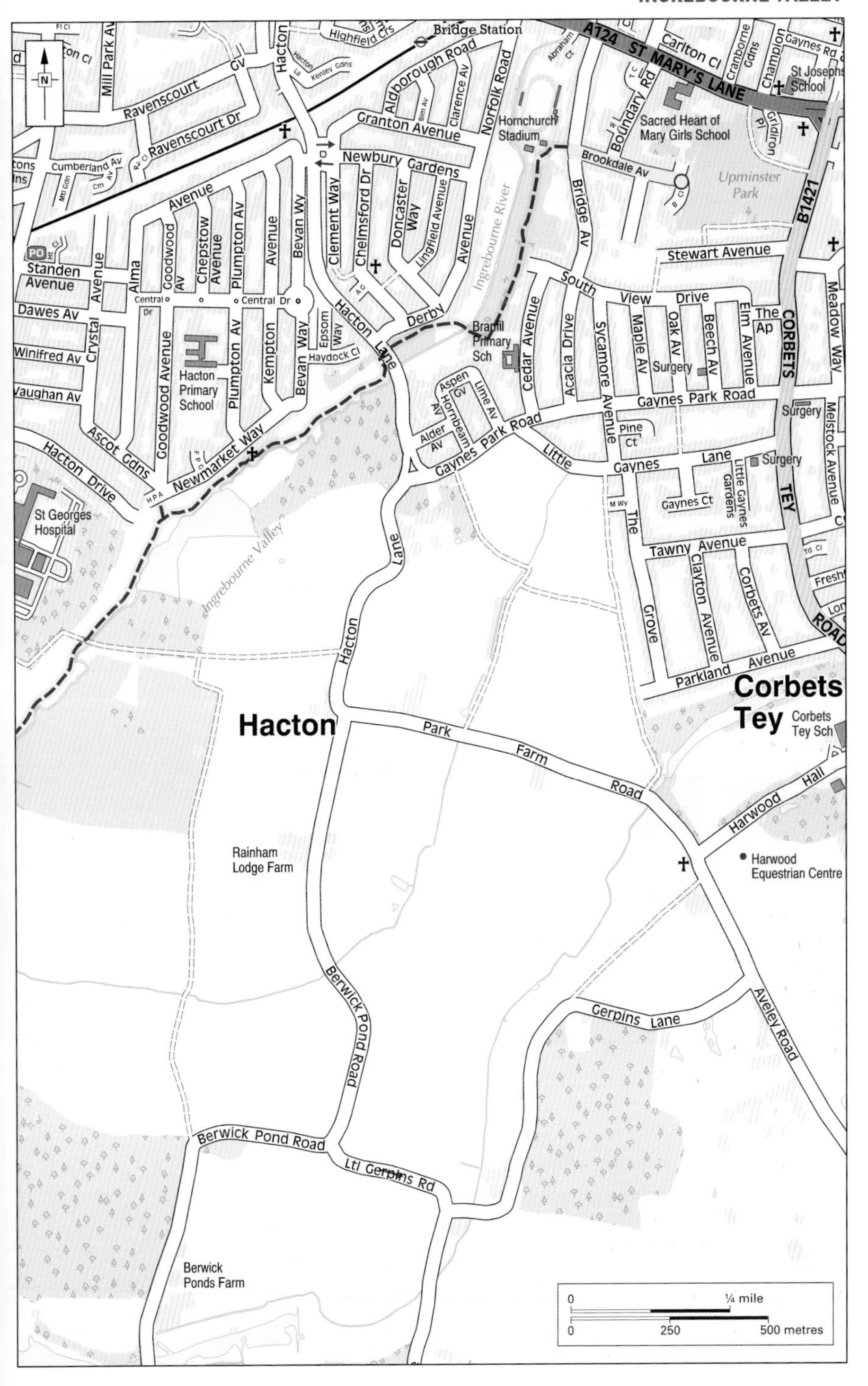
Bridge Station
A124 ST MARY'S LANE
Hornchurch Stadium
Sacred Heart of Mary Girls School
Upminster Park
B1421
St Josephs School
Ingrebourne River
Hacton Primary School
Branfil Primary Sch
St Georges Hospital
Ingrebourne Valley
Hacton
Corbets Tey
Corbets Tey Sch
Rainham Lodge Farm
Harwood Equestrian Centre
Berwick Ponds Farm
Hacton Lane
Park Farm Road
Berwick Pond Road
Ltl Gerpins Rd
Gerpins Lane
Aveley Road
Corbets Tey Road
Harwood Hall
Parkland Avenue
Gaynes Park Road
Little Gaynes Lane
South View Drive
Stewart Avenue
Newmarket Way
Hacton Drive
Surgery
0
¼ mile
0
250
500 metres

LEE VALLEY – WALTHAM ABBEY PARK TO GREENWICH

This is a wonderful ride into London, starting just within the M25 and going alongside reservoirs, canals, nature reserves, through parks, over a tree-lined bridge, between skyscrapers, along the River Thames, over docks and even through a tunnel under the river to finish. The whole route is quite long, but you can just do shorter sections as you please. However, it is fairly straightforward to follow and there is a train station at the end, so you need ride only one way if you wish.

There is an abundance of wildlife along the way, including the rare and elusive bittern hiding in reeds, the blue-tailed damselfly and the beautiful bee orchid. In addition, you have man-made creations, such as 73 full-sized football pitches on Hackney Marsh, lovely Victoria Park (the oldest municipal park in the world, opened to the public in 1845), Green Mile End Bridge, high-rise towers in Canary Wharf, and Mudchute City Farm on the Isle of Dogs.

Lee Valley Regional Park is free to enter and open every day of the year. Twice the size of all of London's royal parks combined, it offers 26 miles (42km) of riverside trails, country parks and nature reserves.

ROUTE INFORMATION

National Route: 1
Start: Waltham Abbey.
Finish: Greenwich Foot Tunnel.
Distance: 17.5 miles (28km).
Grade: Easy.
Surface: Tarmac and grit trails.
Hills: A couple of short little hills towards the end but, overall, nothing significant.

YOUNG & INEXPERIENCED CYCLISTS

A mostly traffic-free route suitable for children and novices, but take care on the road section past Mile End (as you near the Thames).

REFRESHMENTS

- Cafe at Springfield Marina (by Walthamstow reservoirs).
- Cafe at the WaterWorks Nature Reserve visitor centre, by the A104 (Hackney Marshes).
- Mudchute Kitchen, Mudchute City Farm
- Lots of choice in Greenwich.

THINGS TO SEE & DO

- Waltham Abbey Church & Gardens: award-winning site steeped in history and set in the grounds of the Abbey at Waltham, the last to be dissolved by Henry VIII and thought to be the burial site of King Harold, who was killed at the Battle of Hastings in 1066; open 7 days a week; 01992 767897; www.walthamabbeychurch.co.uk
- Royal Gunpowder Mills, Waltham Abbey: established in the 17th century to make explosives; set in 170 acres of natural parkland with 20 historic buildings; 01992 707370; www.royalgunpowdermills.com
- Hayes Hill Farm, Stubbins Hall Lane, Waltham Abbey: rare breed pigs, sheep, cows, rabbits, scaly reptiles and llamas; 01992 892781; www.leevalleypark.org.uk
- Cornmill Meadows Dragonfly Sanctuary, Waltham Abbey: Site of Special Scientific Interest (SSSI), where over half of Britain's native species of dragonfly can be seen between May and September; 01992 717711; www.leevalleypark.org.uk
- Mudchute City Farm: the largest inner city farm in Europe, with a variety of animals, including many rare British breeds; 020 7515 5901; www.mudchute.org
- The *Cutty Sark*, Greenwich: 85-m (279-ft) long clipper ship, built in 1869, now used as

Salmon Lane Lock on Regent's Canal at Mile End

a museum; currently closed for conservation work until 2011; 020 8858 2698; www.cuttysark.org.uk

TRAIN STATIONS

Waltham Cross; Greenwich; and various others in between.

Note that the DLR (Docklands Light Railway) only allows folding bicycles in carrying cases.

BIKE HIRE

- **Lee Valley Cycle Hire, Broxbourne, Hertfordshire:** 01992 630127
- **City Bike Service, Shoreditch, London:**

020 7247 4151;
www.citybikeservice.co.uk

FURTHER INFORMATION

- To view or print National Cycle Network routes, visit www.sustrans.org.uk
- Maps for this area are available to buy from www.sustransshop.co.uk
- Transport for London (TfL): contact for free maps (nos. 2, 4 and 7); 020 7222 1234; www.tfl.gov.uk
- Lee Valley Park Information: 01992 702200; www.leevalleypark.org.uk
- London Tourist Information: 0870 156 6366; www.visitlondon.com

ROUTE DESCRIPTION

Starting at Waltham Abbey, the route heads south along National Route 1 (you follow the signs until the end of the ride at the Greenwich Foot Tunnel). The route quickly leaves the urban surroundings, passing through Gunpowder Park, then running alongside King George's and William Girling reservoirs, for just over 3 miles (5km). Passing some smaller reservoirs, this pleasant stretch of trail then brings you to Springfield Park by the River Lea and Springfield Marina. This attractive park was built on the grounds of three 19th-century houses, one of which remains and is now a cafe. Just over the River Lea at this point is Walthamstow Marsh Nature Reserve, one of the last remaining marshes along the Lea. A Site of Special Scientific Interest (SSSI), it is home to over 300 species of plants.

Further along you pass Hackney Marshes, home to the largest collection of football fields in Europe and where you can see 100 football matches being played in one place on one day. (After the Olympic Games of 2012, a bridge will cross the motorway and connect the Marshes to the Olympic Park, making them one of the best-equipped sporting venues in London.) Cross Victoria Park to Regent's Canal and go over Mile End Road via the 'green' bridge covered in grass and lined with trees, to the Mile End Ecology Park, with good views of Canary Wharf. After reaching the River Thames and passing Canary Wharf, cross over Millwall Dock and enter Mudchute Park, home to Europe's largest city farm. At Island Gardens, at the tip of the Isle of Dogs, there are seats from which to appreciate the views over the Thames, before crossing under the river via the Greenwich Foot Tunnel – bikes must be pushed – to emerge by the *Cutty Sark* (closed until 2011), where there are plenty of refreshment options and Greenwich train station.

Note that the lifts down to the Foot Tunnel normally operate Monday to Saturday, 7am to 7pm, and Sunday, 10am to 5.30pm. The tunnel is open 24 hours a day, but it is a long walk down a spiral staircase. If you miss the last lift, take National Route 1 north to Canary Wharf Pier and catch the ferry (www.thamesclippers.com) to Hilton Docklands Pier (Rotherhithe).

NEARBY CYCLE ROUTES

The Lee Valley Park has miles of shared-use pathways that are perfect for family cycling. At the end of the route, National Route 4 heads west into London, or east, along the River Thames, into Kent.

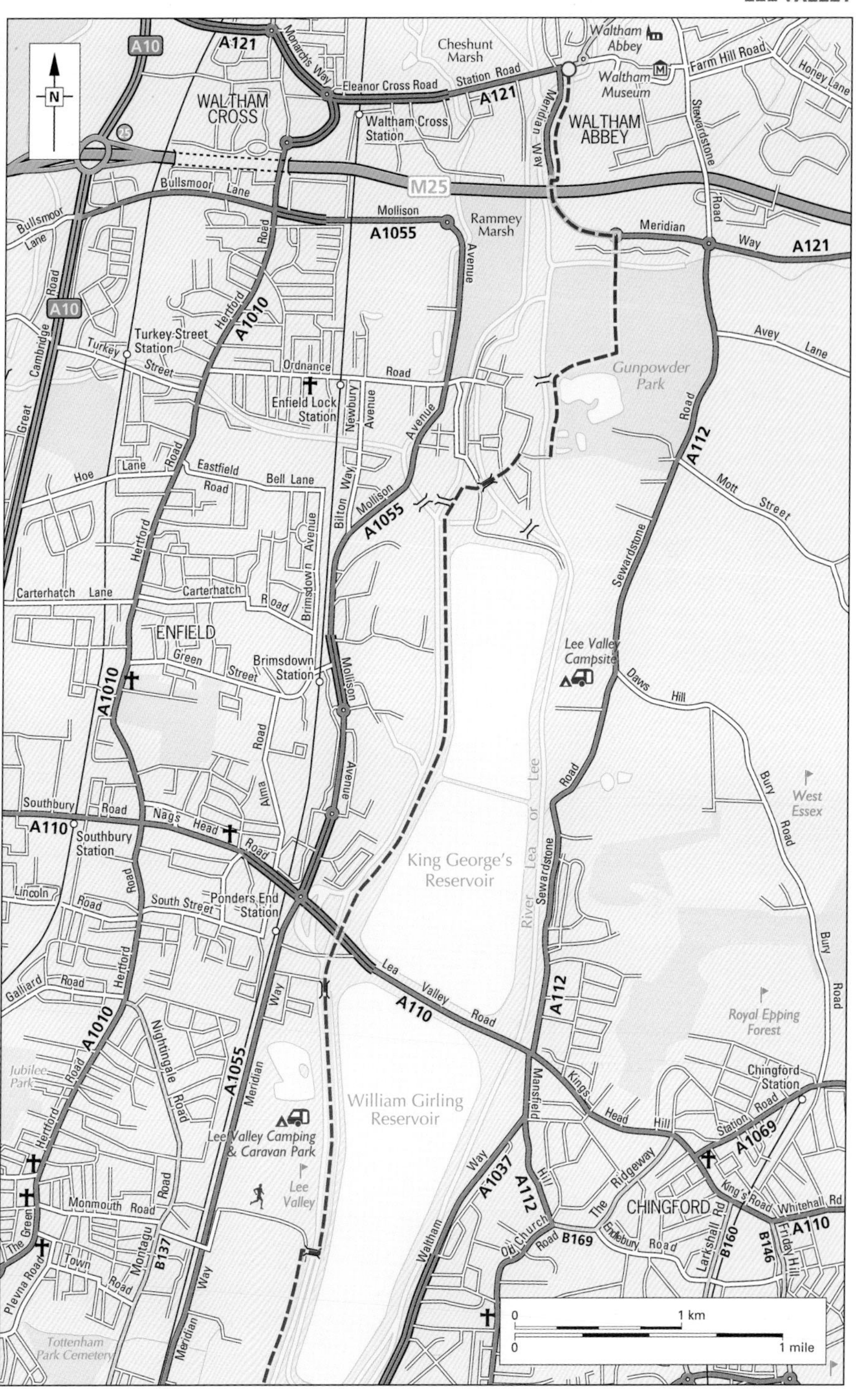

WALTHAM CROSS
WALTHAM ABBEY
Waltham Abbey
Waltham Museum
Cheshunt Marsh
Rammey Marsh
Gunpowder Park
ENFIELD
King George's Reservoir
William Girling Reservoir
Lee Valley Campsite
Lee Valley Camping & Caravan Park
Lee Valley
West Essex
Royal Epping Forest
CHINGFORD
Chingford Station
Jubilee Park
Tottenham Park Cemetery
Turkey Street Station
Enfield Lock Station
Brimsdown Station
Southbury Station
Ponders End Station
Waltham Cross Station
M25
A10
A121
A1055
A1010
A110
A112
A1037
A1069
B169
B160
B146
B137
River Lea or Lee
0
1 km
0
1 mile

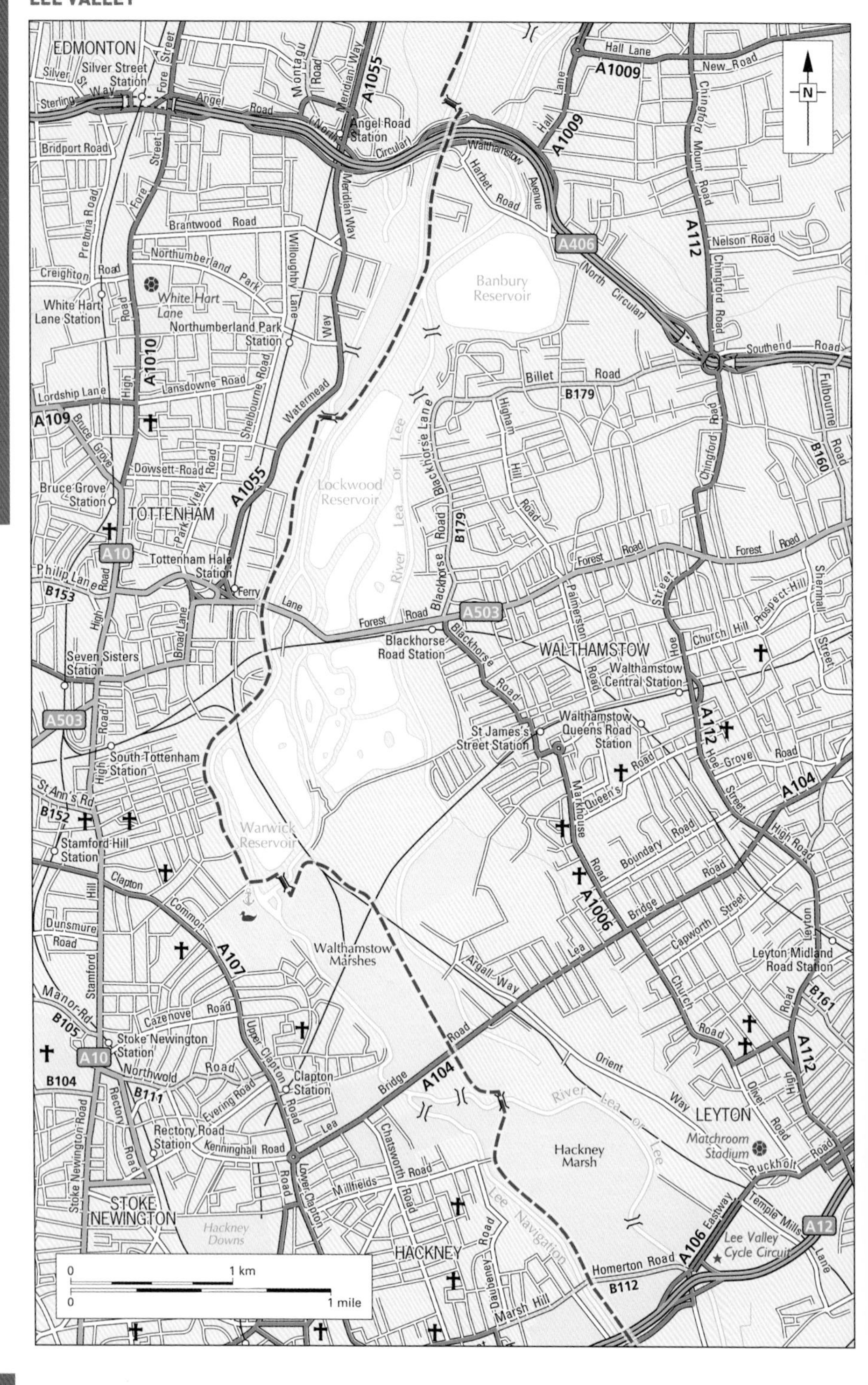
EDMONTON
Silver Street Station
Angel Road Station
North Circular
Meridian Way
A1055
A1009
Hall Lane
New Road
Chingford Mount Road
N
Walthamstow Avenue
Harbet Road
A406
Bridport Road
Pretoria Road
Fore Street
Brantwood Road
Willoughby Lane
Northumberland Park
Creighton Road
White Hart Lane Station
White Hart Lane
Northumberland Park Station
Banbury Reservoir
A112
Nelson Road
Chingford Road
Southend Road
Billet Road
B179
Lordship Lane
A109
A1010
Lansdowne Road
Shelbourne Road
Watermead Way
Lockwood Reservoir
River Lea or Lee
Blackhorse Lane
Higham Hill Road
Fulbourne Road
B160
Bruce Grove
Bruce Grove Station
Dowsett Road
Park View Road
TOTTENHAM
A10
Tottenham Hale Station
Ferry Lane
Forest Road
Philip Lane
B153
A503
Blackhorse Road Station
WALTHAMSTOW
Palmerston Road
Hoe Street
Church Hill
Prospect Hill
Shernhall Street
Seven Sisters Station
Broad Lane
High Road
Walthamstow Central Station
Walthamstow Queens Road Station
St James's Street Station
Blackhorse Road
South Tottenham Station
St Ann's Rd
B152
Stamford Hill Station
Warwick Reservoir
Queen's Road
Markhouse Road
Hoe Grove
A104
Boundary Road
Clapton Common
A107
A1006
Walthamstow Marshes
Dunsmure Road
Lea Bridge Road
Capworth Street
Leyton Midland Road Station
Argall Way
Manor Rd
B105
Stamford Hill
Cazenove Road
Church Road
B161
Stoke Newington Station
Upper Clapton Road
Orient Way
B104
Northwold Road
Clapton Station
Evering Road
B111
River Lea or Lee
LEYTON
Hackney Marsh
Matchroom Stadium
Rectory Road
Rectory Road Station
Kenninghall Road
Lower Clapton Road
Chatsworth Road
Millfields Road
Ruckholt Road
Stoke Newington Road
STOKE NEWINGTON
Hackney Downs
Lee Navigation
Temple Mills Lane
A12
A106 Eastway
Lee Valley Cycle Circuit
HACKNEY
Homerton Road
B112
Daubeney Road
Marsh Hill
0
1 km
1 mile

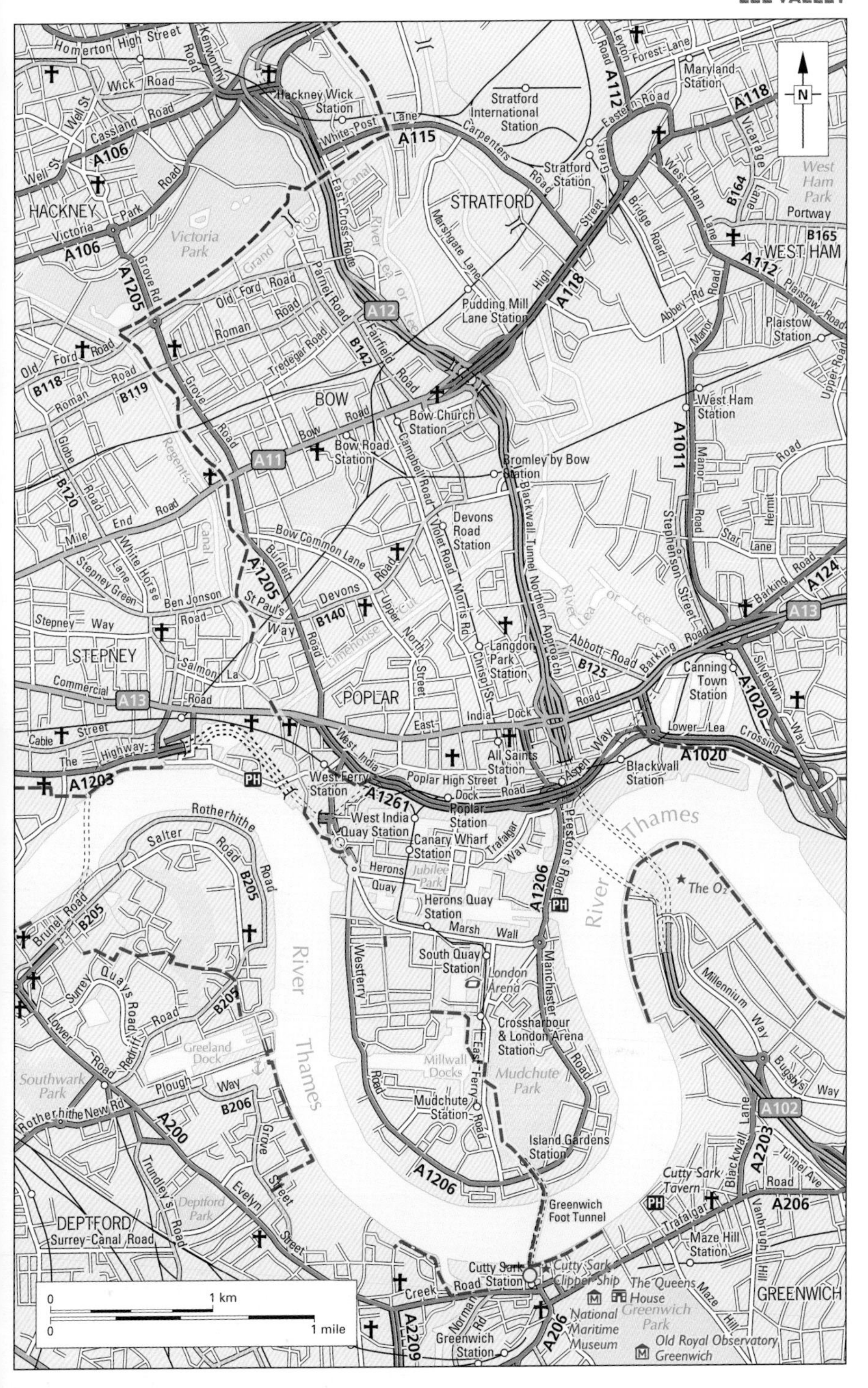
N
Homerton High Street
Wick Road
Hackney Wick Station
Kenworthy Road
White Post Lane
A115
Stratford International Station
Carpenters Road
Stratford Station
STRATFORD
Forest Lane
Leyton Road
A112
Maryland Station
Eastern Road
A118
Great Eastern Road
West Ham Park
Portway
B165
WEST HAM
Vicarage Lane
B164
West Ham Lane
Bridge Road
Well St
Cassland Road
A106
HACKNEY
Victoria Park Road
Victoria Park
Grand Union Canal
East Cross Route
River Lea or Lee
Marshgate Lane
High Street
A118
Pudding Mill Lane Station
A12
Abbey Rd
Manor Road
Plaistow Road
Plaistow Station
Upper Road
A1205
Grove Rd
Old Ford Road
Parnell Road
Roman Road
Tredegar Road
B142
Fairfield Road
Old Ford Road
B118
B119
Roman Road
Grove Road
BOW
Bow Road
Bow Church Station
Bow Road Station
Campbell Road
A11
Regent's Canal
Bromley by Bow Station
West Ham Station
A1011
Manor Road
Globe Road
B120
Mile End Road
White Horse Lane
Stepney Green
Bow Common Lane
Burdett Road
Devons Road Station
Violet Road
Blackwall Tunnel Northern Approach
Stephenson Street
Hermit Road
Star Lane
Barking Road
A124
A13
Ben Jonson Road
St Paul's Way
Devons Road
B140
Limehouse Cut
Upper North Street
Morris Rd
Langdon Park Station
Chrisp St
River Lea or Lee
Abbott Road
B125
Stepney Way
STEPNEY
Salmon La
Commercial Road
A13
POPLAR
East India Dock Road
Canning Town Station
A1020
Silvertown Way
Lower Lea Crossing
Cable Street
The Highway
A1203
PH
West India
All Saints Station
Poplar High Street
Aspen Way
Blackwall Station
A1020
West Ferry Station
A1261
Dock Road
Poplar Station
West India Quay Station
Canary Wharf Station
Trafalgar Way
River Thames
Rotherhithe Road
Salter Road
B205
Brunel Road
Herons Quay
Jubilee Park
Herons Quay Station
Marsh Wall
A1206
Preston's Road
PH
River
The O₂
Millennium Way
Westferry Road
South Quay Station
London Arena
Manchester Road
River Thames
Surrey Quays Road
B205
Lower Road
Redriff Road
Greeland Dock
Plough Way
Crossharbour & London Arena Station
Millwall Docks
Mudchute Park
East Ferry Road
Bugsby's Way
A102
Southwark Park
Rotherhithe New Rd
A200
B206
Grove Street
Mudchute Station
Island Gardens Station
A1206
Blackwall Lane
A2203
Tunnel Ave
Road
Trundley's Road
Deptford Park
Evelyn Street
Greenwich Foot Tunnel
Cutty Sark Tavern
PH
Trafalgar
A206
DEPTFORD
Surrey Canal Road
Maze Hill Station
Vanbrugh Hill
Cutty Sark Road Station
Cutty Sark Clipper Ship
The Queens House
Maze Hill
GREENWICH
0
1 km
0
1 mile
Creek Road
A2209
Norman Rd
Greenwich Station
A206
National Maritime Museum
Greenwich Park
Old Royal Observatory Greenwich

RAINHAM MARSHES

Rainham Marshes, closed to the public for over 100 years and used as a military firing range, was acquired by the RSPB in 2000, who set about transforming it into a reserve. Not only is it now an important place for nature, it is a great place to visit – expect to see breeding wading birds in spring and summer, and large flocks of wild ducks in winter. Birds of prey, water voles and dragonflies are not uncommon either.

With all the wildlife around the marshes, this is a flat and tranquil ride that can be done as a straight route finishing at the RSPB centre, or it can be easily extended by doubling back to the start in Rainham.

The famous Thames concrete barges can be found just off the shores of Rainham Marshes. During World War II, steel was in short supply and new barges were made of concrete. In 1953, these barges were used to bolster the flood defences that had been damaged by a huge storm and surge tide, causing the worst Thames floods in living memory. Today, the barges lie abandoned on the Rainham mud flats.

The cycle route linking the villages of Rainham and Purfleet runs beside the reserve, following the river, looping round and passing the concrete barges.

Rainham Marshes RSPB reserve

Female reed bunting

ROUTE INFORMATION

National Route: 13
Start: Rainham train station.
Finish: RSPB Environment Centre, Purfleet.
Distance: 5 miles (8km). Longer option, returning via the marshes 8.5 miles (13.5km).
Grade: Easy.
Surface: Tarmac cycle track.
Hills: None.

YOUNG & INEXPERIENCED CYCLISTS

Apart from the little bit of road to reach the stations at the start and finish, this is an excellent ride for young children and novices.

REFRESHMENTS

- Lots of choice in Rainham.
- Snacks and drinks at the RSPB Environment Centre, Purfleet.

THINGS TO SEE & DO

- Rainham Marshes RSPB Reserve: see a variety of interesting, sometimes rare, birds, mammals, reptiles and amphibians, as well as bugs and beasties of all kinds; nature trails and over 3 miles (5km) of nature boardwalks; one bird hide and several open viewing areas; shop, cafe, wildlife garden and children's adventure play area; open daily

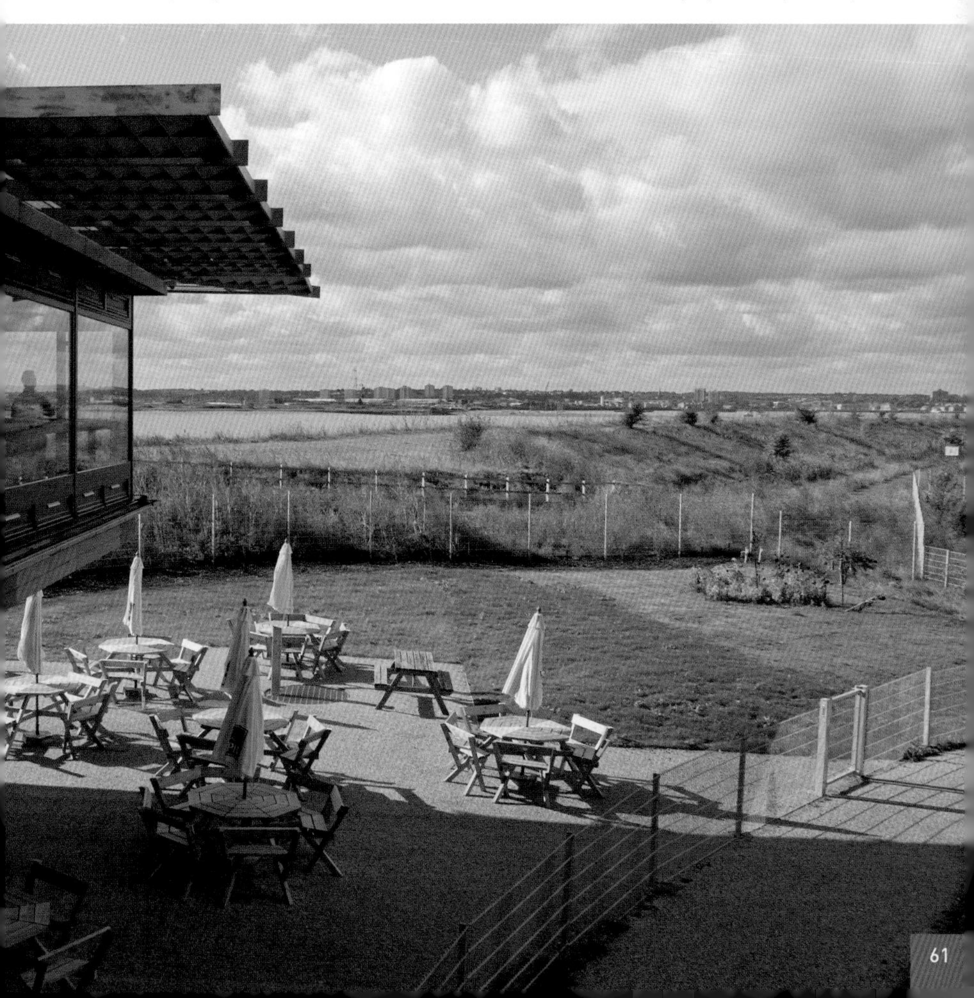

from 9.30am to 4.30pm; 01708 899840; www.rspb.org.uk

TRAIN STATIONS

Rainham; Purfleet.

BIKE HIRE

None locally.

FURTHER INFORMATION

- To view or print National Cycle Network routes, visit www.sustrans.org.uk
- Maps for this area are available to buy from www.sustransshop.co.uk
- **Transport for London (TfL):** contact for free map (no. 8); 020 7222 1234; www.tfl.gov.uk
- **London Tourist Information:** 0870 156 6366; www.visitlondon.com

ROUTE DESCRIPTION

From Rainham train station, head south, past the A13, on the 'London Loop' trail. Go left into Rainham Marshes, where a short, quiet road section leads you down to the banks of the Thames. The trail then follows the edge of the river, where the stone barges lie dormant on the Rainham mud banks. The trail bears left near the industrial buildings. After running

Concrete barges on the Thames shore

parallel with the road for a while, bear right to the outskirts of Purfleet, where you will find the Rainham RSPB visitor centre.

National Route 13 follows the Mar Dyke, back to the river's edge, and on to Purfleet and the train station. Alternatively, you could retrace your steps back to the junction near the industrial road, but bear right this time, to head back along Route 13, keeping beside the road, and through the middle of the Marshes.

You will soon come across the trail you originally entered the Marshes on, leading you back to the A13 crossing, and eventually back into Rainham.

NEARBY CYCLE ROUTES

National Route 1, on the other side of the Thames, heads back into London, along the river, to the *Cutty Sark* in Greenwich, where you have further choices.

The Ingrebourne Valley ride (see page 48) runs just north of Rainham. There is also the new Ingrebourne Hill Cycle Circuit, which offers waymarked cycle routes suitable for riders of all abilities.

RAINHAM MARSHES

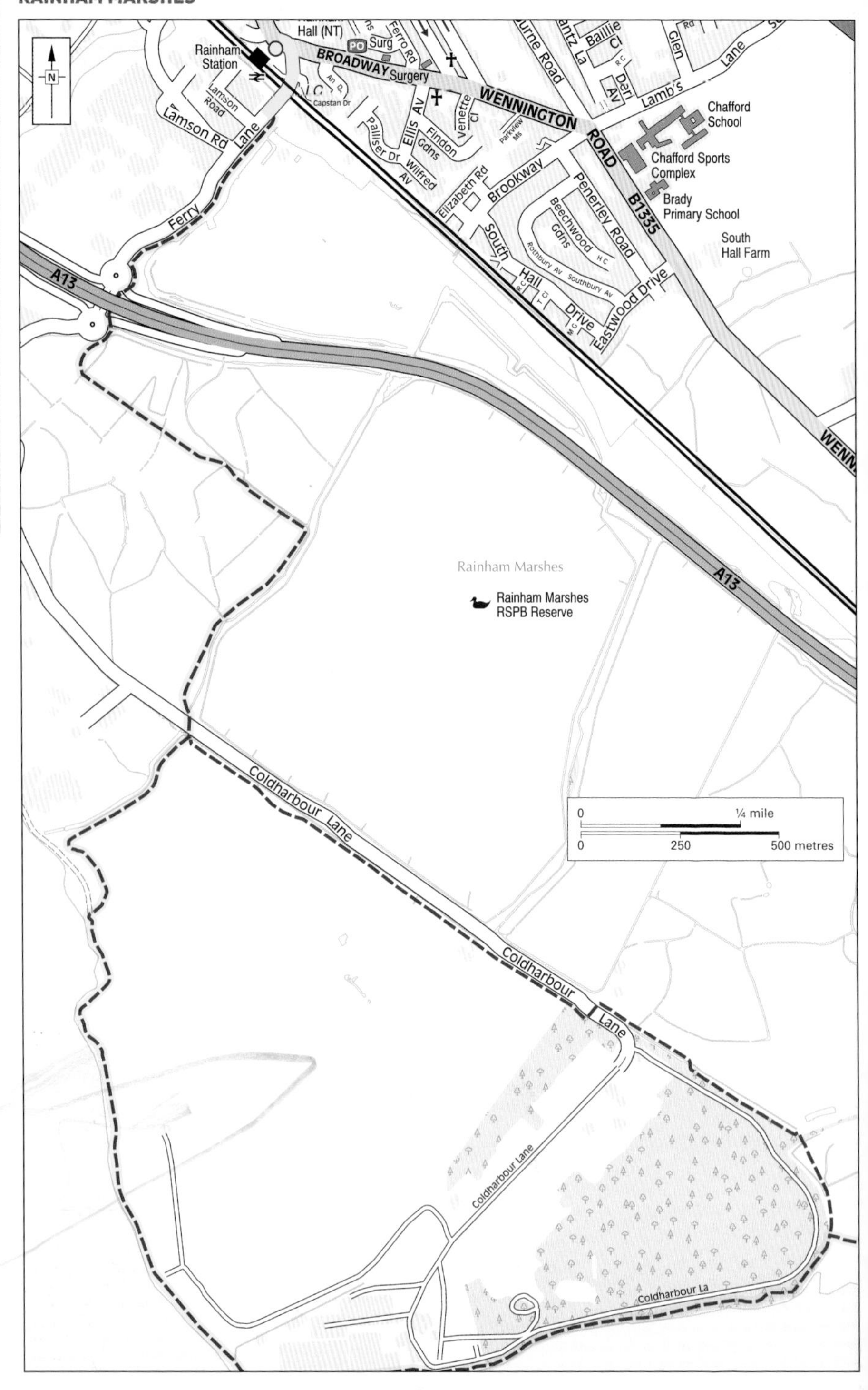

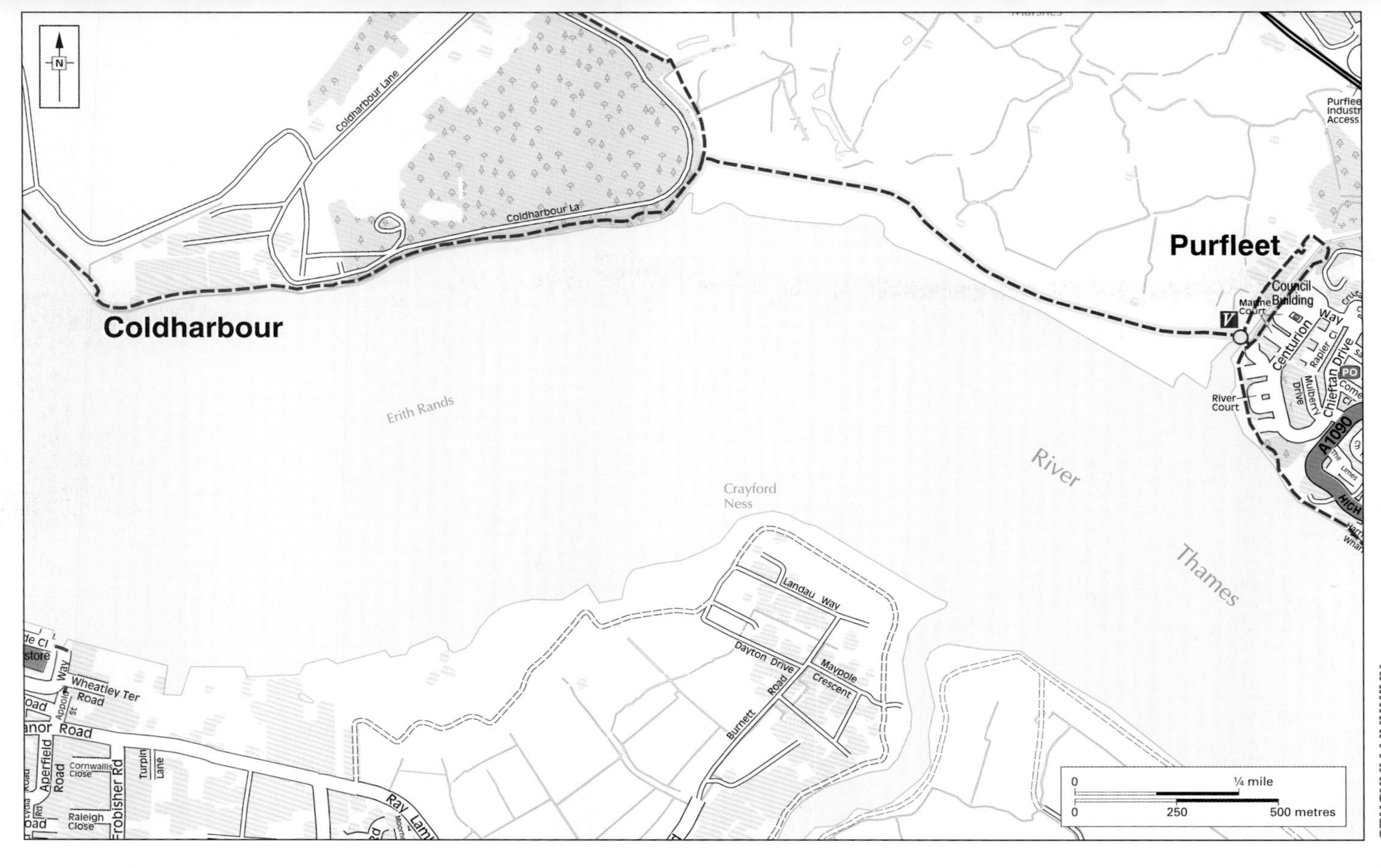
N
Coldharbour Lane
Coldharbour La
Coldharbour
Purfleet
Purfleet Industrial Access
Council Building
Marine Court
Centurion Way
Rapier Cl
Chieftan Drive
Mulberry Drive
PO
River Court
A1090
The Limes
HIGH
Erith Rands
Crayford Ness
River
Thames
Landau Way
Dayton Drive
Maypole Crescent
Burnett Road
Wheatley Ter Road
Way
Road
Aperfield Road
Cornwallis Close
Raleigh Close
Frobisher Rd
Turpin Lane
0
¼ mile
0
250
500 metres

ROYAL ALBERT DOCK TO VICTORIA PARK

The vast Royal Albert Dock was constructed east of the earlier Victoria Dock in 1880, when it was considered the finest dock system in the world, with over 3 miles (5km) of quay and dry docks, and machine shops. In the 1980s, this and all of the other royal docks were closed to commercial traffic. Today, it is used for water sports, such as rowing and windsurfing, but the main feature is London City Airport – its single runway strip covers the length of the southern side of the dock.

With views of Canary Wharf, this route starts by the impressive, modern University of East London campus on the Royal Albert Dock, and heads west along an easy-to-follow greenway to Victoria Park. This is probably one of the less well-known London parks, but it is a lovely place and a great finish to the ride.

University of East London

ROUTE INFORMATION

Start: University of East London, Royal Albert Dock.
Finish: Victoria Park, Hackney.
Distance: 6 miles (9.5km).
Grade: Easy.
Surface: Good tarmac tracks for most of the ride, with tarmac roads at the start and finish.
Hills: None.

YOUNG & INEXPERIENCED CYCLISTS

There are some sections of road at the start and end of the ride, but they aren't too busy. Most of the ride (along the greenway) is traffic-free and therefore great for children and beginners.

REFRESHMENTS

- There is nothing on the route itself, but there are plenty of options just off-route.

THINGS TO SEE & DO

- London City Airport, southern side of the Royal Albert Dock: in good view from the route for watching planes land and take off; www.londoncityairport.com
- Royal Albert Dock: now home to the Raging Dragons dragon boat racing club, which can be seen training on the water every Sunday between 10 and 11am; www.royaldockstrust.org.uk; www.ragingdragons.co.uk
- ExCel London, Royal Victoria Dock: world-class international exhibition and conference centre, over 100 acres, with four arenas; will host a number of events at the 2012 Olympic Games, such as boxing, weightlifting and table tennis; 020 7069 5000; www.excel-london.co.uk
- Newham City Farm, Stansfield Road, near the Royal Albert Dock: established in 1977, offering educational and leisure activities, with a wide collection of farm animals, including a number of rare breeds; 020 7474 4960; www.newham.gov.uk
- Victoria Park, Hackney: London's first public park, opened in 1845 with the aim to be east London's version of Hyde Park, complete with its own Speakers' Corner; contains a deer enclosure, lakes, fountain area, paddling pool, adventure playground and model boating lake.

TRAIN STATIONS

None.
Note that the DLR (Docklands Light Railway) only allows folding bicycles in carrying cases.

BIKE HIRE

- **Go Pedal!:** delivery to most areas of London; 07850 796320; www.gopedal.co.uk
- **City Bike Service, Shoreditch:** 020 7247 4151; www.citybikeservice.co.uk

FURTHER INFORMATION:

- To view or print National Cycle Network routes, visit www.sustrans.org.uk
- Maps for this area are available to buy from www.sustransshop.co.uk
- **Transport for London (TfL):** contact for free map (no. 7); 020 7222 1234; www.tfl.gov.uk
- **London Tourist Information:** 0870 156 6366; www.visitlondon.com

ROUTE DESCRIPTION

From the University of East London campus, head east on University Way, along National Route 13. After passing the pumping station, turn north to leave the docks behind you and take to the trails, cycling along good tracks between the houses and trees. After a short section alongside the A1020, take a left turn and head west on the elevated greenway.

Follow the greenway for a straight, easy-to-navigate journey. This 'green' trail goes on for an amazing 5 miles (8km) along well-surfaced, traffic-free, enjoyable tracks through London. At the end of the trail, at Wick Lane by the A12, shortly after crossing a bridge over the Hertford Union Canal, go under the A12 and over the bridge to Victoria Park.

NEARBY CYCLE ROUTES

National Route 13 runs along the northern edge of the Royal Victoria Docks, past the ExCel exhibition centre. At the end of the ride, in Victoria Park, Route 1 runs north and south. Heading north will take you along the Lea Valley route, past Hackney Marsh and onwards, to the numerous reservoirs. Going south will lead you back to the Thames, passing Canary Wharf, through The Isle of Dogs to the Greenwich Foot Tunnel (see page 54).

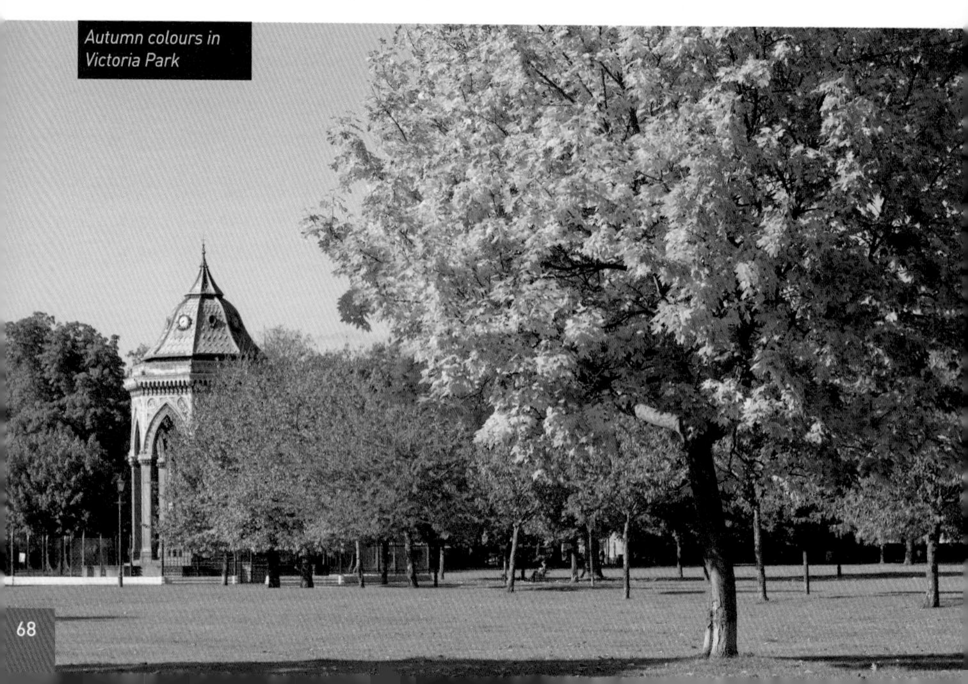

Autumn colours in Victoria Park

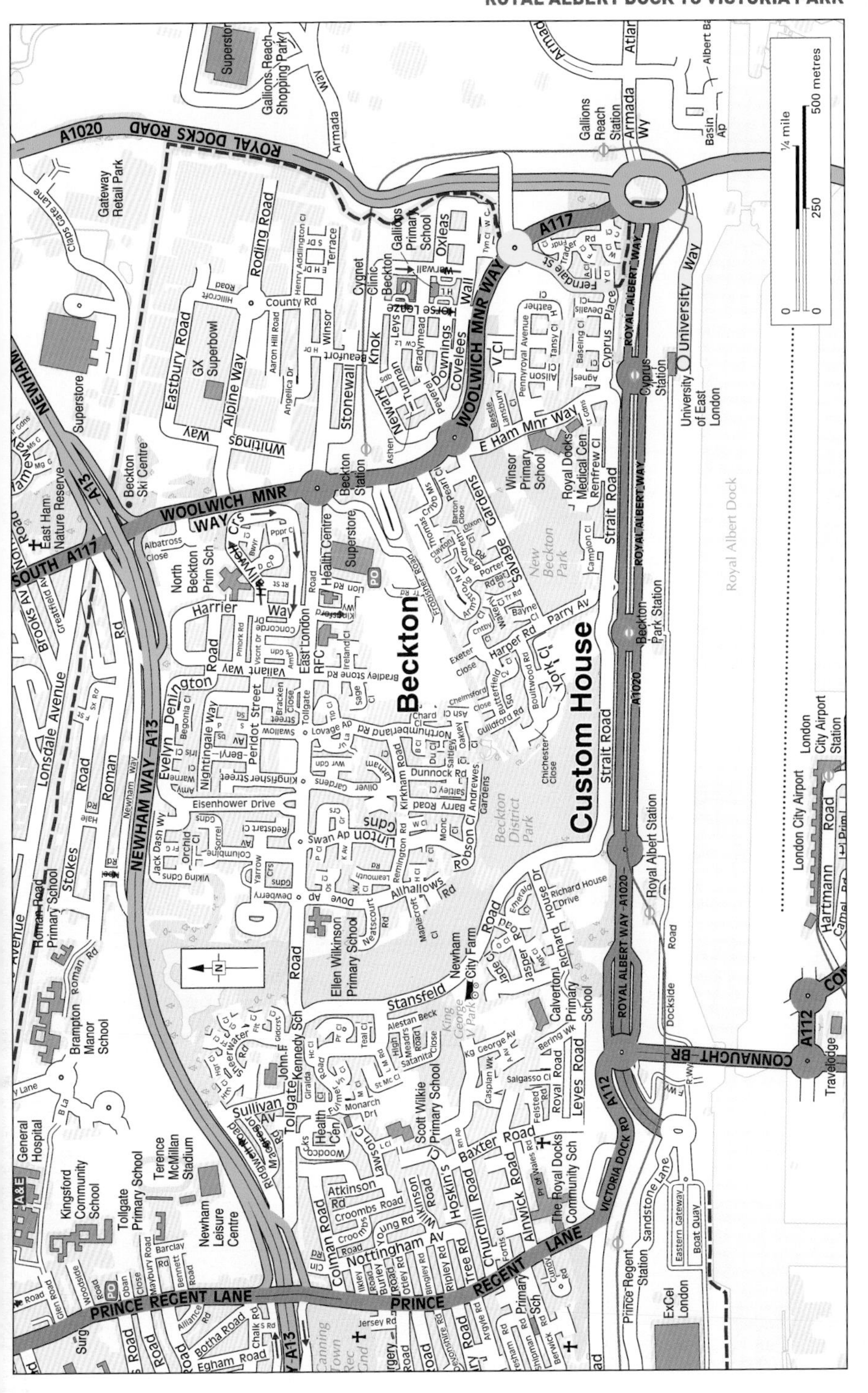

Beckton
Custom House
ROYAL DOCKS ROAD
A1020
WOOLWICH MNR WAY
A117
NEWHAM WAY A13
PRINCE REGENT LANE
VICTORIA DOCK RD
A112
CONNAUGHT BR
ROYAL ALBERT WAY
Royal Albert Dock
Gallions Reach Shopping Park
Gateway Retail Park
Beckton Station
Cyprus Station
Gallions Reach Station
Beckton Park Station
Royal Albert Station
Prince Regent Station
London City Airport
London City Airport Station
University of East London
ExCeL London
Beckton District Park
New Beckton Park
Newham City Farm
Beckton Ski Centre
East Ham Nature Reserve
Newham General Hospital
Newham Leisure Centre
Terence McMillan Stadium
Brampton Manor School
Kingsford Community School
Tollgate Primary School
Ellen Wilkinson Primary School
Scott Wilkie Primary School
The Royal Docks Community Sch
North Beckton Prim Sch
Winsor Primary School
Royal Docks Medical Cen
Travelodge
¼ mile
250
500 metres

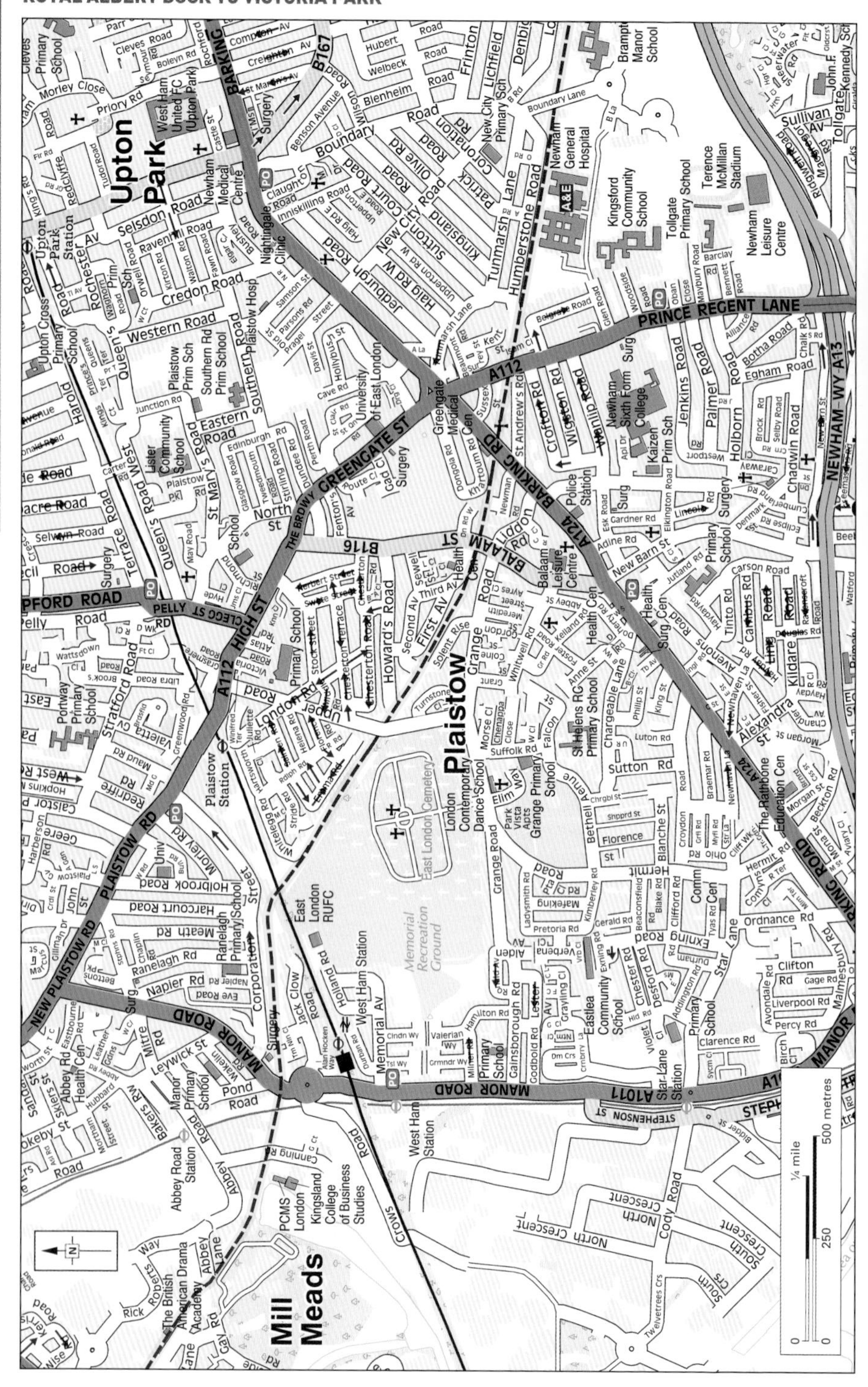
Upton Park
Plaistow
Mill Meads
West Ham United FC (Upton Park)
Newham General Hospital
East London Cemetery
Memorial Recreation Ground
East London RUFC
West Ham Station
Plaistow Station
Upton Park Station
Abbey Road Station
Star Lane Station
PRINCE REGENT LANE
BARKING RD
A124
A112
GREENGATE ST
PLAISTOW RD
NEW PLAISTOW RD
MANOR ROAD
A1011
STEPHENSON ST
BALAAM ST
B116
HIGH ST
NEWHAM WY A13
Boundary Road
Tunmarsh Lane
Humberstone Road
Grange Road
Howard's Road
Chargeable Lane
Alexandra St
Memorial Av
Holland Rd
Jack Clow Road
Corporation Street
Crows Road
Cody Road
North Crescent
South Crescent
Twelvetrees Crs
Newham Leisure Centre
Terence McMillan Stadium
Tollgate Primary School
Kingsford Community School
Newham Sixth Form College
Balaam Leisure Centre
Police Station
The Rathbone Education Cen
Kingsland College of Business Studies
PCMS London
The British American Drama Academy
London Contemporary Dance School
Grange Primary School
St Helens RC Primary School
Eastlea Community School
Star Lane Primary School
Ranelagh Primary School
Portway Primary School
Lister Community School
Greengate Medical Cen
University of East London
Nightingale Clinic
Plaistow Hosp
Newham Medical Centre
¼ mile
0
250
500 metres
N

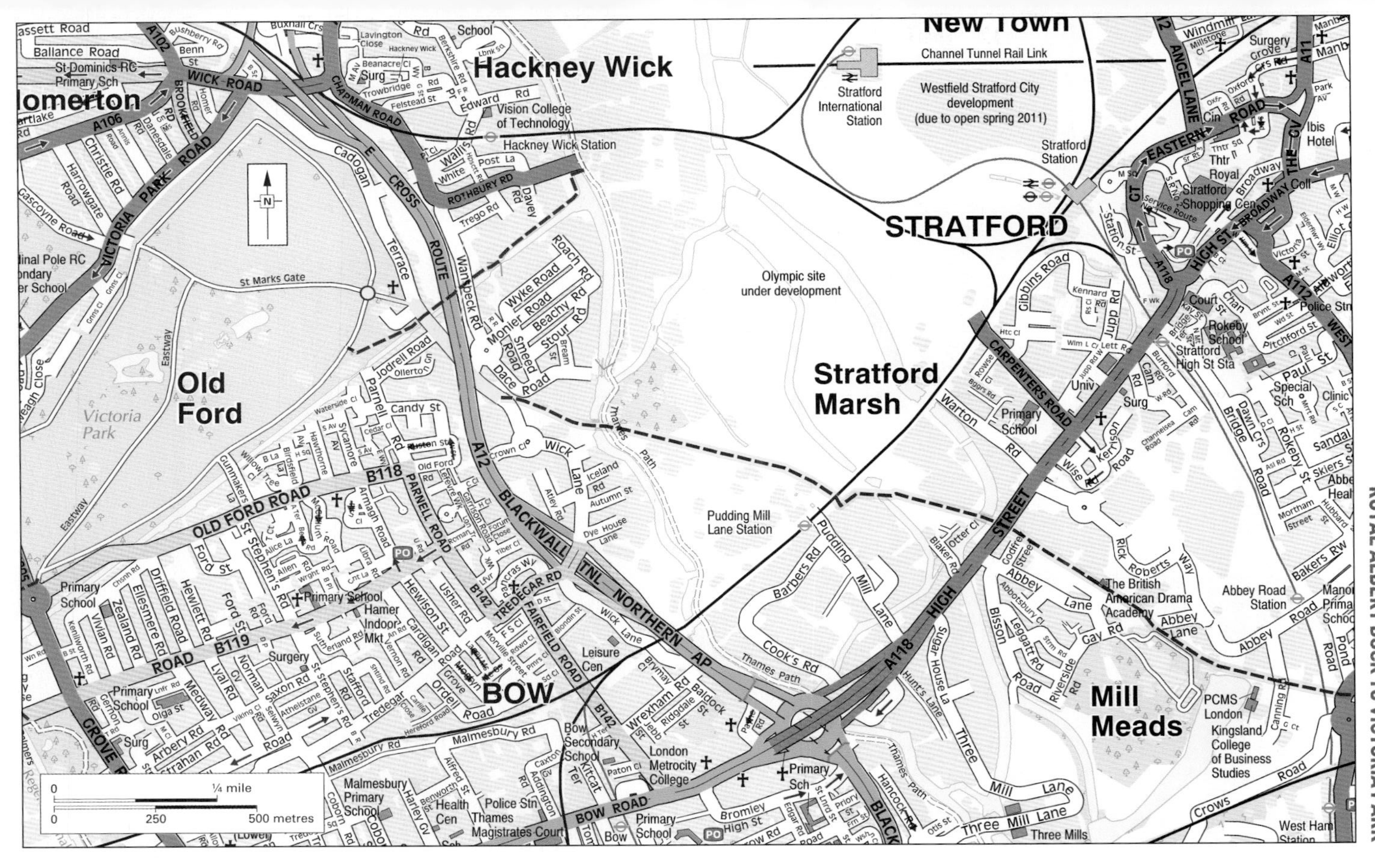

New Town
Channel Tunnel Rail Link
Stratford International Station
Westfield Stratford City development (due to open spring 2011)
Hackney Wick
Vision College of Technology
Hackney Wick Station
Homerton
Stratford Station
STRATFORD
Olympic site under development
Stratford Marsh
Old Ford
Victoria Park
St Marks Gate
Pudding Mill Lane Station
BOW
Mill Meads
The British American Drama Academy
Abbey Road Station
PCMS London Kingsland College of Business Studies
London Metrocity College
Bow Secondary School
Three Mills
West Ham Station
Stratford High St Sta
HIGH STREET
CARPENTERS ROAD
BLACKWALL TNL NORTHERN AP
EAST CROSS ROUTE
OLD FORD ROAD
PARNELL ROAD
BOW ROAD
VICTORIA PARK ROAD
WICK ROAD
ANGEL LANE
Thames Magistrates Court
¼ mile
0
250
500 metres

RODING VALLEY WAY

In 2000, the Redbridge branch of the London Cycling Campaign (and other local LCC groups) suggested a route linking the Thames National Cycle Route with the Essex countryside, following the course of the River Roding. The idea was accepted by local councils and, to date, several sections of the route, including this one from Woodford Wells to Ilford, have been completed. Just short of 6 miles (9.5km), this ride is good for commuters yet passes through pleasant countryside and quiet sections. Starting at Roding Valley tube station, the route runs alongside the M11 for a way before joining a long and peaceful section following the River Roding. From here, a short section of the route runs alongside the A406 on the way to Wanstead Park, just close to the end of the ride at Ilford. Although cycling is prohibited in much of Wanstead Park, it is a pleasant place to stop and watch the wildlife. The park, opened to the public in 1882, has been a royal court, a centre of England's government, and home to the world's largest telescope (of its time).

The Temple at Wanstead Park

ROUTE INFORMATION

Start: Roding Valley tube station.
Finish: Romford Road, Ilford.
Distance: 6 miles (9.5km).
Grade: Easy.
Surface: Mostly good cycle tracks, with some sections of road and rougher terrain.
Hills: None – the ride is slightly downhill.

YOUNG & INEXPERIENCED CYCLISTS

There are some busy road crossings and sections along roads.

REFRESHMENTS

- Refreshment kiosk in Wanstead Park, by the Wanstead Park Avenue/Northumberland Avenue entrance, off the route.

THINGS TO SEE & DO

- Queen Elizabeth's Hunting Lodge, Chingford: built for Henry VIII in 1543 as a grandstand for guests to view or participate in the hunt by shooting their crossbows from the high vantage point; display of Tudor foods and (replica) kitchenware, Tudor carpentry and costume; great views from the upper floors; 020 8529 6681 (during opening hours); 020 8529 7090 (outside opening hours); www.cityoflondon.gov.uk
- Wanstead Park: ideal for relaxing, although cycling is not permitted throughout; www.wansteadpark.org.uk

TRAIN STATIONS

Ilford. Roding Valley tube station (note that bicycles are allowed only as far as Leyton heading into London).

BIKE HIRE

- Redbridge Cycling Centre, Redbridge: 020 8500 9359; www.hoghill.co.uk
- Tri and Run, Chigwell: 020 8500 4841; www.triandrun.com

Queen Elizabeth's Hunting Lodge

FURTHER INFORMATION

- To view or print National Cycle Network routes, visit www.sustrans.org.uk
- Maps for this area are available to buy from www.sustransshop.co.uk
- Transport for London (TfL): contact for free map (no. 5); 020 7222 1234; www.tfl.gov.uk
- London Tourist Information: 0870 156 6366; www.visitlondon.com

ROUTE DESCRIPTION

From Roding Valley tube station, go right on Cherry Tree Ride, following the roads leading to the sports ground. Cut across the sports ground to a footbridge over the River Roding, to the M11. The route heads south, alongside the M11, crossing underneath it at the A113,

continued on page 76

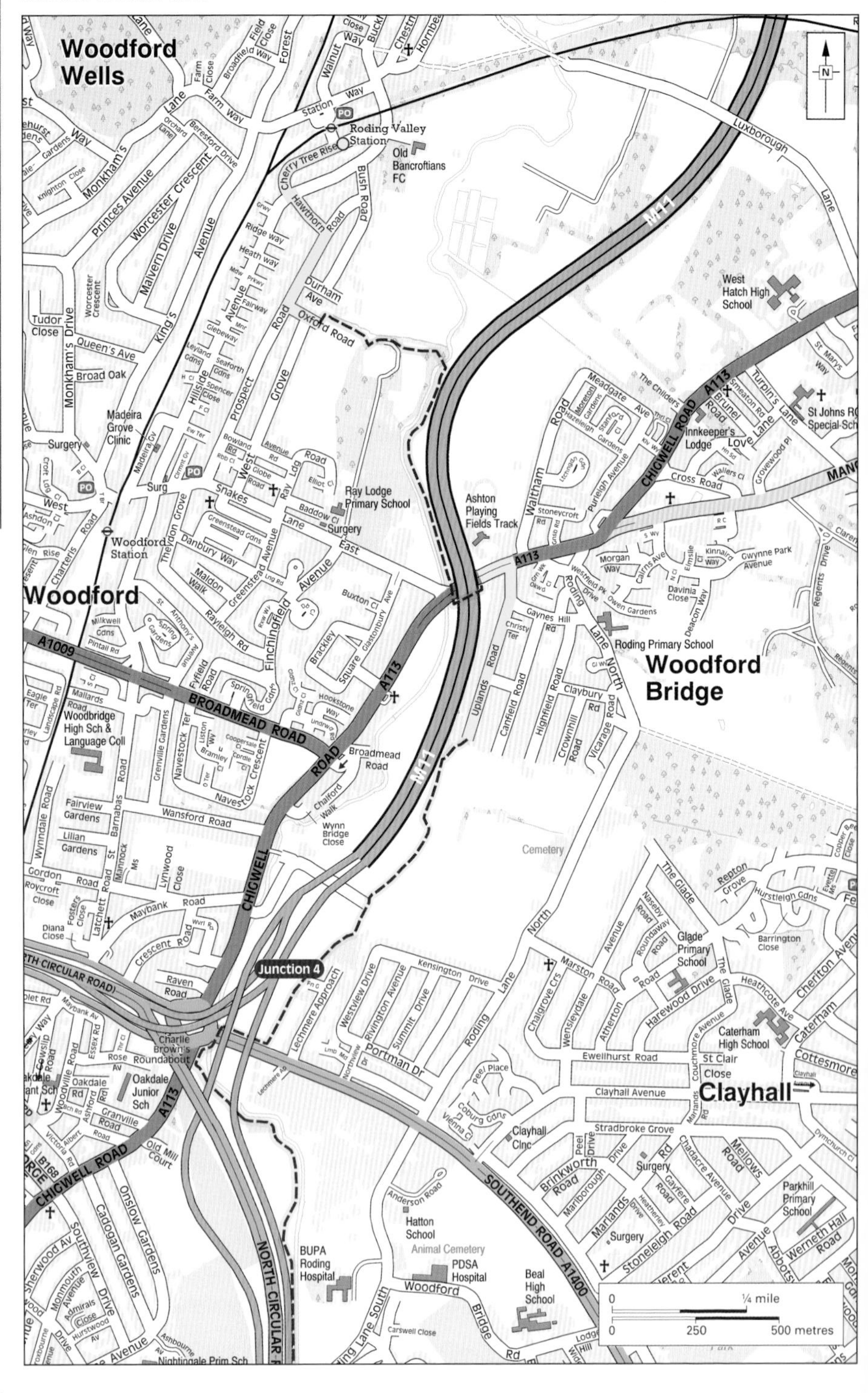
Woodford Wells
Woodford
Woodford Bridge
Clayhall
Roding Valley Station
Woodford Station
Old Bancroftians FC
West Hatch High School
St Johns RC Special Sch
Innkeeper's Lodge
Ashton Playing Fields Track
Ray Lodge Primary School
Madeira Grove Clinic
Surgery
Roding Primary School
Woodbridge High Sch & Language Coll
Cemetery
Glade Primary School
Caterham High School
Junction 4
Charlie Brown's Roundabout
Oakdale Junior Sch
Clayhall Clnc
Parkhill Primary School
BUPA Roding Hospital
Hatton School
Animal Cemetery
PDSA Hospital
Beal High School
Nightingale Prim Sch
M11
A113
A1009
BROADMEAD ROAD
CHIGWELL ROAD
NORTH CIRCULAR ROAD
SOUTHEND ROAD A1400
Luxborough Lane
Roding Lane North
Roding Lane South
Woodford Bridge Rd
Broadmead Road
Oxford Road
Hawthorn Road
Bush Road
Cherry Tree Rise
Station Way
Prospect Avenue
Grove Road
Snakes Lane East
Finchingfield Avenue
Greenstead Avenue
Rayleigh Rd
Danbury Way
Maldon Walk
Theydon Grove
Monkham's Drive
Monkham's Lane
Princes Avenue
Worcester Crescent
Malvern Drive
King's Avenue
Queen's Ave
Broad Oak
Tudor Close
Wansford Road
Fairview Gardens
Lilian Gardens
Gordon Road
Roycroft Close
Maybank Road
Crescent Road
Raven Road
Uplands Road
Canfield Road
Highfield Road
Crownhill Road
Vicarage Road
Claybury Rd
Gaynes Hill Rd
Waltham Road
Purleigh Avenue
Meadgate Ave
Cross Road
Love Lane
Turpin's Lane
Morgan Way
Cairns Ave
Davinia Close
Deacon Way
Gwynne Park Avenue
Kensington Drive
Rivington Avenue
Summit Drive
Westview Drive
Lechmere Approach
Portman Dr
Ewellhurst Road
Clayhall Avenue
Stradbroke Grove
Brinkworth Road
Marlborough Road
Marlands Road
Stoneleigh Road
Mellows Road
Chadacre Avenue
Gayfere Road
Harewood Drive
Heathcote Ave
The Glade
Repton Grove
Barrington Close
Cheriton Ave
Cottesmore
St Clair Close
Peel Place
Coburg Gdns
Anderson Road
Carswell Close
Onslow Gardens
Cadogan Gardens
Granville Road
Oakdale Rd
Rose Av
Old Mill Court
0 ¼ mile
0 250 500 metres

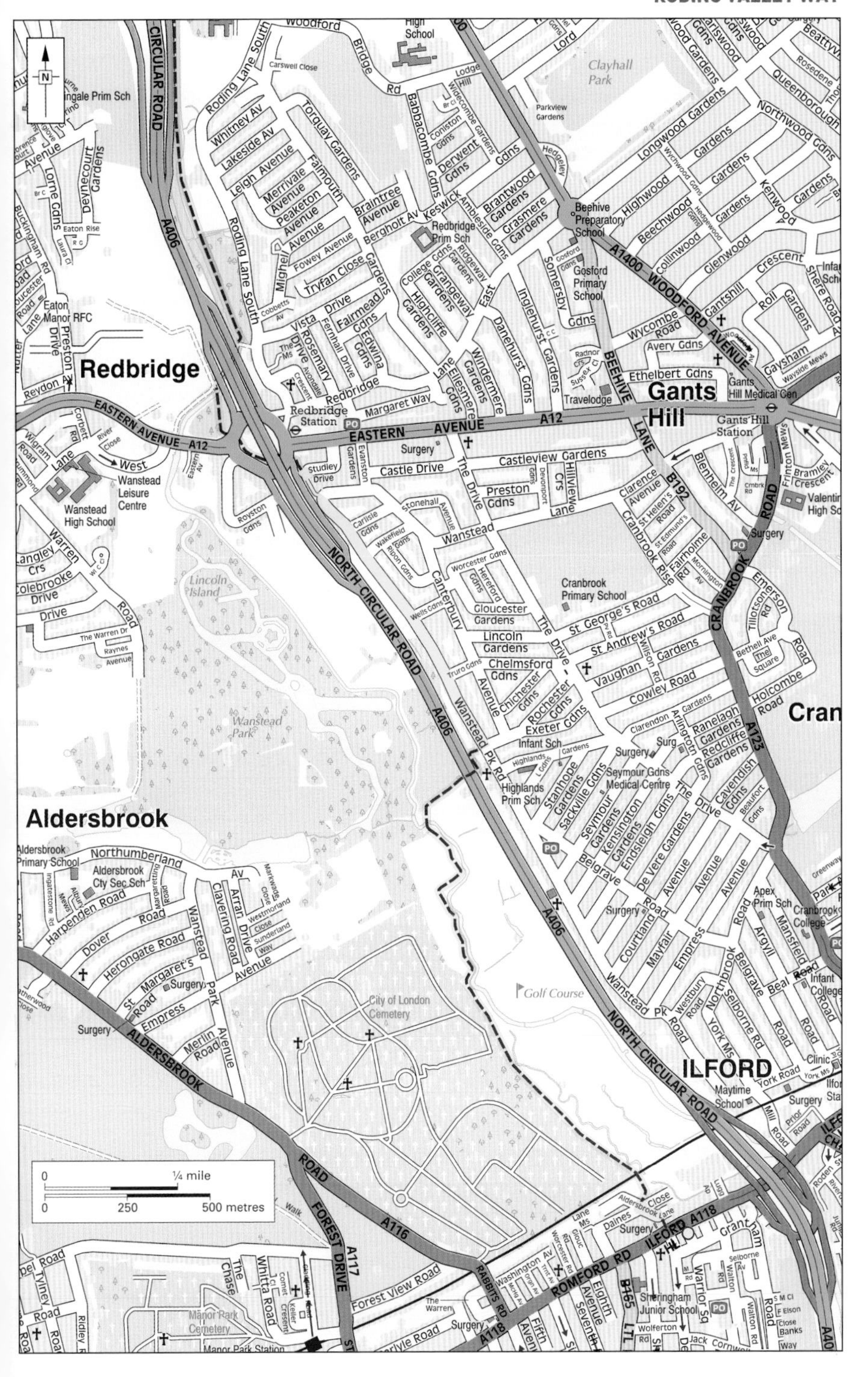
N
Redbridge
Gants Hill
Aldersbrook
ILFORD
Cran
CIRCULAR ROAD
A406
NORTH CIRCULAR ROAD
EASTERN AVENUE A12
EASTERN AVENUE
A12
A1400 WOODFORD AVENUE
BEEHIVE LANE
B192
CRANBROOK ROAD
A123
ALDERSBROOK ROAD
FOREST DRIVE
A117
A116
ROMFORD RD
A118
ILFORD A118
RABBITS RD
B165
Clayhall Park
High School
Woodford Bridge Rd
Lodge Hill
Lord
Parkview Gardens
Roding Lane South
Carswell Close
Whitney Av
Lakeside Av
Leigh Avenue
Torquay Gardens
Babbacombe Gdns
Coniston Gdns
Derwent Gdns
Merrivale Avenue
Peaketon Avenue
Falmouth
Braintree Avenue
Berghoit Av
Keswick
Redbridge Prim Sch
Ambleside Gdns
Brantwood Gardens
Grasmere Gardens
Fowey Avenue
Tryfan Close
Mighell Avenue
Cobbetts Av
Vista Drive
Fairmead Gdns
Rosemary Drive
Edwina Gdns
Crangeway Gardens
Highcliffe Gardens
Ridgeway Gardens
College Gdns
Danehurst Gdns
Windermere Gardens
Ellesmere Gdns
Inglehurst Gardens
Somersby Gdns
Gosford Primary School
Beehive Preparatory School
Highwood
Beechwood
Collinwood
Glenwood
Longwood Gardens
Northwood Gdns
Queenborough
Crescent
Wycombe Road
Gantshill
Avery Gdns
Ethelbert Gdns
Gaysham
Roll Gardens
Shere Road
Gants Hill Medical Cen
Gants Hill Station
Travelodge
Redbridge Station
Margaret Way
Redbridge
Surgery
Castleview Gardens
Castle Drive
Studley Drive
Evanston Gardens
The Drive
Preston Gdns
Hillview Crs
Clarence Avenue
Blenheim Av
Frinton Mews
Bramley Crescent
Valentines High Sch
Eaton Manor RFC
Preston Drive
Reydon Av
Corbett Rd
River Close
Wigram Road
West
Wanstead Leisure Centre
Wanstead High School
Warren Road
Langley Crs
Colebrooke Drive
The Warren Dr
Raynes Avenue
Royston Gdns
Eastern Av
Wanstead
Stonehall Avenue
Carlisle Gdns
Wakefield Gdns
Ripon Gdns
Canterbury Avenue
Worcester Gdns
Hereford Gdns
Gloucester Gardens
Lincoln Gardens
Chelmsford Gdns
Chichester Gdns
Rochester Gdns
Exeter Gdns
Infant Sch
Cranbrook Primary School
St George's Road
St Andrew's Road
Vaughan Gardens
Cowley Road
Fairholme Rd
Cranbrook Rise
Emerson Rd
Tillotson Rd
Bethell Ave
The Square
Holcombe Road
Lincoln Island
Wanstead Park
Wanstead Pk Rd
Highlands Prim Sch
Stanhope Gardens
Sackville Gdns
Seymour Gardens
Seymour Gdns Medical Centre
Kensington Gardens
Endsleigh Gdns
Ranelagh Gardens
Redcliffe Gardens
Cavendish Gdns
Belgrave Road
De Vere Gardens
Courtland Avenue
Mayfair Avenue
Empress Avenue
Apex Prim Sch
Cranbrook College
Argyll Road
Mansfield Road
Northbrook Road
Selborne Rd
York Ms
Westbury Road
Beal Road
Infant College
Clinic
York Road
Maytime School
Mill Road
Prior Road
Golf Course
Wanstead Pk Road
Aldersbrook Primary School
Northumberland Av
Aldersbrook Cty Sec Sch
Harpenden Road
Dover Road
Herongate Road
Clavering Road
Arran Drive
Westmorland Close
Sunderland Way
Wanstead Park Avenue
St Margaret's Road
Empress Avenue
Merlin Road
City of London Cemetery
Aldersbrook Lane
Daines Close
Forest View Road
The Chase
Whitta Road
Keller Crescent
Manor Park Cemetery
Manor Park Station
The Warren
Washington Av
Sheringham Junior School
Warrior Sq
Wolferton Rd
Jack Cornwell
Grantham
Walton Rd
Banks Way
0
¼ mile
250
500 metres

Wanstead Park is a haven for wildlife

to continue along the opposite side of the motorway, cycling down a residential street before exiting into the countryside, still following close to the motorway.

You need to walk the section along the southern side of Charlie Brown's Roundabout in Woodford, but soon there is a good track on the left, running alongside the A406 and then alongside the River Roding, giving a long, traffic-free section. After navigating your way around the footpaths at Redbridge roundabout and a section along Wanstead Park Road, beside the A406, you cross over the A406 via a bridge, to Wanstead Park. Running parallel to the City of London Cemetery, the track passes under the railway, to Romford Road (A118) in Ilford and the end of the route.

NEARBY CYCLE ROUTES

National Route 1, heading south, goes into London along the Lee Valley (see page 54).

The Redbridge Cycling Centre in Hainault has 1.2 miles (2km) of road and 1.8 miles (3km) of off-road cycle tracks, ideal for adults and children wanting to develop their skills. There's also a good pump track. Visit www.vision-rcl.org.uk/redbridge_cycle_centre for more information.

Nearby Epping Forest offers a good choice of riding, from wide, well-surfaced forest tracks suitable for families (but be careful of the few road crossings along the way), to challenging off-road riding for mountain bikers.

WIMBLEDON TO SUTTON

This route starts at Wimbledon town centre and heads down quiet roads to Bushy Mead and Joseph Hood Recreation Ground. From here, the ride goes southeast, passing through Morden Park and finishing in Sutton town centre.

Although not part of the ride, Wimbledon Common – famous for its Wombles – is worth a visit, as it contains various recreational areas, woodland, scrubland, heathland, numerous ponds, bridal paths and two golf courses. Note that it is also possible to cycle to Richmond Park from Wimbledon Common, crossing the busy A3 via a new bridge.

ROUTE INFORMATION

National Route: Not part of the National Route Network but can be linked up with National Route 20 (The Wandle Trail).
Start: Wimbledon train station.
Finish: Sutton High Street.
Distance: 6 miles (9.5km).
Grade: Easy.
Surface: Tarmac roads and pathways.
Hills: None, apart from a small climb at the end.

YOUNG & INEXPERIENCED CYCLISTS

Due to the sections of road along this route, it is not very suitable for young children. A better option would be to stay on Wimbledon Common or go to Richmond Park (see Tamsin Trail, on page 82).

REFRESHMENTS

- Lots of choice in Wimbledon town centre and village.
- Windmill Tea Rooms, Wimbledon Common.
- The Crooked Billet pub, Wimbledon Common.
- Cafe at Rosehill Recreation Ground, near Sutton.
- Lots of choice in Sutton.

THINGS TO SEE & DO

- **Wimbledon Lawn Tennis Museum, Church Road, Wimbledon:** displays of trophies,

Rushmere Pond on Wimbledon Common

The famous tennis courts at Wimbledon

champions' kits and other memorabilia; cinema screen; 'walk-through' of a re-creation of the men's dressing room in the 1980s with a ghost-like image of John McEnroe; 020 8946 6131; www.wimbledon.org

- Wimbledon Windmill, Wimbledon Common: built in 1817; has a museum attached, depicting the history of windmills and milling using working models, machinery and tools; children can also do some milling themselves; 020 8947 2825; www.wimbledonwindmillmuseum.org.uk
- Cannizaro Park, Wimbledon Common: beautiful parkland with rare trees and magnificent plants, open to the public; Cannizaro House is now a hotel; www.cannizaropark.org.uk

TRAIN STATIONS

Wimbledon; Wimbledon Chase; Morden South; Sutton Common; Sutton.

Wimbledon Windmill Museum

BIKE HIRE

- **Smith Brothers, Wimbledon:** 020 8946 2270
- **Tri and Run, Wimbledon:** 020 8500 4841; www.triandrun.com

FURTHER INFORMATION

- To view or print National Cycle Network routes, visit www.sustrans.org.uk
- Maps for this area are available to buy from www.sustransshop.co.uk
- **Transport for London (TfL):** contact for free maps (nos. 10 and 12); 020 7222 1234; www.tfl.gov.uk
- **London Tourist Information:** 0870 156 6366; www.visitlondon.com
- **Wimbledon & Putney Commons:** 020 8788 7655; www.wpcc.org.uk

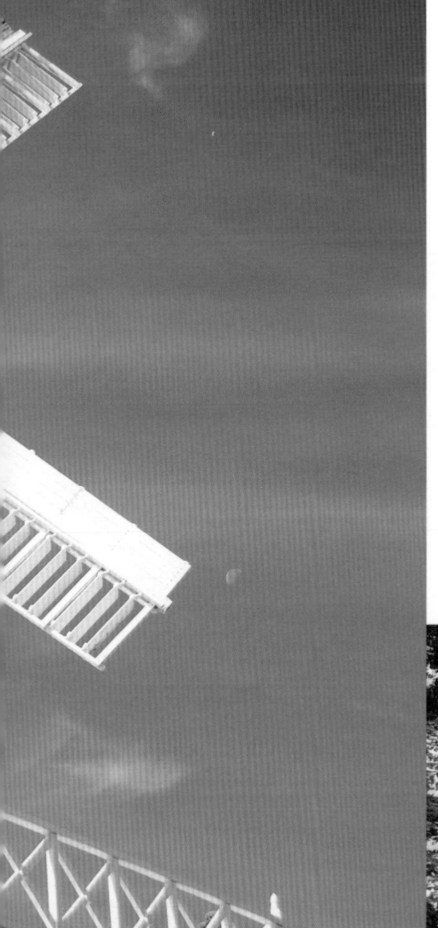

ROUTE DESCRIPTION

From Wimbledon train station, head south along quiet roads and a short traffic-free section, past Wimbledon Chase to Cannon Hill Common in Bushy Mead. Turn left at the playground, then bear right by the paddling pools, into the trees, then left, alongside a lake. Cross the road to join Cherrywood Lane and follow the quiet roads to attractive Morden Park, which makes a good stopping point and is where you join a traffic-free path. Push on, past various recreational grounds, to Rosehill. Cross the recreation ground, then join some quiet roads, heading south, to arrive at Sutton town centre and the end of the ride.

NEARBY CYCLE ROUTES

National Route 4 passes through Richmond Park, heading south to Weybridge and on to Windsor Great Park. Eastwards, Route 4 goes into central London and beyond, passing the London Eye en route. The Tamsin Trail is a 7-mile (11-km) circular route in Richmond Park (see page 82).

Wimbledon Common has many permitted cycle paths (blue 'Cycle Route' signs are fixed to posts along the paths). A map of these is displayed at various points on the common, and copies are available from the Ranger's Office (020 8788 7655).

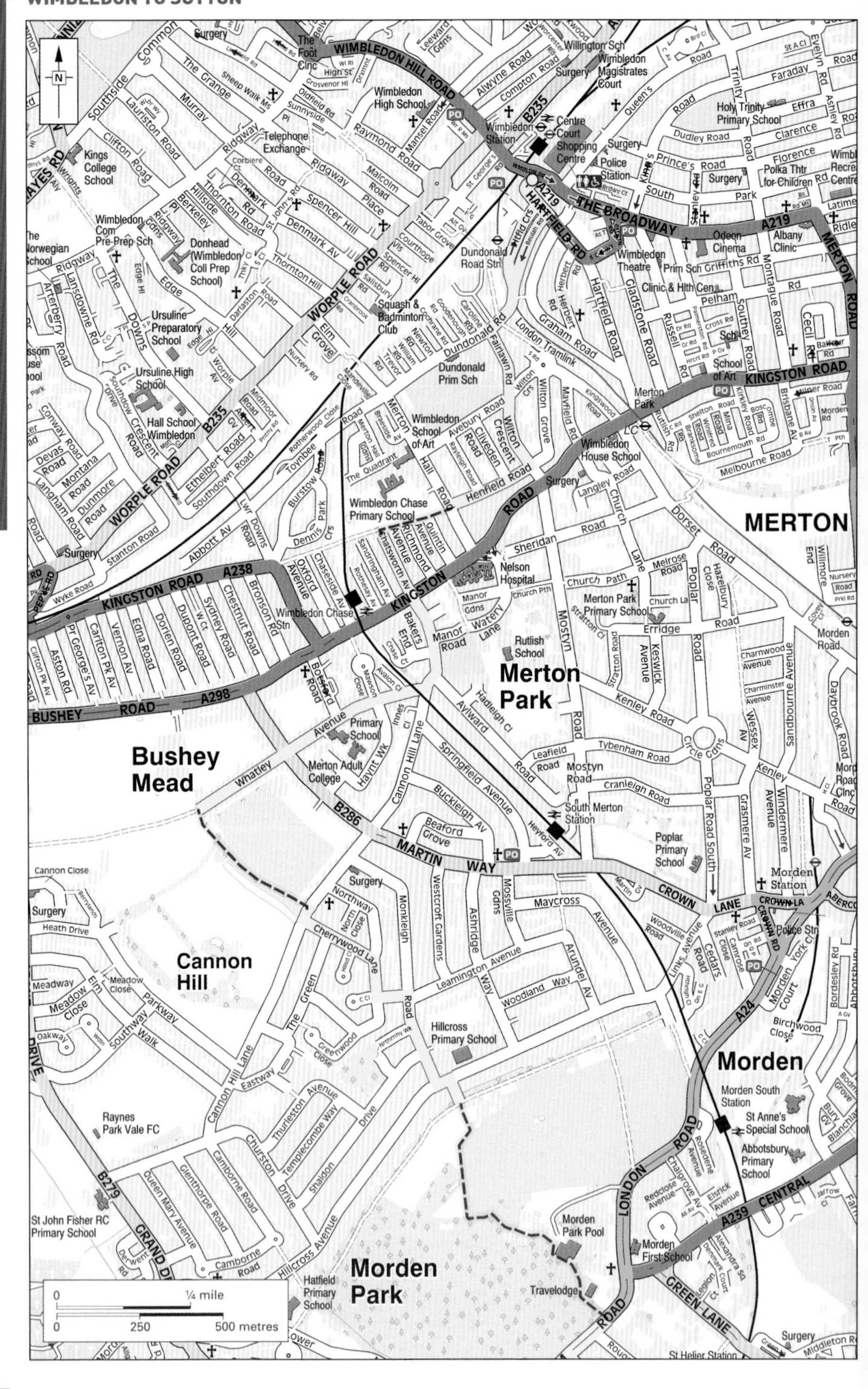
N
WIMBLEDON HILL ROAD
Surgery
The Foot Clinc
High St
Wimbledon High School
Willington Sch
Wimbledon Magistrates Court
Centre Court Shopping Centre
Wimbledon Station
B235
Telephone Exchange
Kings College School
Southside Common
The Grange
Murray
Lauriston Road
Clifton Road
Ridgway
Thornton Road
Spencer Hill
Denmark Av
Raymond Road
Malcolm Road
Alwyne Road
Compton Road
Queen's Road
Police Station
Surgery
Prince's Road
THE BROADWAY
A219
HARTFIELD RD
Wimbledon Theatre
Odeon Cinema
Albany Clinic
Holy Trinity Primary School
Faraday Rd
Dudley Road
Clarence Road
Florence Road
Polka Thtr for Children
MERTON ROAD
Wimbledon Com Pre-Prep Sch
The Norwegian School
Donhead (Wimbledon Coll Prep School)
Ursuline Preparatory School
Ursuline High School
Hall School Wimbledon
WORPLE ROAD
Squash & Badminton Club
Dundonald Road Stn
Dundonald Prim Sch
London Tramlink
Graham Road
Hartfield Road
Gladstone Road
Prim Sch
Clinic & Hlth Cen
Griffiths Rd
Pelham
Russell Rd
Southey Rd
Montague Road
Sch
School of Art
KINGSTON ROAD
Merton Park
Wimbledon School of Art
Wimbledon House School
Wilton Crescent
Wilton Grove
Mayfield Rd
Melbourne Road
Bournemouth Rd
MERTON
Wimbledon Chase Primary School
Henfield Road
Surgery
Nelson Hospital
Sheridan Road
Church Lane
Dorset Road
Kingston Road
A238
Wimbledon Chase Stn
Merton Park Primary School
Erridge Road
Rutlish School
Merton Park
Mostyn Road
Kenley Road
Poplar Road
Morden Road
BUSHEY ROAD
A298
Bushey Mead
Primary School
Merton Adult College
Whatley Avenue
Cannon Hill Lane
Springfield Avenue
Tybenham Road
Cranleigh Road
South Merton Station
Poplar Primary School
B286
MARTIN WAY
CROWN LANE
Morden Station
Police Stn
Cannon Close
Surgery
Heath Drive
Cannon Hill
Meadway
Parkway
Southway Walk
Northway
Cherrywood Lane
Westcroft Gardens
Ashridge Way
Maycross Avenue
Leamington Avenue
Woodland Way
Arundel Av
Hillcross Primary School
Morden
A24
Morden South Station
St Anne's Special School
Abbotsbury Primary School
Raynes Park Vale FC
B279
GRAND DRIVE
St John Fisher RC Primary School
Queen Mary Avenue
Camborne Road
Churston Drive
Templecombe Way
Hillcross Avenue
Hatfield Primary School
Morden Park
Morden Park Pool
Travelodge
LONDON ROAD
A239 CENTRAL
Morden First School
GREEN LANE
Surgery
St Helier Station
0 ¼ mile
0 250 500 metres

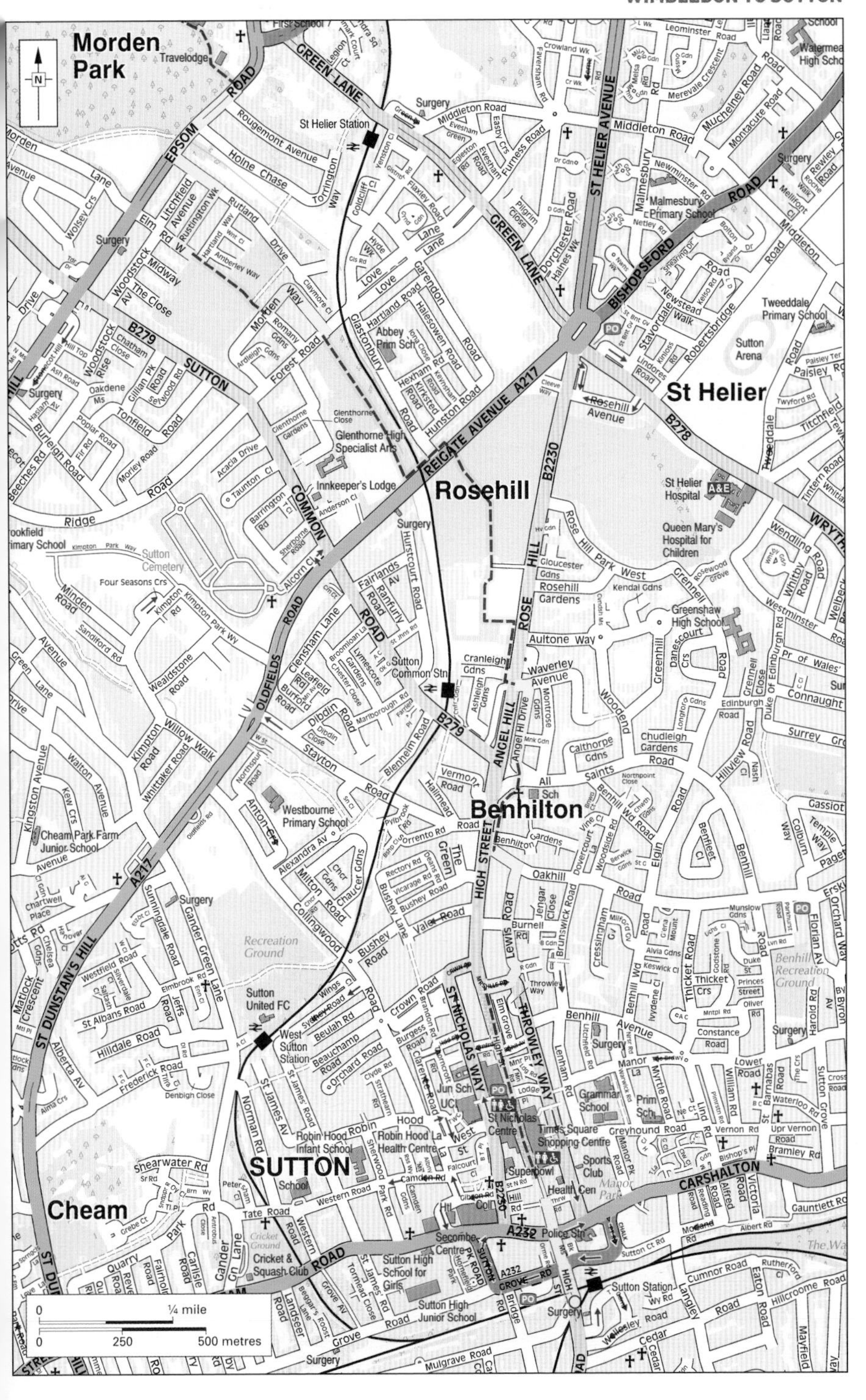

Morden Park
St Helier
Rosehill
Benhilton
SUTTON
Cheam
St Helier Station
Sutton Common Stn
West Sutton Station
Sutton Station
St Helier Hospital
Queen Mary's Hospital for Children
Sutton United FC
Recreation Ground
Sutton Cemetery
St Nicholas Centre
Times Square Shopping Centre
0 ¼ mile
0 250 500 metres

TAMSIN TRAIL – RICHMOND PARK

Created through the generosity of an anonymous donor and named after his daughter, the Tamsin Trail is a beautiful 7-mile (11-km) circular route through London's largest royal park, which covers an impressive 2,500 acres and boasts amazing views of the city.

Richmond Park has been designated a Site of Special Scientific Interest (SSSI) and a National Nature Reserve (NNR). There is much wildlife to see, including large populations of red and fallow deer, introduced to the park by Charles I in the 1630s.

ROUTE INFORMATION

National Route: Links with National Route 4, running through the centre of Richmond Park.
Start and Finish: As the route is circular, the ride can be started at any point.
Distance: 7.5 miles (12km). Shorter option 5 miles (8km).
Grade: Medium.
Surface: Gravel and tarmac tracks.
Hills: There are a couple of steep hills between Kingston and Wimbledon Gates, and from Broomfield Hill to Robin Hood Gate, where

Cyclists on the Tamsin Trail

cyclists may need to dismount. On the shorter ride, there is an incline up to and passing White Lodge.

YOUNG & INEXPERIENCED CYCLISTS

There are some road crossings along the route, so children should be closely supervised, but otherwise this traffic-free route makes a great day out for everyone.

REFRESHMENTS

- Refreshment points at each of the car parks, around the edge of the park.
- Ice-cream van in the car park, Kingston Gate.
- Take-away van (with good bacon butties) at Broomfield car park.
- Roehampton Cafe, by Roehampton Gate.
- Pembroke Lodge cafe, near Richmond Gate.

THINGS TO SEE & DO

- Pembroke Lodge, near Richmond Gate: once the home of the Prime Minister, Lord John Russell, this recently refurbished Georgian mansion is now a popular restaurant and picnic area; 11 acres of landscaped gardens, where King Henry VIII's Mound, the highest point in the park, is located; from here, you can see St Paul's Cathedral; 020 8940 8207;

Pembroke Lodge, Richmond Park

www.pembroke-lodge.co.uk

- **Children's playground by Petersham Gate.**
- **Wildlife Watch:** there are hundreds of red deer and fallow deer, and over 1,000 different types of beetle (including the stag beetle) to look out for in the area; www.royalparks.org.uk/parks/richmond_park

TRAIN STATIONS

Kingston upon Thames; Richmond.

There is a link route from Mortlake station, which leads south to Richmond Park (Sheen Gate) and Route 4.

BIKE HIRE

- **Sterling Concessions, Roehampton Gate car park:** bicycle hire (including tandems and tag-alongs for children) available from April to September or by arrangement out of season; very popular, especially at weekends, so arrive early or book ahead; 07922 237700; cyclehire@sterlinggroupltd.com
- **Go Pedal!:** delivery to most areas of London; 07850 796320; www.gopedal.co.uk
- **Dutch Bike Hire, Hyde Park:** delivers and collects bicycles; 07809 155577; www.dutchbikehire.com

FURTHER INFORMATION

- To view or print National Cycle Network routes, visit www.sustrans.org.uk
- Maps for this area are available to buy from www.sustransshop.co.uk
- **Transport for London (TfL):** contact for free map (no. 9); 020 7222 1234; www.tfl.gov.uk

A herd of deer in Richmond Park

- **Richmond Park Information:** www.richmondparklondon.co.uk
- **London Tourist Information:** 0870 156 6366; www.visitlondon.com

ROUTE DESCRIPTION

There are various points (car parks) around the park that make good starting places for the Tamsin Trail. You can ride it in either direction, although clockwise seems to be the most common, and it makes sense to go with the flow. Note that the Tamsin Trail is a shared path with walkers, and there is a 10mph (16km/hr) speed limit. This route can be easily shortened to 5 miles (8km) by cutting across the park on National Route 4 at Sheen Gate.

NEARBY CYCLE ROUTES

National Route 4 passes through Richmond Park, heading back into London, or continues southwest along the River Thames to Weybridge and beyond.

Keen cyclists can extend their ride from Richmond Park, via Robin Hood Gate, to Wimbledon Common.

Confident road cyclists can also use the 7-mile (11-km) long road running around the edge of the park. It's best ridden anticlockwise to minimize stopping at the five roundabouts. Note that there is a 20mph (32km/h) road speed limit throughout the park.

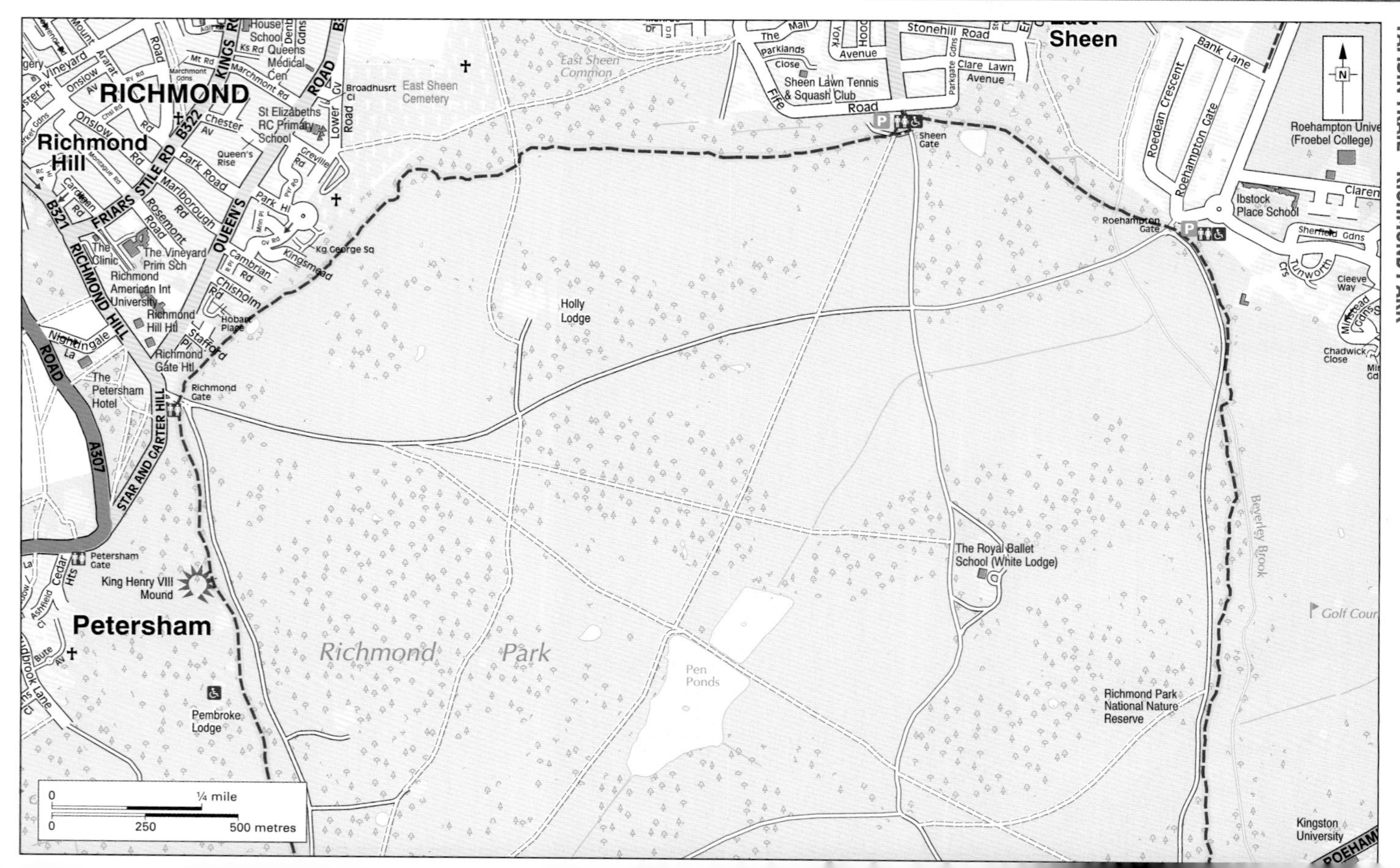
RICHMOND
Richmond Hill
East Sheen
East Sheen Common
East Sheen Cemetery
Sheen Lawn Tennis & Squash Club
Sheen Gate
Roehampton Gate
Roedean Crescent
Roehampton Gate
Bank Lane
Ibstock Place School
Holly Lodge
Richmond Gate
The Petersham Hotel
STAR AND CARTER HILL
RICHMOND HILL
A307
B321
B322
QUEEN'S
KINGS
FRIARS STILE RD
Petersham Gate
King Henry VIII Mound
Petersham
Pembroke Lodge
Richmond Park
Pen Ponds
The Royal Ballet School (White Lodge)
Richmond Park National Nature Reserve
Beverley Brook
Kingston University
0
¼ mile
250
500 metres

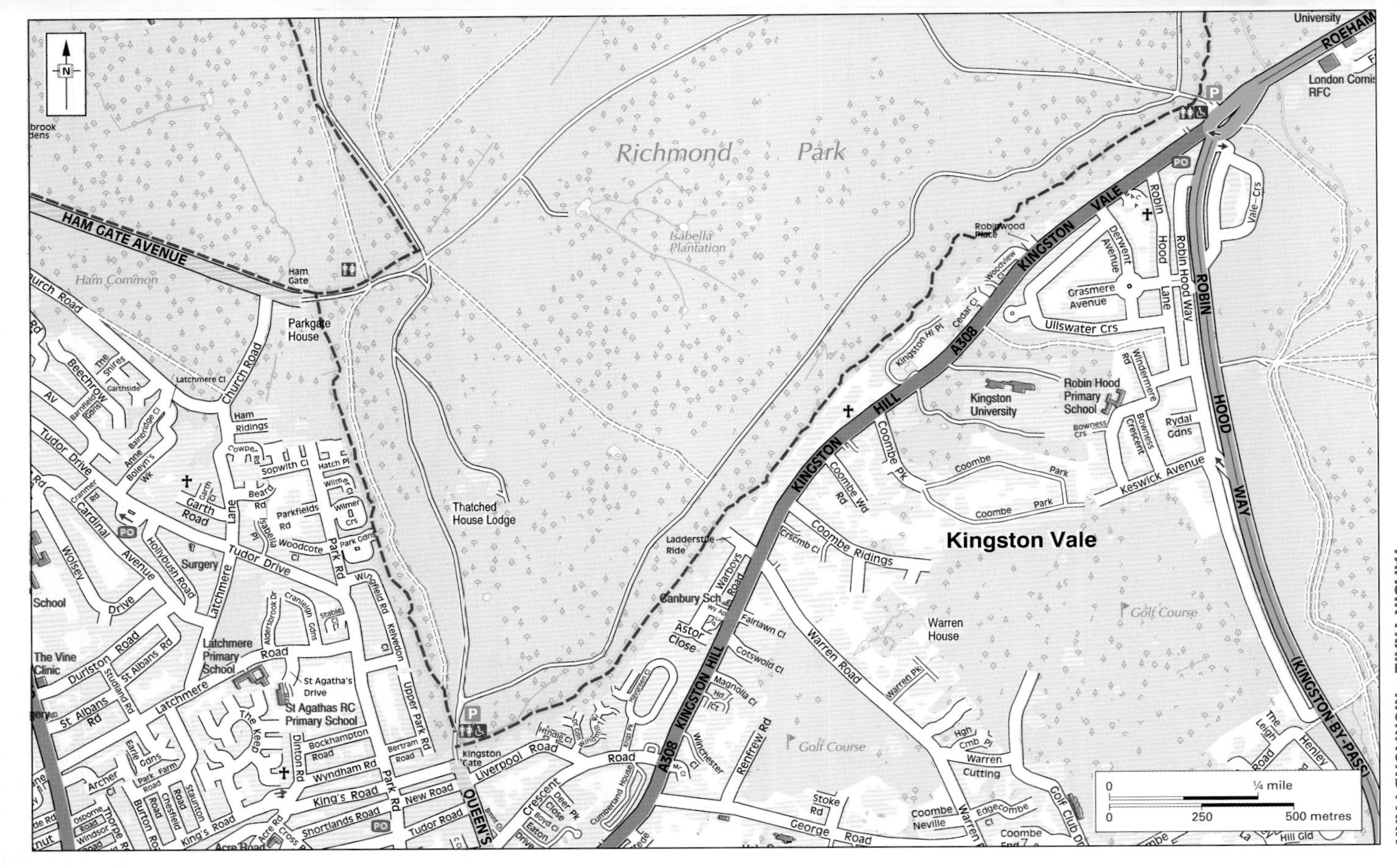

Kingston Vale
Richmond Park
Isabella Plantation
Ham Common
HAM GATE AVENUE
ROBIN HOOD WAY
(KINGSTON BY-PASS)
KINGSTON VALE
A308
KINGSTON HILL
QUEEN'S
Robin Hood Way
Robin Hood Lane
Derwent Avenue
Grasmere Avenue
Ullswater Crs
Windermere Rd
Bowness Crescent
Rydal Gdns
Keswick Avenue
Robin Hood Primary School
Kingston University
London Cornis
RFC
Coombe Park
Coombe Pk
Coombe Wd Rd
Coombe Ridings
Warren House
Warren Road
Golf Course
Golf Club Dr
Warren Cutting
Coombe Neville
George Road
Renfrew Rd
Ladderstile Ride
Canbury Sch
Astor Close
Winchester Cl
Cumberland House
Kingston Gate
Liverpool Road
Deer Pk Close
Eaton Drive
Thatched House Lodge
Upper Park Rd
Kelvedon Cl
Park Rd
Wingfield Rd
Parkgate House
Ham Gate
Church Road
Ham Ridings
Tudor Drive
Latchmere Lane
Latchmere Road
Latchmere Primary School
St Agatha's Drive
St Agathas RC Primary School
Dinton Rd
The Keep
Bockhampton Road
Wyndham Rd
King's Road
Shortlands Road
New Road
Tudor Road
Surgery
Hollybush Road
Cardinal Avenue
Wolsey Drive
School
The Vine Clinic
St Albans Rd
Durlston Road
Staunton Road
Chesfield Road
Burton Road
Earle Gdns
Archer Cl
¼ mile
500 metres
250
N

HAMPTON COURT TO PUTNEY BRIDGE

Forming part of National Route 4, which runs all the way from West Wales to the capital, this splendid green and leafy corridor offers plenty of interest, including Hampton Court Palace, boating at Teddington Lock, deer in Richmond Park and the Wetlands Centre at Barnes. The Palace was originally built for Cardinal Wolsey but it passed to Henry VIII when he fell out of favour with the king. It was at Hampton Court Palace that the King James Bible has its origins, and during the Civil War, Charles I was held prisoner here for three months before escaping. There is a striking contrast between the highly managed pleasure boat section of river to Teddington Lock and the wide, untamed tidal Thames that lies beyond.

Just off the route, but connected to Route 4 via traffic-free paths, are the Royal Botanic Gardens at Kew and Ham House, owned by the National Trust. Kew Gardens were started in 1759 by Princess Augusta, the mother of George III. They now cover more than 300 acres, and contain over 25,000 species and varieties of plants, as well as statues, glasshouses and an 18th-century pagoda. Ham House is a 17th-century mansion famous for its decorative interiors and restored formal gardens.

ROUTE INFORMATION

National Route: 4
Start: Hampton Court Palace.
Finish: Putney Bridge, south bank.
Distance: 12 miles (19.5km). Shorter options, from Hampton Court Palace to Richmond Park 6 miles (9.5km); to Kingston upon Thames 3 miles (5km).
Grade: Easy.
Surface: Mixture of tarmac and good-quality gravel paths.
Hills: Mostly level with a gentle rolling section through Richmond Park.

Parts of the Thames are highly managed

The busy banks of the Thames

YOUNG & INEXPERIENCED CYCLISTS

The route is a mixture of quiet streets and cyclepaths. The best traffic-free section of the route runs east alongside the river from Hampton Court, crossing the bridge at Kingston upon Thames.

REFRESHMENTS

- Lots of choice all along the route.

THINGS TO SEE & DO

- **Hampton Court Palace:** Tudor palace alongside a baroque palace, steeped in history; attractions include a maze, privy gardens, medieval hall and working Tudor kitchens; 0844 482 7777; www.hrp.org.uk
- **Ham House, Ham (just off the route):** Stuart mansion and gardens on the banks of the River Thames; 17th-century interiors and collections of textiles, furniture and paintings; reputedly the most haunted house in England;
  020 8940 1950; www.nationaltrust.org.uk
- **Royal Botanic Gardens, Kew (just off the route):** 020 8332 5655; www.kew.org
- **The National Archives, Kew (just off the route):** contains almost 1,000 years of history; 020 8876 3444; www.nationalarchives.gov.uk
- **Richmond Park:** the largest Royal Park in London and home to around 650 free-roaming deer; designated a National Nature Reserve (NNR), a Site of Special Scientific Interest (SSSI) and a Special Area of Conservation (SAC); 020 7298 2000; www.royalparks.org.uk
- **Wildfowl & Wetlands Trust (WWT), Barnes:** 020 8409 4400; www.wwt.org.uk

TRAIN STATIONS

Hampton Court; Kingston upon Thames; Barnes; Putney.

BIKE HIRE

- **Go Pedal!:** delivery to most areas of London;

The Royal Botanic Gardens, Kew

07850 796320; www.gopedal.co.uk

- **London Bicycle Tour Company, Gabriel's Wharf:** 020 7928 6838; www.londonbicycle.com
- **Smith Brothers, Wimbledon:** 020 8946 2270
- **Tri and Run, Wimbledon:** 020 8500 4841; www.triandrun.com

FURTHER INFORMATION

- To view or print National Cycle Network routes, visit www.sustrans.org.uk
- Maps for this area are available to buy from www.sustransshop.co.uk
- **Transport for London (TfL):** contact for free maps (nos. 7 and 9); 020 7222 1234; www.tfl.gov.uk
- **London Tourist Information:** 0870 156 6366; www.visitlondon.com

ROUTE DESCRIPTION

Starting at Hampton Court Park, travel along Barge Walk and cross Kingston Bridge, near Kingston train station, where there is a good cycle route. Follow the Route 4 signs as the route threads its way through Kingston upon Thames and along the river to Teddington Lock.

At Teddington Lock, leave the river to go through Ham and Richmond Park. Here, you have the option of completing a totally traffic-free circuit of the park. Leave the park through Roehampton Gate, skirt Barnes Common and go past the London Wetland Centre at Barnes before rejoining the river and following the embankment for a mile or so (1.6km) to the south bank at Putney Bridge.

NEARBY CYCLE ROUTES

The ride described here is the first section of the Thames Valley Cycle Route, which runs from Putney Bridge to Oxford (Route 4 to Reading, then Route 5 from Reading to Oxford). East from Putney Bridge, Route 4 runs right through the heart of London to Greenwich and Route 1 continues on to Dartford. There is also a traffic-free circular ride around Richmond Park (see Tamsin Trail, page 82).

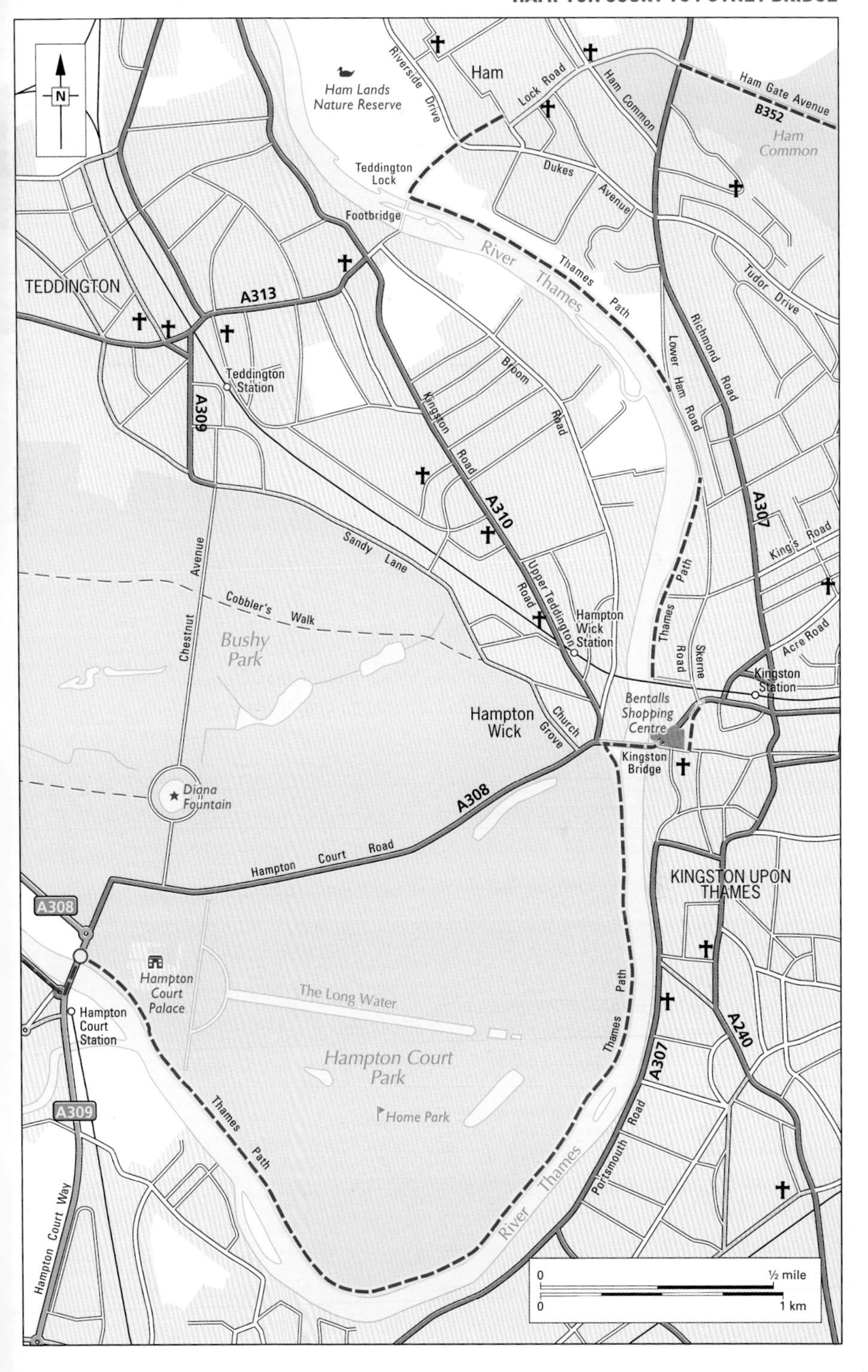
N
Ham
Ham Lands Nature Reserve
Riverside Drive
Lock Road
Ham Common
Ham Gate Avenue
B352
Ham Common
Teddington Lock
Dukes Avenue
Footbridge
River Thames
Thames Path
Tudor Drive
TEDDINGTON
A313
Teddington Station
A309
Broom Road
Kingston Road
Lower Ham Road
Richmond Road
A310
A307
King's Road
Sandy Lane
Chestnut Avenue
Cobbler's Walk
Bushy Park
Upper Teddington Road
Hampton Wick Station
Thames Path
Thames Road
Skerne Road
Acre Road
Kingston Station
Bentalls Shopping Centre
Hampton Wick
Church Grove
Kingston Bridge
Diana Fountain
A308
Hampton Court Road
KINGSTON UPON THAMES
A308
Hampton Court Palace
Hampton Court Station
The Long Water
Thames Path
A240
Hampton Court Park
A307
A309
Home Park
Portsmouth Road
Thames Path
River Thames
Hampton Court Way
0 ½ mile
0 1 km

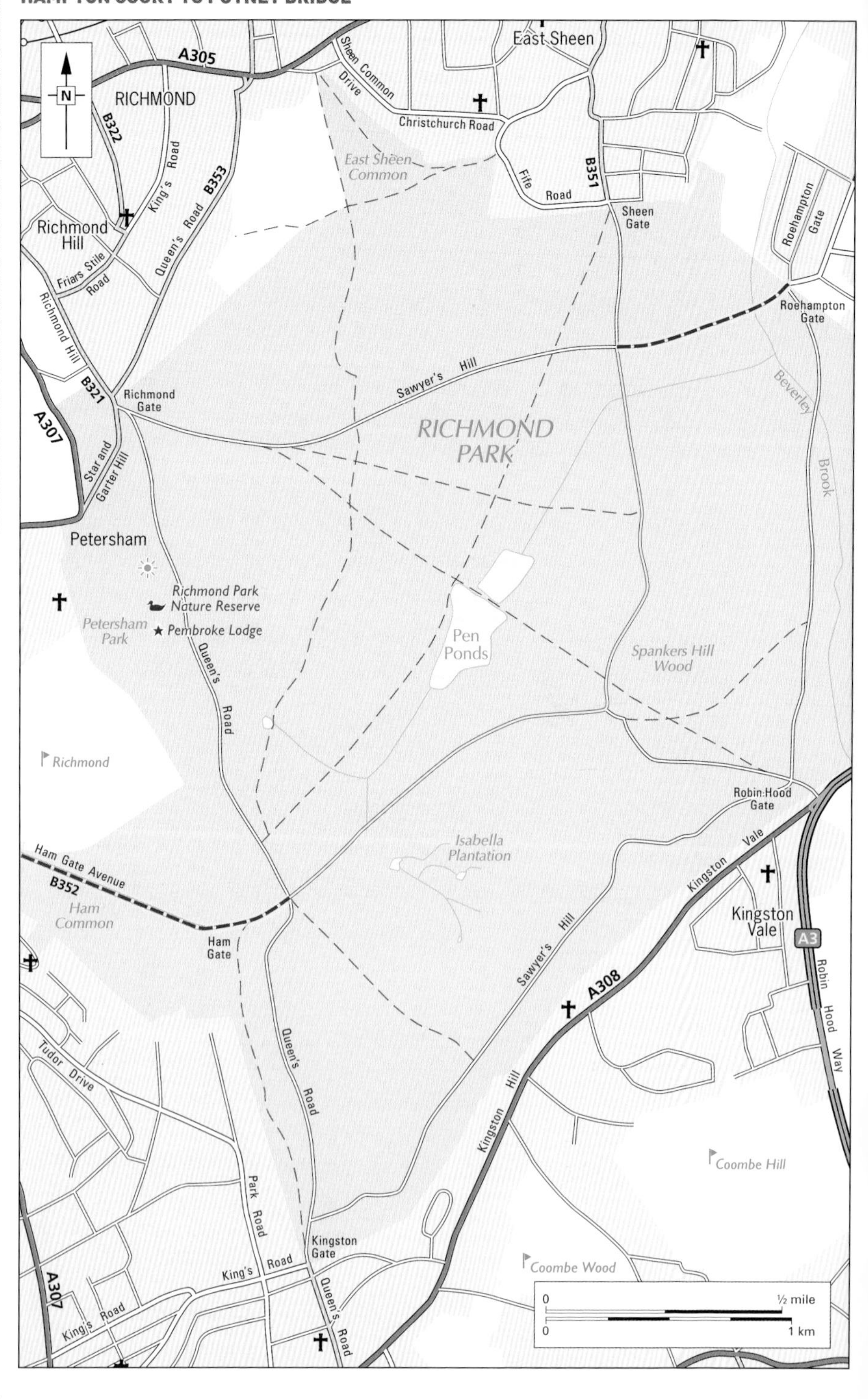
N
A305
East Sheen
RICHMOND
Sheen Common Drive
Christchurch Road
B322
King's Road
B353
Queen's Road
East Sheen Common
Fife Road
B351
Sheen Gate
Roehampton Gate
Richmond Hill
Friars Stile Road
Richmond Hill
Roehampton Gate
Sawyer's Hill
B321
Richmond Gate
A307
Beverley Brook
RICHMOND PARK
Star and Garter Hill
Petersham
Richmond Park Nature Reserve
Petersham Park
Pembroke Lodge
Queen's Road
Pen Ponds
Spankers Hill Wood
Richmond
Robin Hood Gate
Isabella Plantation
Ham Gate Avenue
B352
Kingston Vale
Ham Common
Ham Gate
Sawyer's Hill
Kingston Vale
A3
Robin Hood Way
A308
Tudor Drive
Queen's Road
Kingston Hill
Coombe Hill
Park Road
Kingston Gate
King's Road
Coombe Wood
A307
King's Road
Queen's Road
0
½ mile
0
1 km

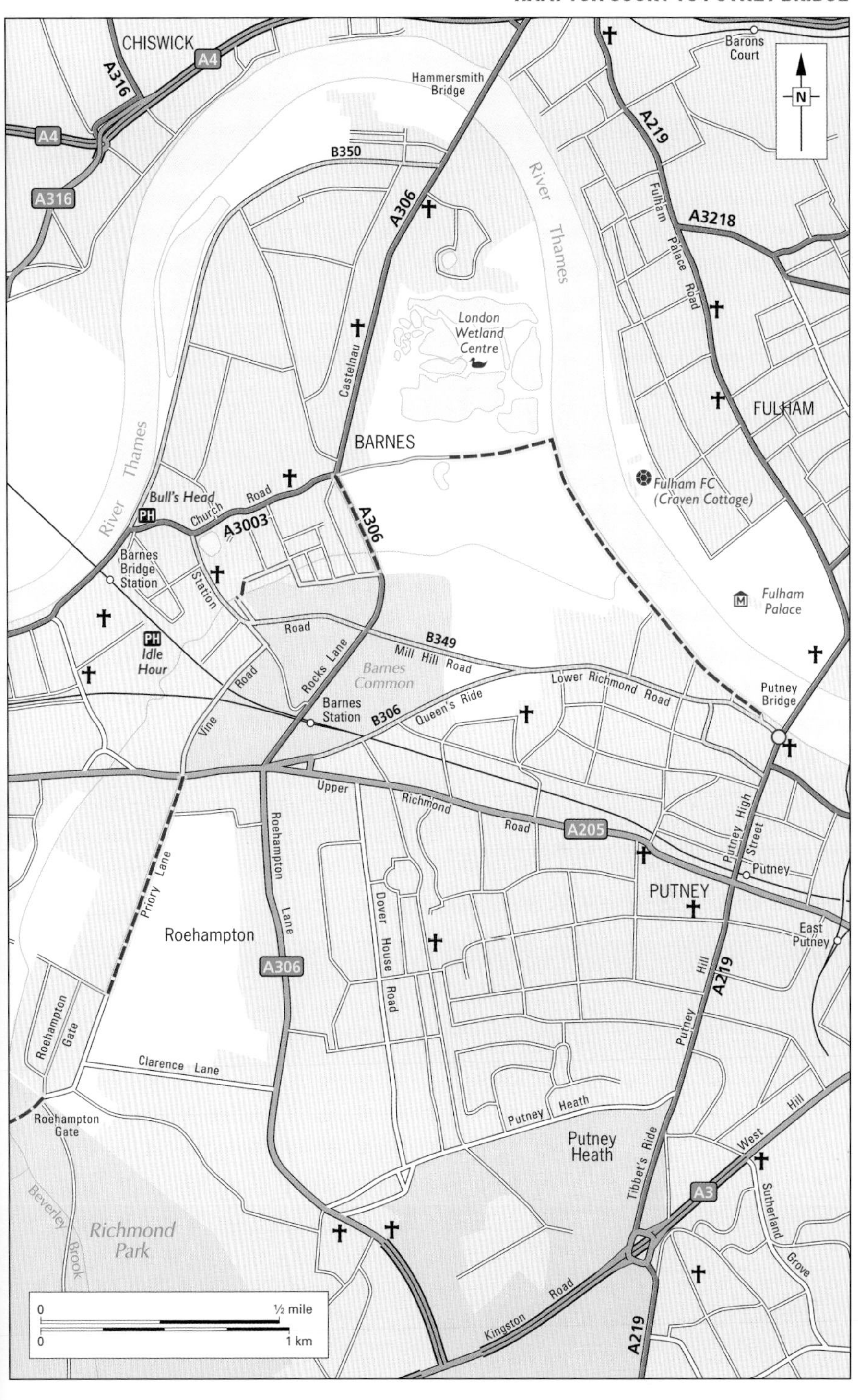
CHISWICK
A4
A316
Hammersmith Bridge
Barons Court
N
A219
B350
A316
River Thames
A306
A3218
Fulham Palace Road
London Wetland Centre
Castelnau
FULHAM
BARNES
Fulham FC (Craven Cottage)
River Thames
Bull's Head
PH
Church Road
A3003
A306
Barnes Bridge Station
Station
Road
Fulham Palace
Idle Hour
Road
B349
Mill Hill Road
Barnes Common
Rocks Lane
Vine Road
Barnes Station
B306
Queen's Ride
Lower Richmond Road
Putney Bridge
Upper Richmond Road
A205
Roehampton Lane
Priory Lane
Roehampton
Dover House Road
Putney High Street
Putney
PUTNEY
East Putney
A306
Putney Hill
A219
Roehampton Gate
Clarence Lane
Putney Heath
Roehampton Gate
Putney Heath
Tibbet's Ride
West Hill
Beverley Brook
Richmond Park
A3
Sutherland Grove
Kingston Road
A219
0
½ mile
0
1 km

THE WANDLE TRAIL

The Wandle Trail follows the River Wandle, really just a chalk stream, from its junction with the Thames in Wandsworth through a series of small riverside parks south to Carshalton. In its industrial prime, the River Wandle was Britain's 'hardest working river' with over 90 mills along its banks. It is one of those rides that improves each time you do it as you begin to memorize the sequences of left, right and straight on that link the green, traffic-free stretches.

There is an excellent coffee/tea stop at the National Trust property in Morden Hall Park, a former deer park with a network of waterways including meadow, wetland and woodland habitats. Morden Hall was built in the mid-18th century by Richard Garth, lord of the manor of Morden. The park also boasts a spectacular rose garden with over 2,000 roses, particularly fragrant from May to September. The historic mills and the 19th-century estate buildings house craft workshops.

ROUTE INFORMATION

National Route: 20
Start: Junction of the River Wandle with the Thames, west of Wandsworth Bridge.
Finish: Carshalton train station.
Distance: 9 miles (14.5km).
Grade: Easy.
Surface: Tarmac or fine gravel and dust path.
Hills: None.

'Viewing Platform' by Andrew Sabin

YOUNG & INEXPERIENCED CYCLISTS

There are several traffic-free sections through parkland linked by short road sections, many of which have safe pelican crossings. The longest traffic-free stretch runs south from Merton High Street to Ravensbury Park, passing through Morden Hall Park.

The Wandle Trail does includes busy sections that younger and less confident cyclists may find challenging, in particular Wandsworth Town and Earlsfield town centres. If necessary, these can easily be navigated on foot. (Sustrans is working to improve cycle facilities not only here but also along the entire Trail.)

REFRESHMENTS

- Lots of choice in the centre of Wandsworth.
- Lots of choice on Merton High Street.
- Merton Abbey Mills.
- Cafe at Morden Hall.
- Surrey Arms pub, Morden Road, just south of Morden Hall Park.
- Lots of choice in the centre of Carshalton.

THINGS TO SEE & DO

- Merton Abbey Mills, Merantum Way, Merton: bustling weekend market specializing in Arts & Crafts, with live music, theatre and craft workshops; www.mertonabbeymills.org.uk
- Deen City Farm, Windsor Avenue, Merton:

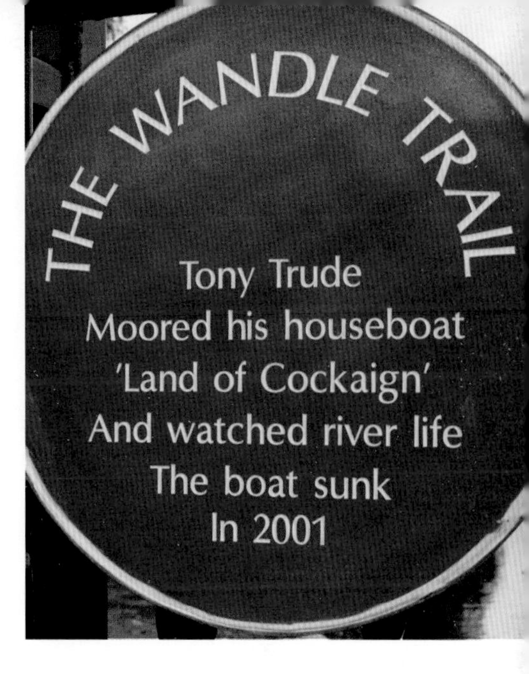
THE WANDLE TRAIL
Tony Trude
Moored his houseboat
'Land of Cockaign'
And watched river life
The boat sunk
In 2001

farm and riding stables, children's events and educational programmes; 020 8543 5300; www.deencityfarm.co.uk
- **Morden Hall Park:** former deer park, now a National Trust property, with a network of waterways, meadows and wetlands; historic snuff mill and craft workshops, including wood turning and furniture restoration; 020 8545 6850; www.nationaltrust.org.uk

TRAIN STATIONS

Wandsworth Town; Earlsfield; Haydons Road; Mitcham Junction; Hackbridge; Carshalton.

BIKE HIRE

- **Go Pedal!:** delivery to most areas of London; 07850 796320; www.gopedal.co.uk
- **London Bicycle Tour Company, Gabriel's Wharf:** 020 7928 6838; www.londonbicycle.com
- **On Your Bike, London Bridge:** 020 7378 6669; www.onyourbike.net
- **Smith Brothers, Wimbledon:** 020 8946 2270
- **Tri and Run, Wimbledon:** 020 8500 4841; www.triandrun.com

FURTHER INFORMATION

- To view or print National Cycle Network routes, visit www.sustrans.org.uk
- Maps for this area are available to buy from www.sustransshop.co.uk
- **Transport for London (TfL):** contact for free maps (nos. 10 and 12); 020 7222 1234; www.tfl.gov.uk

Bridge over the River Wandle, Morden Hall Park

- **Wandle Trail:** www.merton.gov.uk/wandletrail
- **London Tourist Information:** 0870 156 6366; www.visitlondon.com

ROUTE DESCRIPTION

Starting at the Spit, at the mouth of the River Wandle, follow the river past Bell Lane Creek. Follow the route carefully around the Wandsworth one-way system and onto Garratt Lane. Cross the river to enter King George's Park. Leave the park at the end on Acuba Road. Turn left onto Ravensbury Road, left onto Haslemere, then right onto Penwith Road towards Earlsfield Station, where you turn right onto Garratt Lane once more. Turn right onto Summerley Street, then right to cross Trewint Steet Bridge into Garratt Park, where you follow the river. Cross Plough Lane, continue through the park and go under the railway into Wandle Meadow Nature Reserve.

Join Chaucer Way and then turn right onto North Road to follow a road route along East Road, Hanover Road and Leyton Road before rejoining the riverside path. The path passes Merton Abbey Mills and Deen City Farm and goes into Morden Hall Park. Follow the route through the park before crossing Morden Road to reach Ravensbury Park, where once again the route follows the river. There is a short section along Bishopsford Road, left onto Peterborough Road and left again onto Middleton Road to take you around Poulter Park (the walking route goes through the park). Enter Watercress Park and follow the river until you reach Nightingale Road, where you turn right and then left onto The Causeway and left again onto River Gardens past Wilderness Island. Turn right along Denmark Road to reach Carshalton station.

Note that the Wandle Trail for cyclists does not always follow the Wandle Trail for walkers. Please pay close attention to the cycle signs.

NEARBY CYCLE ROUTES

Route 4 of the National Cycle Network, joined at the northern end of the Wandle Trail, runs west from Wandsworth to Putney Bridge, the start of a long, mainly traffic-free section to Weybridge.

Route 20 joins Route 22, which, when completed, will continue south and west through Dorking, Guildford and Farnham, down to the south coast at Portsmouth.
The Tamsin Trail (see page 82) in Richmond Park is a traffic-free circuit around the park's perimeter. The Wandle Trail also forms part of the SW Greenways, a cross-borough network of routes across southwest London.

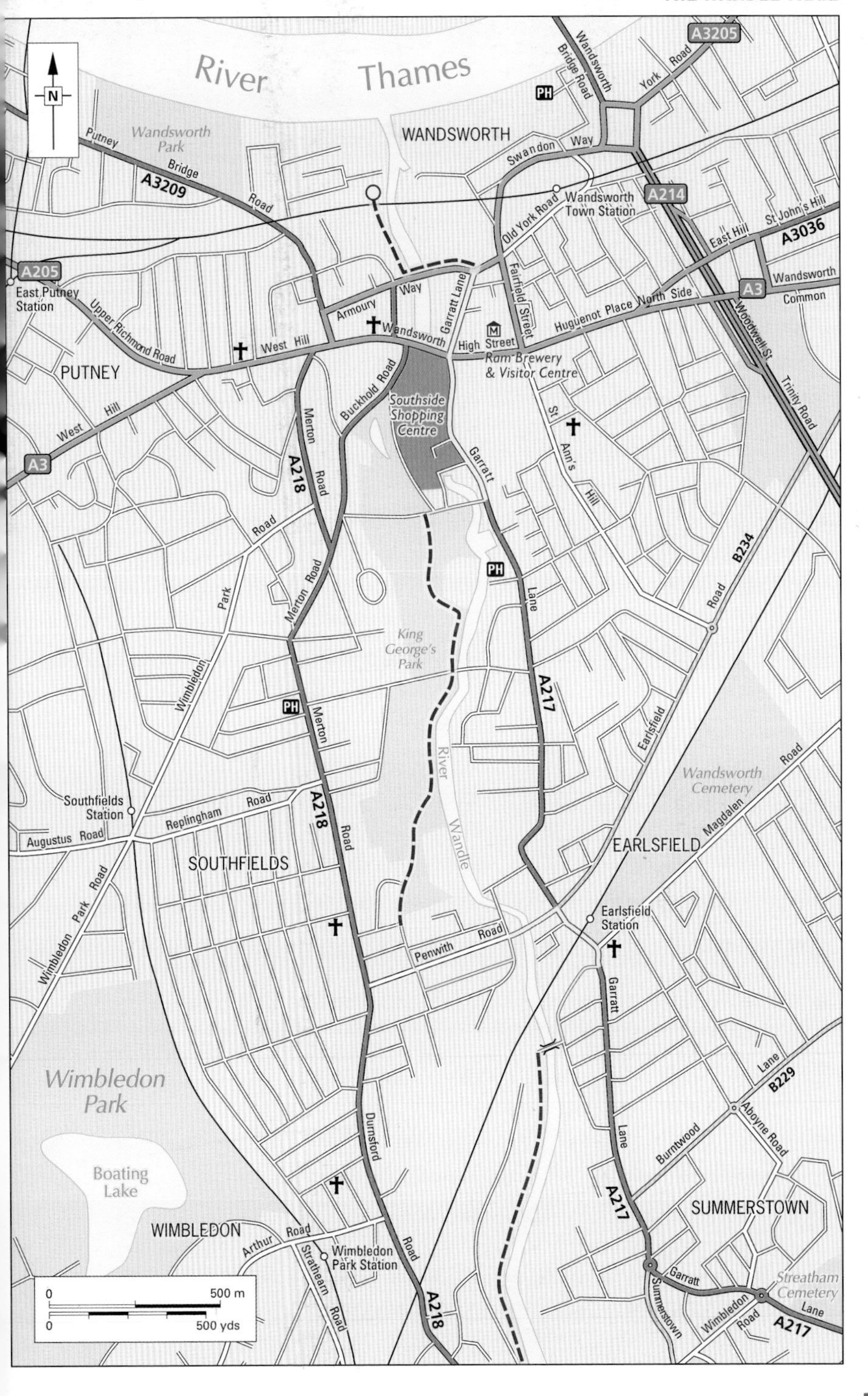
River Thames
WANDSWORTH
Wandsworth Park
PUTNEY
SOUTHFIELDS
EARLSFIELD
SUMMERSTOWN
WIMBLEDON
Wimbledon Park
Boating Lake
King George's Park
Wandsworth Cemetery
Streatham Cemetery
Southside Shopping Centre
Ram Brewery & Visitor Centre
Wandsworth Town Station
East Putney Station
Southfields Station
Earlsfield Station
Wimbledon Park Station
River Wandle
A3209
A3205
A214
A3036
A205
A3
A218
A217
B234
B229
0 500 m
0 500 yds

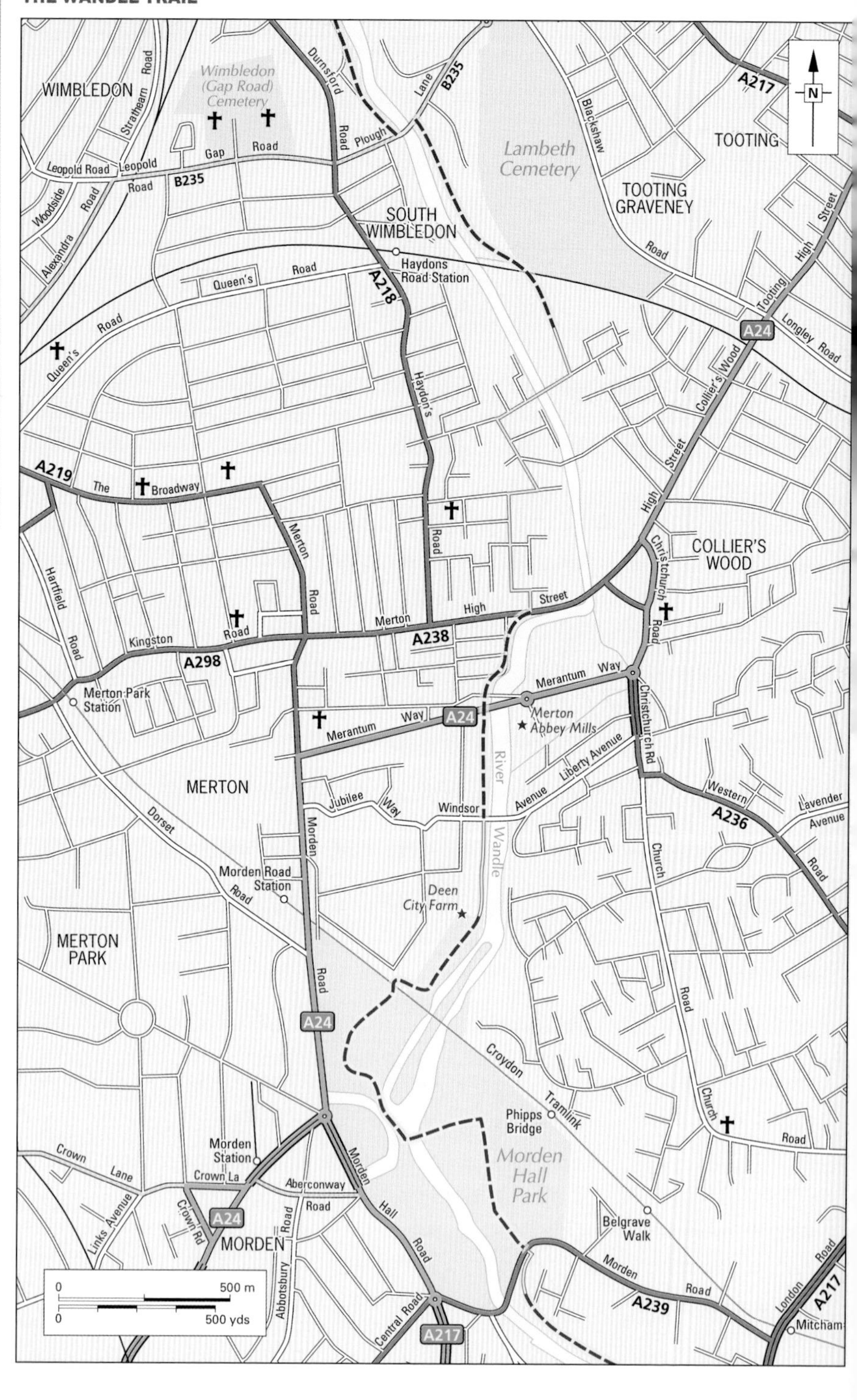

WIMBLEDON
Wimbledon (Gap Road) Cemetery
Lambeth Cemetery
TOOTING
TOOTING GRAVENEY
SOUTH WIMBLEDON
Haydons Road Station
COLLIER'S WOOD
Merton Park Station
Merton Abbey Mills
River Wandle
MERTON
Morden Road Station
Deen City Farm
MERTON PARK
Phipps Bridge
Morden Hall Park
Morden Station
MORDEN
Belgrave Walk
Mitcham
A217
A218
A219
A238
A298
A24
A236
A239
B235
0 500 m
0 500 yds

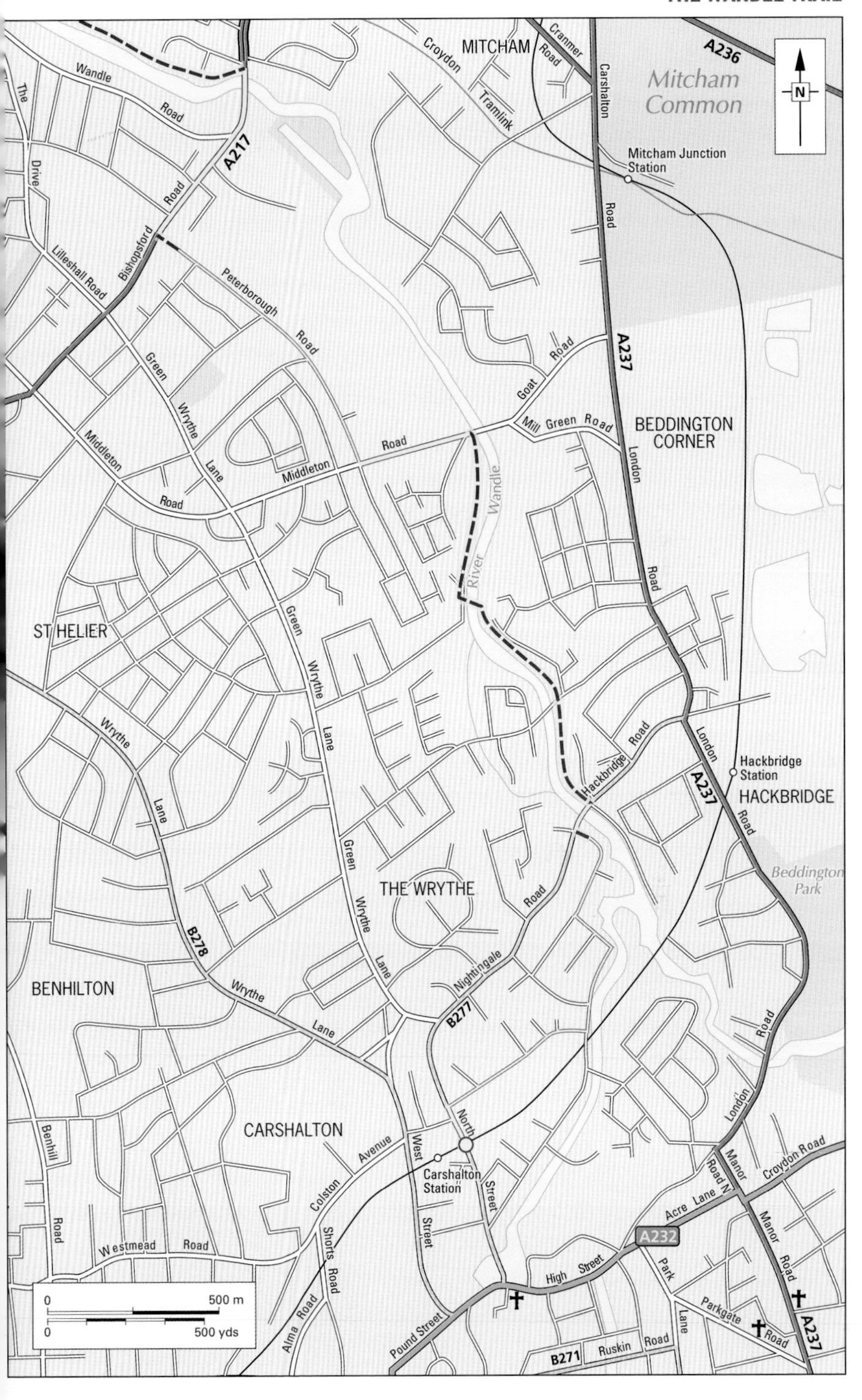
MITCHAM
Mitcham Common
Mitcham Junction Station
BEDDINGTON CORNER
ST HELIER
HACKBRIDGE
Hackbridge Station
Beddington Park
THE WRYTHE
BENHILTON
CARSHALTON
Carshalton Station
River Wandle
Croydon Road
Cranmer Road
Carshalton Road
Tramlink
Wandle Road
The Drive
Bishopsford Road
Lilleshall Road
Peterborough Road
Goat Road
Mill Green Road
Middleton Road
Green Wrythe Lane
Wrythe Lane
London Road
Hackbridge Road
Nightingale Road
North Street
West Street
Colston Avenue
Benhill Road
Westmead Road
Shorts Road
Alma Road
Pound Street
High Street
Acre Lane
Manor Road N
Manor Road
Park Lane
Parkgate Road
Ruskin Road
A217
A236
A237
B278
B277
A232
B271
0 500 m
0 500 yds

COMMONS CIRCULAR – CLAPHAM, WANDSWORTH & TOOTING BEC COMMONS

This circular 5-mile (8-km) route connects Clapham, Wandsworth and Tooting Bec Commons, providing a pleasant way of exploring this part of southwest London.

Clapham Common is a 220-acre triangular area of grassland, with a bandstand in the centre, three ponds, which are historical features, and a modern paddling pool. The two ponds found in the south of the common are used for fishing; the third, Long Pond, is given over to sailing model boats. The common also has basketball courts, playgrounds, areas dedicated to children and families, tennis courts and a bowling green, making it very popular with a wide range of people.

Wandsworth Common is a 73-acre public common, split into lots of parts, with a large area to the east of the railway line used for sports. There is a lake, which can be used for fishing (with a permit), and a number of ponds with geese, ducks, swans and even a heron. The common also boasts various playgrounds, including the Lady Allen Playground designed especially for children with disabilities. There are also tennis courts, a bowling green, a fitness trail, and the Common Ground Cafe Bar.

Named after Bec Abbey in Normandy, 152-acre Tooting Bec Common has at various times also been known as Streatham Common, which causes confusion with the existing common of the same name found just a mile (1.6km) to the southeast. At Tooting Bec Common, you will find formal avenues of trees, a small athletics stadium, tennis courts, lakes, a refreshments kiosk by Bedford Hill (B242) and, most impressively, Tooting Bec Lido, the largest fresh-water open air swimming pool in England.

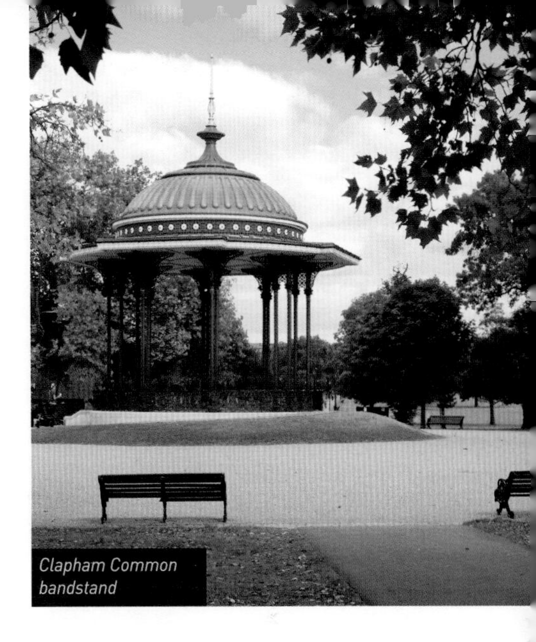
Clapham Common bandstand

ROUTE INFORMATION

National Route: Not part of the National Cycle Network, but can be linked with National Route 20, the Wandle Trail (see page 94).
Start and Finish: As the route is circular, you can start anywhere you like.
Distance: 5.5 miles (9km).
Grade: Medium.
Surface: Park tracks and roads.
Hills: An undulating ride throughout.

YOUNG & INEXPERIENCED CYCLISTS

The road sections and crossings along the route mean that it is not best suited to young children or inexperienced riders riding solo.

REFRESHMENTS

- There are lots of places along the route, from high street cafes and restaurants to cafes and kiosks on the commons.
- The Hope pub, by Wandsworth Common train station.
- The Windmill hotel, Clapham Common South Side.

Swimmers at Tooting Bec Lido

THINGS TO SEE & DO

- Each of the three parks has a variety of things to offer, from large expanses of grassland to play and picnic on to outdoor swimming and fishing (see the introduction).
- Fishing: free on Clapham Common, but a permit is required for Wandsworth Common; 020 8871 6347; www.waterscape.com
- Tooting Bec Lido: the earliest purpose-built open-air pool in London; Art Deco design; also a paddling pool, jacuzzis, saunas, cafe and shaded area; the South London Swimming Club race here on Christmas and New Year's Days, as they have since 1908; 020 8871 7198; www.wandsworth.gov.uk

TRAIN STATIONS

Wandsworth Common; Balham.

BIKE HIRE

- Southbank Cycles, 194 Wandsworth Road: 020 7622 3069; www.southbankcycles.com
- Go Pedal!: delivery to most areas of London; 07850 796320; www.gopedal.co.uk

FURTHER INFORMATION

- To view or print National Cycle Network routes, visit www.sustrans.org.uk

continued on page 104

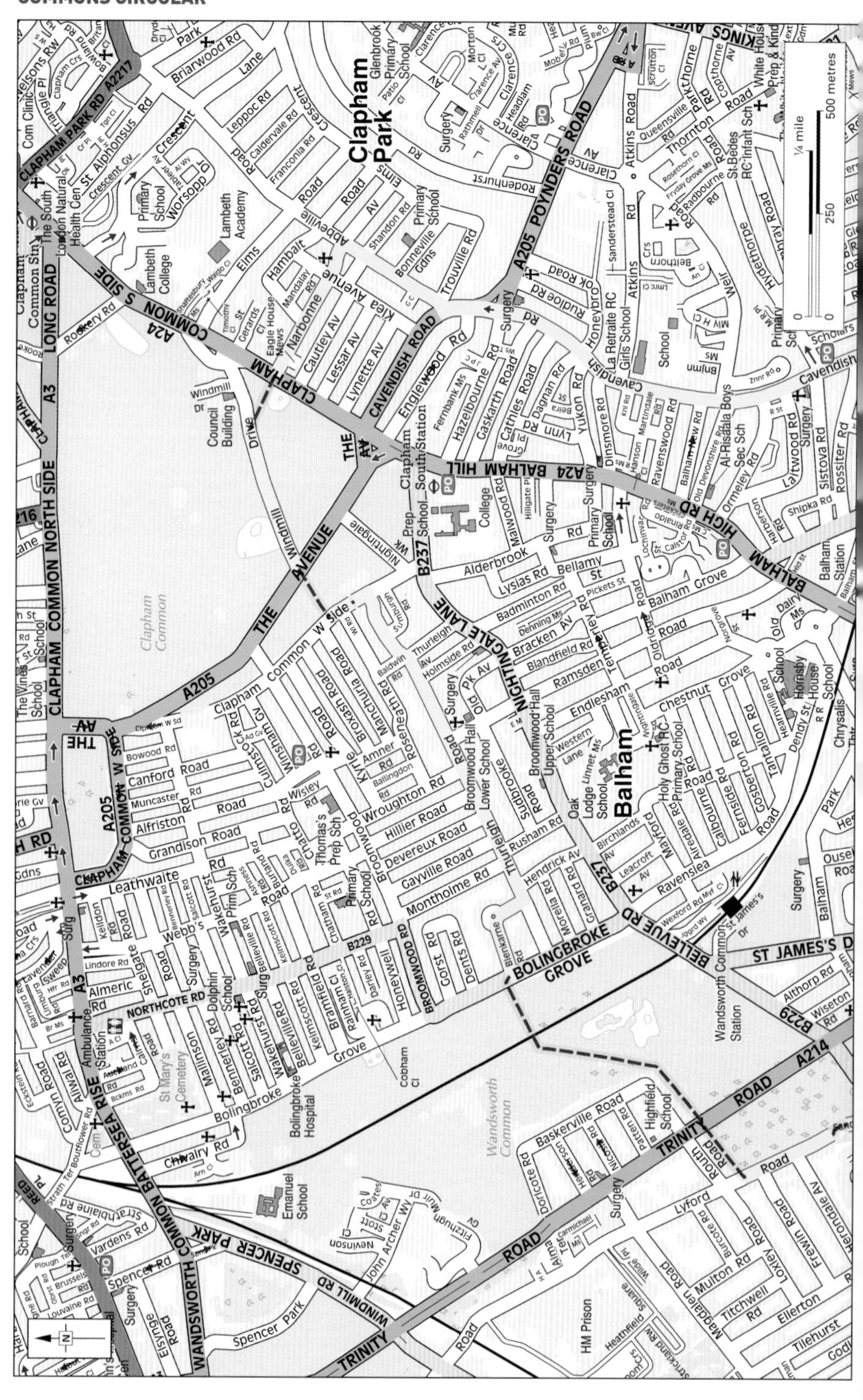
Clapham Park
Clapham Common
Balham
Wandsworth Common
CLAPHAM COMMON NORTH SIDE
LONG ROAD
CLAPHAM COMMON S SIDE
CLAPHAM COMMON W SIDE
THE AVENUE
CAVENDISH ROAD
POYNDERS ROAD
BALHAM HILL
BALHAM HIGH RD
NIGHTINGALE LANE
BOLINGBROKE GROVE
BELLEVUE RD
TRINITY ROAD
BATTERSEA RISE
NORTHCOTE RD
SPENCER PARK
WINDMILL RD
WANDSWORTH COMMON
ST JAMES'S D
Clapham South Station
Wandsworth Common Station
Balham Station
HM Prison
Emanuel School
Bolingbroke Hospital
St Mary's Cemetery
Lambeth College
Lambeth Academy
1/4 mile
500 metres
0
250

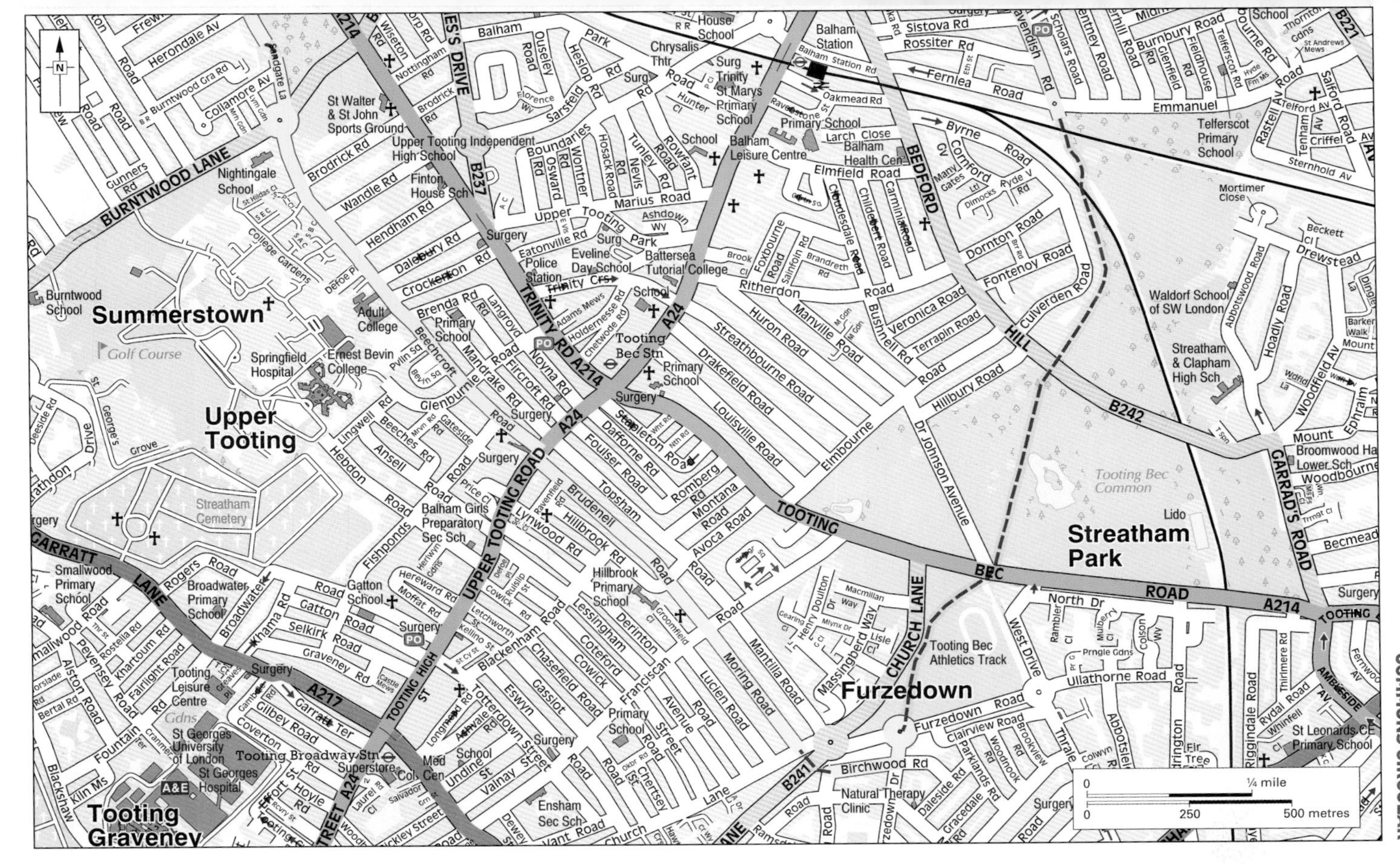
Streatham Park
Furzedown
Summerstown
Upper Tooting
Tooting Graveney
Tooting Bec Common
Lido
Tooting Bec Athletics Track
TOOTING BEC ROAD
A214
UPPER TOOTING ROAD
A24
TRINITY RD A214
BEDFORD HILL
B242
GARRAD'S ROAD
CHURCH LANE
BURNTWOOD LANE
GARRATT LANE
A217
TOOTING HIGH ST
Dr Johnson Avenue
Balham Station
Tooting Bec Stn
Tooting Broadway Stn
Streatham Cemetery
Springfield Hospital
Golf Course
St Georges Hospital
Ernest Bevin College
Waldorf School of SW London
Streatham & Clapham High Sch
Balham Leisure Centre
¼ mile
0
250
500 metres

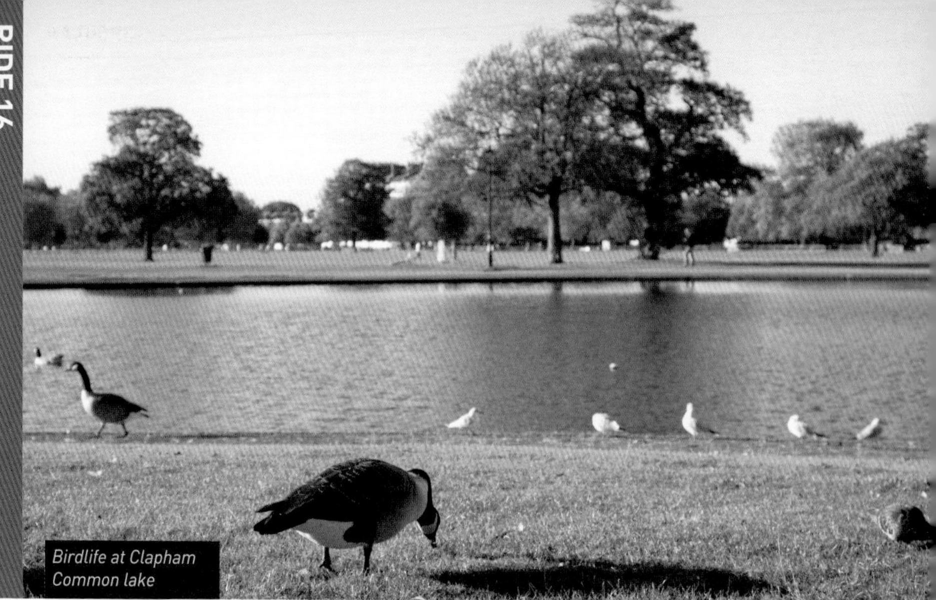

Birdlife at Clapham Common lake

- Maps for this area are available to buy from www.sustransshop.co.uk
- **Transport for London (TfL):** contact for free map (no. 10); 020 7222 1234; www.tfl.gov.uk
- **London Tourist Information:** 0870 156 6366; www.visitlondon.com

ROUTE DESCRIPTION

This ride connects the three commons of Clapham, Wandsworth and Tooting Bec, via some sections of road, so care needs to be taken at various points along the way. If arriving by train, you will start from Wandsworth Common train station. Proceed straight to Wandsworth Common, along St James's Drive. After crossing over the railway in the middle of the common, the route heads south, along the edge of the common, where you exit on Lydford Road to join Beechcroft Road. Keep straight ahead – this road section is easy to navigate – to the roundabout with the B241.

Heading back northwards, pass through Tooting Graveney Common, go past the athletics ground and into Tooting Bec Common, where you will find Tooting Bec Lido – a great place to stop on a hot summer's day. The route exits the park at the northern tip, to join Cavendish Road and Abbeville Road, before heading left on Narbonne Avenue, to enter Clapham Common by Eagle Pond. Here, and at Mount Pond, you can watch anglers reeling in a variety of fish, including carp weighing up to 9.7kg (20lbs). There is also a model boating pond in the northeast and a playground in the northwest of the park. From Clapham Common, it's a short journey along Thurleigh Road, back to Wandsworth Common.

NEARBY CYCLE ROUTES

The Wandle Trail on National Route 20 goes from the Thames to Carshalton station (see page 94). Route 20 continues to join Route 22, which, when completed, will continue south and west through Dorking, Guildford and Farnham, down to the south coast at Portsmouth.

Route 4 of the National Cycle Network, joined at the northern end of the Wandle Trail, runs west from Wandsworth to Putney Bridge, the start of a long, mainly traffic-free section to Weybridge in Surrey.

TOWER BRIDGE TO GREENWICH

This is just short of a 5-mile (8-km) route, starting at the iconic Tower Bridge and finishing at the greatly treasured *Cutty Sark* in Greenwich (closed to the public for conservation work until 2011).

Tower Bridge was constructed in 1894, as London was outgrowing London Bridge, which was originally the only crossing for the Thames. The job of designing the new crossing was opened to the public in 1876 and over 50 designs were submitted, some of which you can see at the Tower Bridge Exhibition. It wasn't until October 1884 that the design put forward by Horace Jones and John Wolfe Barry was chosen. The building of Tower Bridge took eight years and 432 construction workers. Two huge piers were sunk into the river bed to support the construction, and over 11,000 tonnes of steel created the framework, which was then clad in Cornish granite and Portland stone. Tower Bridge was the largest and most sophisticated bascule (French for seesaw) bridge ever completed. Today, the bascules are still operated by hydraulic power, but since 1976 they have been driven by oil and electricity rather than steam. Each section of roadway that moves weighs 1,000 tonnes and takes just one minute to lift. In the first year they were lifted over 6,000 times, while today they are raised only a few times a week. The high-level walkways were designed to let people walk over even when the road was raised, but in 1910 they were closed to the public due to lack of use. However, in 1982 they were reopened and you can walk through the covered walkways and experience the wonderful views.

Further into the ride, the route passes through Greenland Dock, the oldest of London's riverside docks and formerly part of the Surrey Commercial Docks. In the late 1980s, the remaining industrial occupiers were evicted to transform the docks into a residential area. What's left of the dock is now used purely for recreational purposes, with a water sports centre offering sailing, windsurfing, canoeing and dragon boat racing. The ride finishes by the Thames, in Greenwich, where there are plenty of attractions to visit, including Greenwich Park.

ROUTE INFORMATION

National Route: 4
Start: Tower Bridge.
Finish: The *Cutty Sark*, Greenwich.
Distance: 5 miles (8km).
Grade: Medium.
Surface: Roads and tarmac paths.
Hills: There are a few small hills along the route.

YOUNG & INEXPERIENCED CYCLISTS

Due to the changing gradients and road sections along the route, this ride is not suitable for younger children.

REFRESHMENTS

- There are lots of options along the way, including a good choice at the end, by the *Cutty Sark*, in Greenwich.

THINGS TO SEE & DO

- Tower Bridge: see the bridge being raised (at certain times only), then tour the engine rooms and learn how everything works; 020 7403 3761; www.towerbridge.org.uk
- The *Cutty Sark*, Greenwich: 85-m (279-ft) long clipper ship, built in 1869, now dry-docked and used as a museum; closed for conservation until 2011; 020 8858 2698;

Tower Bridge

www.cuttysark.org.uk

- **Greenwich Park:** famous for being bisected by the Greenwich meridian, the line to which time across the globe is referenced; large area of formal parkland, with 'the wilderness', an area enclosed for deer; several historic buildings are in or near the park, including the Old Royal Observatory, the Old Royal Naval College, the National Maritime Museum and the Queen's House; www.royalparks.org.uk

TRAIN STATIONS

London Bridge; Greenwich.

BIKE HIRE

- **On Your Bike, Tooley Street:** 020 7378 6669; www.onyourbike.com
- **Greenwich Cycle Hire:** 020 8858 6677; www.flightcentregreenwich.co.uk
- **Go Pedal!:** delivery to most areas of London; 07850 796320; www.gopedal.co.uk

FURTHER INFORMATION:

- To view or print National Cycle Network routes, visit www.sustrans.org.uk
- Maps for this area are available to buy from www.sustransshop.co.uk
- **Transport for London (TfL):** contact for free maps (nos. 7 and 8); 020 7222 1234; www.tfl.gov.uk
- **London Tourist Information:** 0870 156 6366; www.visitlondon.com

Old Royal Observatory

ROUTE DESCRIPTION

Leaving the hustle and bustle of Tower Bridge, the ride heads away on National Route 4, going east along roads to Bermondsey, with the River Thames to your left. From here, the route uses some traffic-free paths and leaves the Thames again to cut the corner. Using more traffic-free cycling, it passes through the Russia Dock Woodland, to rejoin the Thames by Greenland Dock. A short section along the road takes you past Greenwich Dock and on to a traffic-free section alongside the Thames.

It isn't long, however, before the route has to head away from the river to join a road around the back of an industrial site (Convoy's Wharf). There are plans for a route that runs along the edge of the Thames here and over Deptford Creek, so keep a look out for any developments. The trail soon heads back to the river and joins traffic-free paths to Greenwich Pier and the location of the *Cutty Sark*, where the route ends.

NEARBY CYCLE ROUTES

National Route 4 continues west from Tower Bridge, past the London Eye, London Aquarium, the Houses of Parliament and Big Ben.

Route 1 heads east along the River Thames, past the Thames Barrier (see page 116) and north, through the Greenwich Foot Tunnel, to the Isle of Dogs (see page 20), all the way along the Lee Valley and into Essex (see page 54).

Route 21 from Greenwich heads southbound to South Norwood Country Park (see page 110).

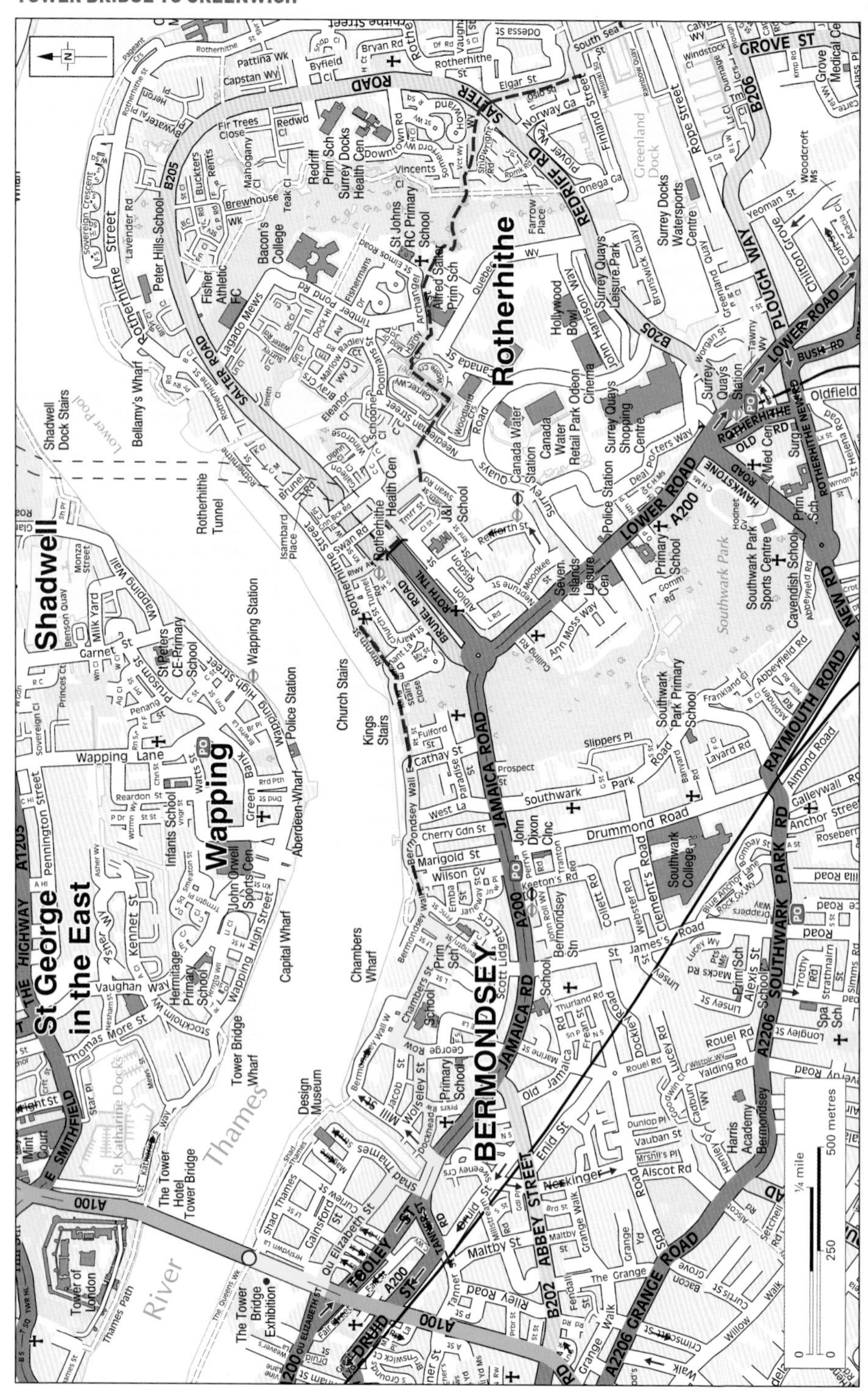
St George in the East
Shadwell
Wapping
Rotherhithe
BERMONDSEY
River Thames
Tower of London
The Tower Bridge Exhibition
The Tower Hotel Tower Bridge
St Katharine Docks
Design Museum
Chambers Wharf
Capital Wharf
Aberdeen Wharf
Tower Bridge Wharf
Church Stairs
Kings Stairs
Isambard Place
Rotherhithe Tunnel
Shadwell Dock Stairs
Bellamy's Wharf
Wapping Station
Police Station
Canada Water Station
Surrey Quays Station
Bermondsey Stn
Canada Water Retail Park
Odeon Cinema
Surrey Quays Shopping Centre
Hollywood Bowl
Surrey Quays Leisure Park
Surrey Docks Watersports Centre
Greenland Dock
Southwark Park
Southwark Park Sports Centre
Southwark College
Harris Academy Bermondsey
Fisher Athletic FC
Bacon's College
Peter Hills School
Surrey Docks Health Cen
Redriff Prim Sch
Seven Islands Leisure Cen
JAMAICA ROAD
LOWER ROAD
SALTER ROAD
REDRIFF RD
PLOUGH WAY
GROVE ST
TOOLEY ST
ABBEY STREET
GRANGE ROAD
SOUTHWARK PARK RD
RAYMOUTH ROAD
NEW RD
THE HIGHWAY
E SMITHFIELD
ROTHERHITHE NEW RD
BRUNEL ROAD
A100
A200
A1205
A2206
B202
B205
B206
0
250
500 metres
0
¼ mile
N

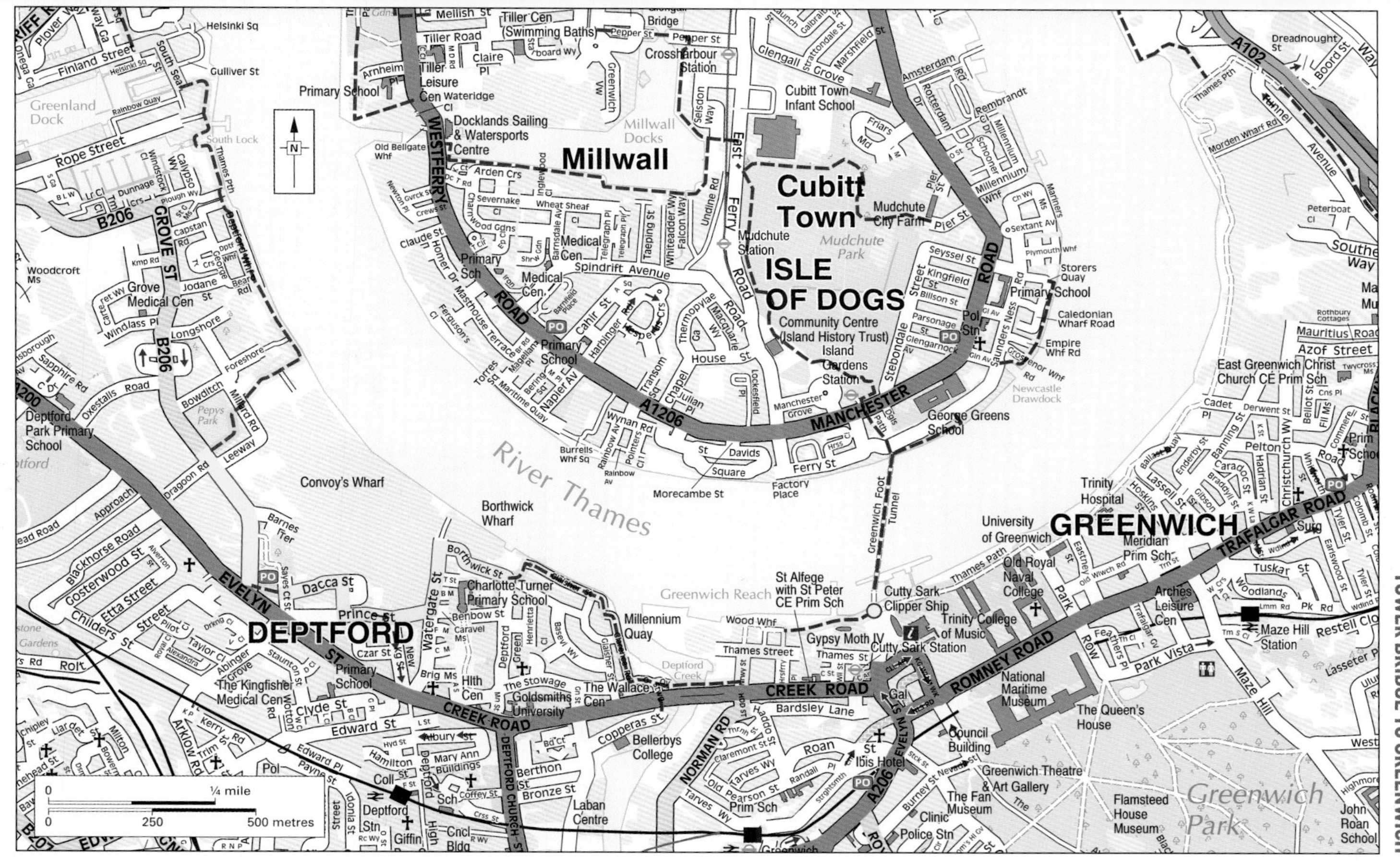

Millwall
Cubitt Town
ISLE OF DOGS
GREENWICH
DEPTFORD
River Thames
Greenwich Park
Greenwich Reach
Millwall Docks
Mudchute Park
Greenland Dock
Pepys Park
Convoy's Wharf
Borthwick Wharf
Millennium Quay
Docklands Sailing & Watersports Centre
Cubitt Town Infant School
Mudchute City Farm
Community Centre (Island History Trust)
Island Gardens Station
Mudchute Station
Crossharbour Station
George Greens School
Greenwich Foot Tunnel
Cutty Sark Clipper Ship
Gypsy Moth IV
Cutty Sark Station
St Alfege with St Peter CE Prim Sch
University of Greenwich
Old Royal Naval College
Trinity College of Music
Trinity Hospital
National Maritime Museum
The Queen's House
Flamsteed House Museum
Greenwich Theatre & Art Gallery
The Fan Museum
Council Building
Ibis Hotel
Maze Hill Station
Arches Leisure Cen
Charlotte Turner Primary School
Goldsmiths University
Bellerbys College
Laban Centre
Deptford Stn
Deptford Park Primary School
East Greenwich Christ Church CE Prim Sch
John Roan School
WESTFERRY ROAD
MANCHESTER ROAD
A1206
TRAFALGAR ROAD
ROMNEY ROAD
CREEK ROAD
EVELYN ST
A206
NORMAN RD
DEPTFORD CHURCH ST
GROVE ST
B206
A102
A200
East Ferry Road
¼ mile
250
500 metres

WATERLINK WAY – GREENWICH TO SOUTH NORWOOD COUNTRY PARK

Part of National Route 21, the Waterlink Way is a gentle ride connecting green spaces in southeast London, while following the Pool and Ravensbourne rivers. It runs through parks, under and over bridges, over suspended walkways and through a tunnel. There are a large number of train stations along the route, which makes it very accessible.

The ride starts at the River Thames, by the *Cutty Sark* clipper ship. Built in 1869, she served as a merchant vessel, then a training ship until she was put on public display in 1954. In May 2007, she was badly damaged in a fire and is now undergoing restoration and conservation work. She is planned to be reopened to the public in 2011.

South Norwood Country Park at the end of the ride was formerly a sewage farm (among many other things), but it is now a lovely park with a designated cycle track and a visitor centre providing refreshments, which makes a perfect end to the ride.

ROUTE INFORMATION

National Route: 4, 21
Start: The *Cutty Sark*, Greenwich.
Finish: South Norwood Country Park.
Distance: 8.5 miles (13.5km).
Grade: Easy.
Surface: Mixture of well-surfaced, traffic-free paths and quiet lanes.
Hills: Slightly uphill to the end, but not really noticeable.

YOUNG & INEXPERIENCED CYCLISTS

The route is suitable for families if care is taken at a few points (see Route description). More than half of it is traffic-free, with some good long stretches completely off-road.

REFRESHMENTS

- Lots of choice in Greenwich and various urban places along the way.
- Cafe in Ladywell Fields, Lewisham.
- Refreshments at South Norwood Country Park visitor centre.

THINGS TO SEE & DO

- The *Cutty Sark*, Greenwich: 85-m (279-ft) long clipper ship, built in 1869, now dry-docked and used as a museum; closed for conservation until 2011; 020 8858 2698; www.cuttysark.org.uk
- Greenwich Park: famous for being bisected by the Greenwich meridian, the line to which time across the globe is referenced; large area of formal parkland, with an area enclosed for deer; several historic buildings are in or near the park, including the Old

Compass on the dome of Old Royal Naval College

Royal Observatory, the Old Royal Naval College, the National Maritime Museum and the Queen's House; www.royalparks.org.uk

- **Ladywell Fields:** one of the main centres for outdoor sports in Lewisham, with a children's playground.
- **South Norwood Country Park:** a pleasant area to finish and relax at the end of the ride; visitor centre, pitch and putt, lake and children's playground; 020 8656 5947

TRAIN STATIONS

Greenwich; Elmers End; and a number of other train stations in between.
Note that the DLR (Docklands Light Railway) only allows folding bicycles in carrying cases.

BIKE HIRE

- **Greenwich Cycle Hire:** 020 8858 6677; www.flightcentregreenwich.co.uk
- **Go Pedal!:** delivery to most areas of London; 07850 796320; www.gopedal.co.uk

FURTHER INFORMATION

- To view or print National Cycle Network routes, visit www.sustrans.org.uk
- Maps for this area are available to buy from www.sustransshop.co.uk
- **Transport for London (TfL):** contact for free maps (nos. 7 and 10); 020 7222 1234; www.tfl.gov.uk
- **London Tourist Information:** 0870 156 6366; www.visitlondon.com

Greenwich Park and Old Royal Observatory

The O2 Arena

Greenwich's famous old clipper ship

ROUTE DESCRIPTION

Starting at Greenwich, by the *Cutty Sark*, head west on National Route 4, crossing the Wharf (Deptford Creek), then turn left onto Route 21 (Copperas Street).

Route 21 soon starts to run alongside the River Ravensbourne on good traffic-free trails, through Brookmill Park. Take care in Lewisham, around the back of the train station, where the trail leaves the riverside for a short stretch. Soon after, you leave the riverside again for a section along the B236 in Ladywell, where care is also needed, before rejoining the traffic-free trail alongside the river.

The trail follows the river for a good distance now, with Ladywell Fields making a pleasant (and popular) place to stop for a rest and refreshment break.

At Catford, there is just a short road section, then it's back on traffic-free paths along the River Pool. Continue past an Industrial estate and through Cator Park, while keeping an ear out for the local parakeets.

There is a section along Kings Hall Road that requires some care. Follow Churchfields Road, through Elmers End, to South Norwood Country Park. Here you will find a visitor centre serving refreshments, toilets, picnic tables, children's playground, a lake, and a pitch and putt course. There is also a designated cyclepath around the park to follow, before you make your way to Elmers End train station, which is just at the edge of the park.

NEARBY CYCLE ROUTES

From Greenwich, National Route 4 continues west into central London, past Tower Bridge (see page 105) and on to the London Eye, Houses of Parliament and Big Ben.

Route 1 heads east along the River Thames, past the Thames Barrier (see page 116), and north, through the Greenwich Foot Tunnel, to the Isle of Dogs (see page 20), all the way along the Lee Valley and into Essex (see page 54).

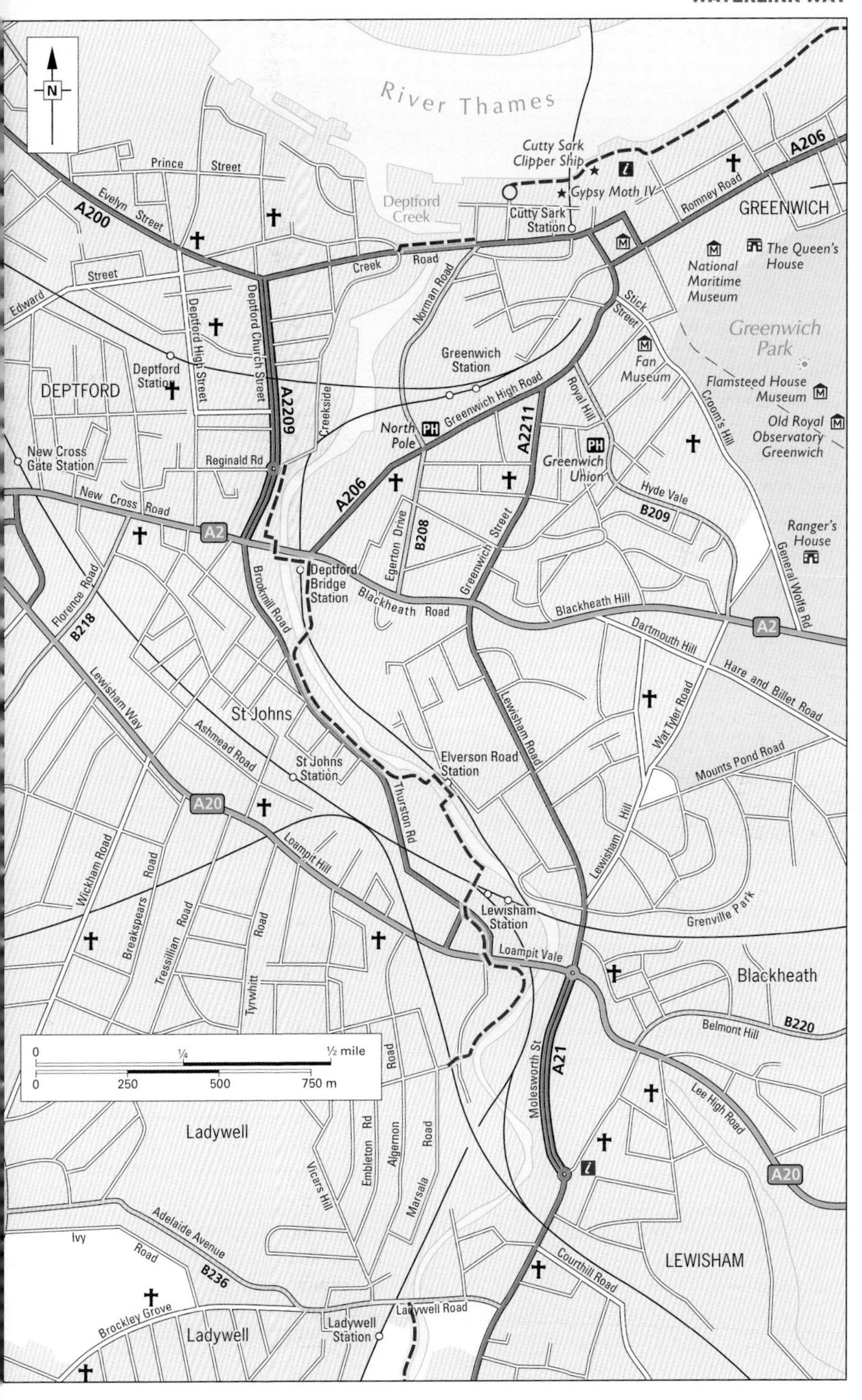
N
River Thames
Cutty Sark Clipper Ship
Gypsy Moth IV
Cutty Sark Station
Deptford Creek
Prince Street
Evelyn Street
A200
Edward Street
Creek Road
Norman Road
Romney Road
A206
GREENWICH
National Maritime Museum
The Queen's House
Stick Street
Greenwich Park
Fan Museum
Greenwich Station
Greenwich High Road
Deptford Station
DEPTFORD
Deptford High Street
Deptford Church Street
A2209
Creekside
North Pole
A2211
Royal Hill
Croom's Hill
Flamsteed House Museum
Old Royal Observatory Greenwich
Greenwich Union
New Cross Gate Station
Reginald Rd
New Cross Road
A2
A206
Egerton Drive
B208
Greenwich Street
Hyde Vale
B209
Ranger's House
General Wolfe Rd
Florence Road
B218
Deptford Bridge Station
Brookmill Road
Blackheath Road
Blackheath Hill
Dartmouth Hill
Hare and Billet Road
Lewisham Way
St Johns
Ashmead Road
St Johns Station
Elverson Road Station
Lewisham Road
Wat Tyler Road
Mounts Pond Road
Thurston Rd
A20
Loampit Hill
Lewisham Hill
Wickham Road
Breakspears Road
Tressillian Road
Tyrwhitt Road
Lewisham Station
Grenville Park
Loampit Vale
Blackheath
Belmont Hill
B220
0
¼
½ mile
250
500
750 m
Road
Molesworth St
A21
Lee High Road
Ladywell
Vicars Hill
Embleton Rd
Algernon Road
Marsala Road
A20
Adelaide Avenue
Ivy Road
B236
Courthill Road
LEWISHAM
Brockley Grove
Ladywell Road
Ladywell Station
Ladywell

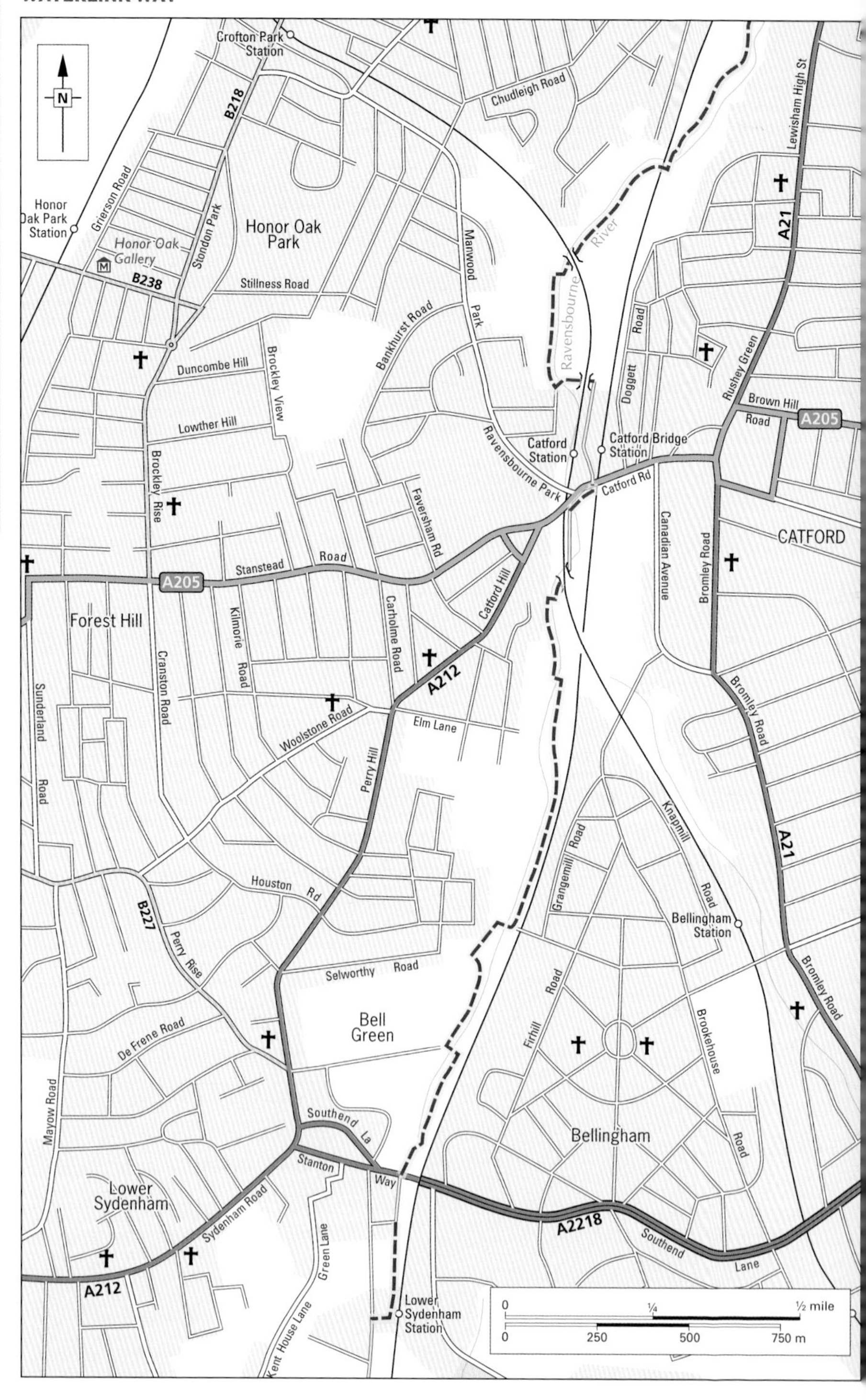
N
Crofton Park Station
Chudleigh Road
Lewisham High St
B218
Honor Oak Park Station
Grierson Road
Stondon Park
Honor Oak Park
Honor Oak Gallery
B238
Stillness Road
Manwood Park
Ravensbourne River
A21
Road
Doggett
Rushey Green
Bankhurst Road
Brockley View
Duncombe Hill
Lowther Hill
Brown Hill Road
A205
Catford Station
Catford Bridge Station
Ravensbourne Park
Catford Rd
Brockley Rise
Faversham Rd
Canadian Avenue
Bromley Road
CATFORD
Stanstead Road
A205
Catford Hill
Forest Hill
Kilmorie Road
Carholme Road
Cranston Road
A212
Sunderland Road
Woolstone Road
Elm Lane
Perry Hill
Bromley Road
Knapmill Road
Grangemill Road
A21
Houston Rd
B227
Perry Rise
Bellingham Station
Selworthy Road
Bell Green
Firhill Road
Brookehouse Road
Bromley Road
De Frene Road
Mayow Road
Southend La
Bellingham
Stanton Way
Lower Sydenham
Sydenham Road
Green Lane
A2218
Southend Lane
A212
Kent House Lane
Lower Sydenham Station
0
¼
½ mile
0
250
500
750 m

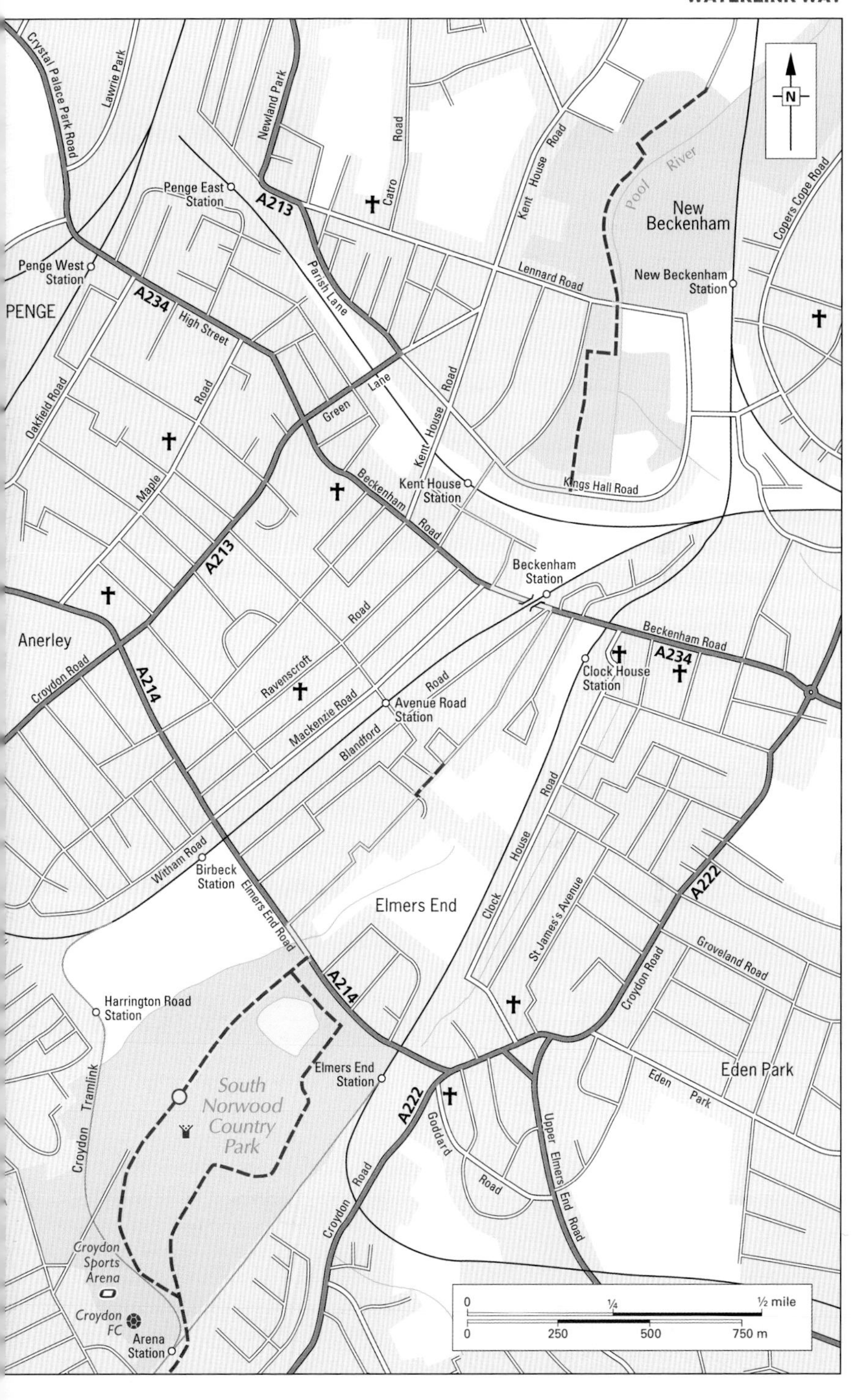

Crystal Palace Park Road
Lawrie Park
Newland Park
Road
Catro
Kent House Road
Pool River
New Beckenham
Copers Cope Road
Penge East Station
A213
Penge West Station
PENGE
A234
High Street
Parish Lane
Lennard Road
New Beckenham Station
Oakfield Road
Road
Maple
Green Lane
Kent House Road
Kent House Station
Kings Hall Road
Beckenham Road
Beckenham Station
A213
Anerley
Croydon Road
A214
Ravenscroft Road
Mackenzie Road
Blandford Road
Avenue Road Station
Beckenham Road
A234
Clock House Station
Witham Road
Birbeck Station
Elmers End Road
Elmers End
Clock House Road
St James's Avenue
A222
Groveland Road
Croydon Road
A214
Harrington Road Station
Elmers End Station
South Norwood Country Park
A222
Goddard Road
Upper Elmers End Road
Eden Park
Eden Park
Croydon Tramlink
Croydon Road
Croydon Sports Arena
Croydon FC
Arena Station
0
¼
½ mile
0
250
500
750 m

THAMESMEAD TO GREENWICH

This is a lovely route, following a good, long, traffic-free trail alongside the River Thames, with wonderful views and some interesting and impressive landmarks.

Perhaps the most striking, famous and important of these is the Thames Barrier near Woolwich, designed to protect London from flooding. The Environment Agency began construction in 1974, and the official opening came ten years later. The nine stainless steel piers span 520m (1,706ft) across the river, and there are ten movable gates. Each gate has a curved face that lies in a recessed chamber in the river bed when the barrier is open, and rotates 90 degrees to a close in less than 30 minutes. When raised, the main gates are as high as a five-storey building, as wide as the opening of Tower Bridge, and weigh 3,300 tonnes.

Next along the route is the Millennium Dome, now the O2 Arena, built to hold a major exhibition celebrating the beginning of the 2000 millennium. This multi-purpose indoor arena is the largest domed structure in the world and can accommodate 20,000 people.

Greenwich, at the end of the ride, has been designated a World Heritage Site because of its architectural, scientific and royal associations. There are many things to do and see here (see below).

ROUTE INFORMATION

National Route: 1
Start: Thamesmead. On the bank of the Thames near Greenhaven Drive.
Finish: The *Cutty Sark*, Greenwich.
Distance: 9 miles (14.5km).
Grade: Easy.
Surface: Well-surfaced (cycle) tracks, with some cobbled streets.
Hills: None.

YOUNG & INEXPERIENCED CYCLISTS

This ride is perfect for families and novices, with most of the ride traffic-free.

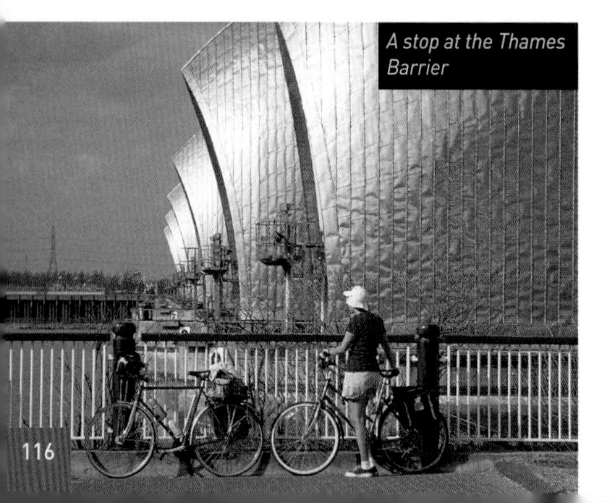

A stop at the Thames Barrier

REFRESHMENTS

- Lots of choice in Thamesmead.
- Cafe at the information centre by the Thames Barrier.
- Lots of choice in the O2 Arena.
- Lots of choice in Greenwich.

THINGS TO SEE & DO

- **Thames Barrier, near Woolwich:** one of the largest movable flood barriers in the world, spanning the river Thames, to protect London from flooding; www.environment-agency.gov.uk
- **The *Cutty Sark*, Greenwich:** 85-m (279-ft) long clipper ship, built in 1869, now dry-docked and used as a museum; closed for conservation until 2011; 020 8858 2698; www.cuttysark.org.uk
- **The O2, Greenwich:** world-class entertainment venue in the iconic Millennium Dome; home to live music and sporting events; includes 11 cinema screens, exhibition centre and wide variety of restaurants; 020 8463 2627; www.theo2.co.uk
- **National Maritime Museum, Greenwich:** created in 1934, the museum is the leading

Thames Barrier and the O2 Arena

maritime museum in the UK and has the world's largest maritime historical reference library, with books dating back to the 15th century; 020 8858 4422; 020 8312 6565 (recorded information line); www.nmm.ac.uk

- **The Queen's House, Greenwich:** former royal residence built between 1614 and 1617; now part of the National Maritime Museum; 020 8858 4422; 020 8312 6565 (recorded information line); www.nmm.ac.uk
- **The Royal Observatory, Greenwich:** situated on the hill in Greenwich Park; commissioned in 1675 and the first purpose-built scientific research facility in Britain; now part of the National Maritime Museum; 020 8858 4422; 020 8312 6565 (recorded information line); www.nmm.ac.uk

TRAIN STATIONS

Abbey Wood; Greenwich.

Note that the DLR (Docklands Light Railway) only allows folding bicycles in carrying cases.

BIKE HIRE

- **Greenwich Cycle Hire:** 020 8858 6677; www.flightcentregreenwich.co.uk
- **Go Pedal!:** delivery to most areas of London; 07850 796320; www.gopedal.co.uk

FURTHER INFORMATION

- To view or print National Cycle Network routes, visit www.sustrans.org.uk
- Maps for this area are available to buy from www.sustransshop.co.uk
- **Transport for London (TfL):** contact for free maps (nos. 7 and 8); 020 7222 1234; www.tfl.gov.uk
- **Greenwich Tourist Information:** 0870 608 2000; www.greenwich.gov.uk
- **Greenwich Park:** www.royalparks.org.uk
- **London Tourist Information:** 0870 156 6366; www.visitlondon.com

ROUTE DESCRIPTION

This lovely ride is very easy to follow, following National Route 1 westwards along the edge of the River Thames, to London. The traffic-free trail along the river provides a good track with great views, to just before the Thames Barrier, where it has to leave the riverside briefly to join a road. It then rejoins the riverside by the Thames Barrier, enabling you to appreciate this impressive engineering feat at close range. There is also a small visitor centre, cafe and toilets here.

The route continues along the Thames, passing various jetties and wharves, virtually all traffic-free, to the O2, which you cycle around

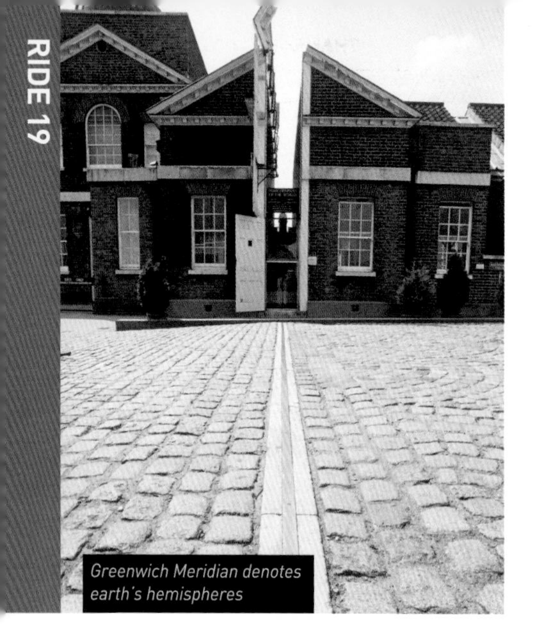
Greenwich Meridian denotes earth's hemispheres

closely, allowing you to really appreciate its size. The trail leaves the riverside for a while, first staying on traffic-free tracks, then on-road, past the Queen's House on Park Row. Turn right here towards the Thames, by the Old Royal Naval College (now part of the University of Greenwich); alternatively, turn left for the National Maritime Museum and Greenwich Park, where you will find the Old Royal Observatory. The last part of the route follows a new shared-use path through the Old Royal Naval College, adjacent to the Thames, finishing at the *Cutty Sark*.

Note that if you are getting to the start of the ride by train, Abbey Wood station is the closest. From here, you can follow the Green Chain Walk trail from Lesnes Abbey, which heads north to meet the River Thames.

NEARBY CYCLE ROUTES

National Route 4 goes west into central London, past Tower Bridge (see page 105) and on to the London Eye, Houses of Parliament and Big Ben.
From Greenwich, Route 1 heads north through the Greenwich Foot Tunnel to the Isle of Dogs (see page 20), all the way along the Lee Valley and into Essex (see page 54).

Route 21 from Greenwich, southbound, goes to South Norwood Country Park (see page 110).

Royal Naval College and Queen's House

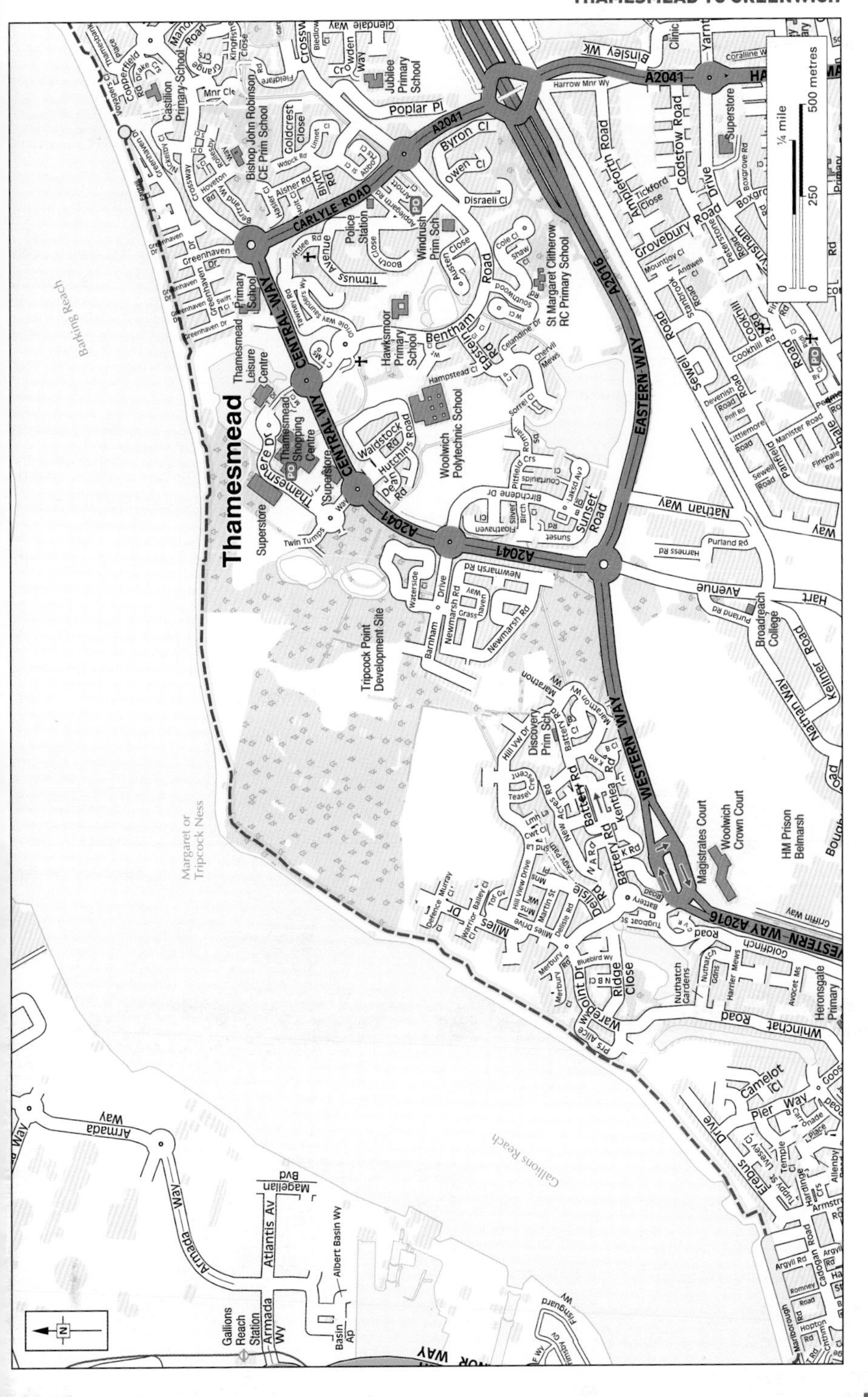
Thamesmead
Thamesmead Shopping Centre
Thamesmead Leisure Centre
Superstore
Twin Tumps
Barking Reach
Margaret or Tripcock Ness
Gallions Reach
Tripcock Point Development Site
Woolwich Polytechnic School
Hawksmoor Primary School
Windrush Prim Sch
Police Station
St Margaret Clitherow RC Primary School
Bishop John Robinson CE Prim School
Castilion Primary School
Jubilee Primary School
Discovery Prim Sch
Broadreach College
Magistrates Court
Woolwich Crown Court
HM Prison Belmarsh
Gallions Reach Station
CENTRAL WAY
CENTRAL WY
CARLYLE ROAD
EASTERN WAY
WESTERN WAY
WESTERN WAY A2016
A2016
A2041
Harrow Mnr Wy
Binsley Wk
Poplar Pl
Byron Cl
Owen Cl
Disraeli Cl
Titmuss Avenue
Bentham Road
Hampstead Cl
Waldstock Rd
Hutchins Road
Sunset Road
Nathan Way
Harness Rd
Purland Rd
Avenue
Hart
Kellner Road
Newmarsh Rd
Barnham Drive
Waterside Cl
Battery Rd
Kentlea Rd
Marathon Way
Hill View Drive
Miles Dr
Defence Cl
Ridge Close
Tugboat St
Nuthatch Gardens
Harrier Mews
Goldfinch
Whinchat Road
Heronsgate Primary
Camelot Cl
Pier Way
Erebus Drive
Armada Way
Atlantis Av
Magellan Bvd
Albert Basin Wy
Basin Ap
Armada Wy
Greenhaven Dr
Goldcrest Close
Amplefortn Road
Tickford Close
Godstow Road
Grovebury Road
Drive
Sewell Road
Cookhill Rd
Superstore
Clinic
¼ mile
0
250
500 metres
N

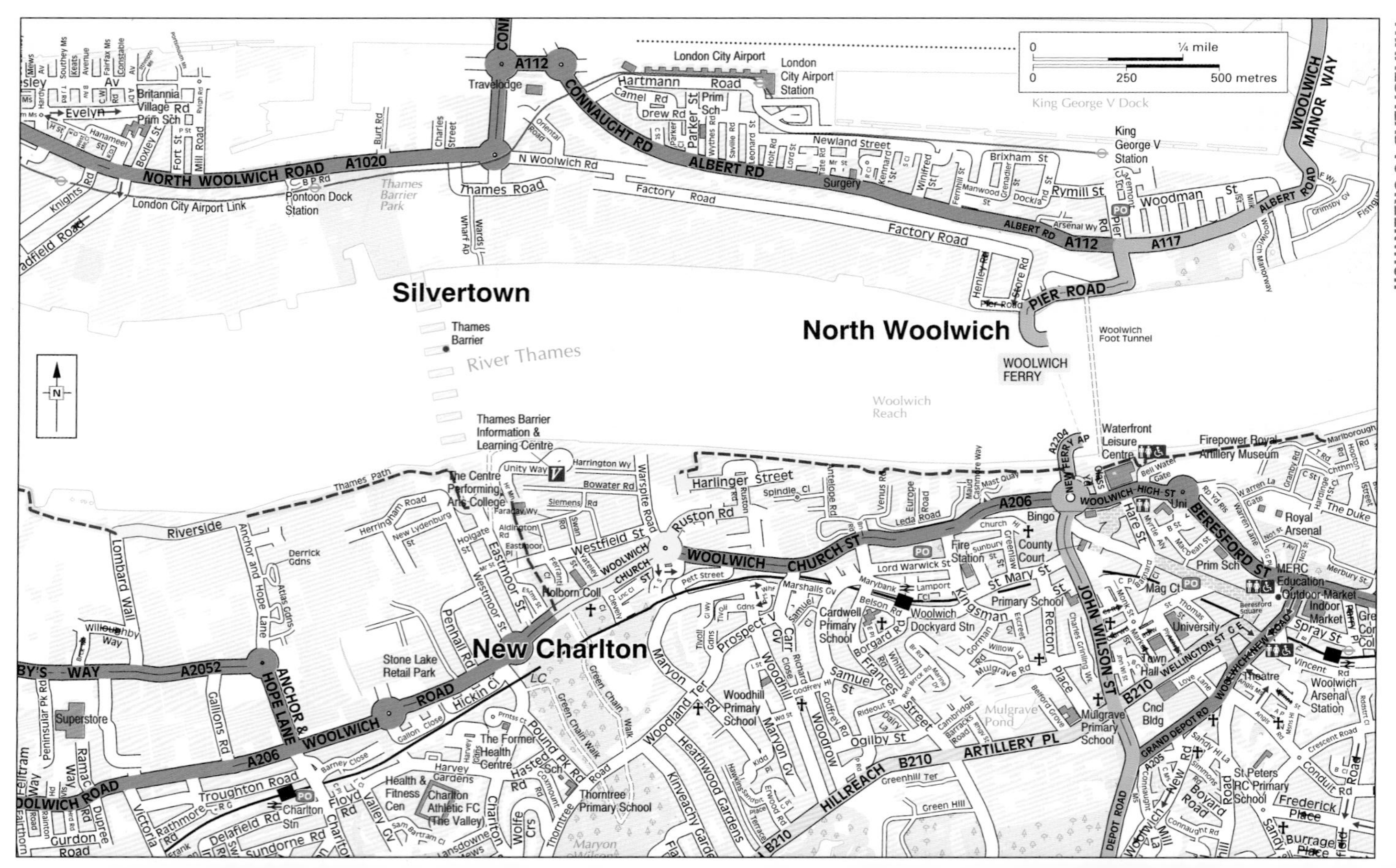

North Woolwich
Silvertown
New Charlton
River Thames
Woolwich Reach
WOOLWICH FERRY
Woolwich Foot Tunnel
Thames Barrier
Thames Barrier Information & Learning Centre
Thames Barrier Park
Thames Path
King George V Dock
King George V Station
London City Airport
London City Airport Station
Pontoon Dock Station
London City Airport Link
WOOLWICH MANOR WAY
ALBERT ROAD
ALBERT RD
A117
A112
PIER ROAD
CONNAUGHT RD
NORTH WOOLWICH ROAD
A1020
Factory Road
Hartmann Road
Newland Street
Thames Road
Firepower Royal Artillery Museum
Waterfront Leisure Centre
WOOLWICH HIGH ST
BERESFORD ST
JOHN WILSON ST
WOOLWICH CHURCH ST
WOOLWICH ROAD
ANCHOR & HOPE LANE
A206
A2052
ARTILLERY PL
HILLREACH
B210
GRAND DEPOT RD
DEPOT ROAD
Woolwich Arsenal Station
Woolwich Dockyard Stn
Anchor and Hope Lane
Riverside
Lombard Wall
Stone Lake Retail Park
Charlton Athletic FC (The Valley)
Charlton Stn
Superstore
Green Chain Walk
Heathwood Gardens
Mulgrave Pond
Rectory Place
Warspite Road
Harlinger Street
Ruston Rd
Eastmoor St
Westmoor St
Penhall Rd
Gallions Rd
Troughton Road
Woodland Ter
Maryon Rd
Frances Street
Samuel St
Ogilby St
Woodrow
Kingsman
St Mary St
0 ¼ mile
0 250 500 metres
N

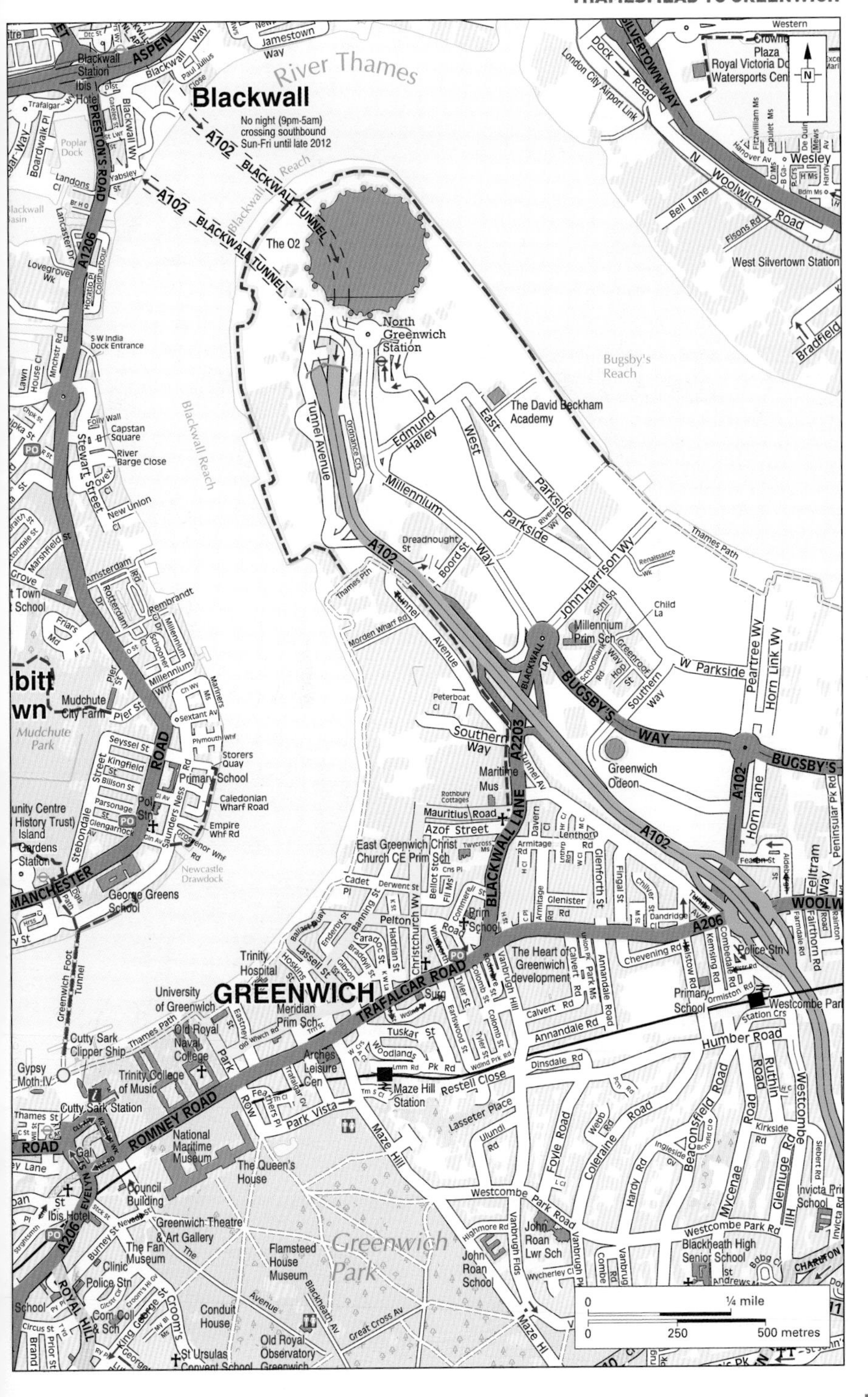

River Thames
Blackwall
No night (9pm-5am) crossing southbound Sun-Fri until late 2012
A102 BLACKWALL TUNNEL
Blackwall Station
Ibis Hotel
ASPEN WAY
PRESTON'S ROAD
A1206
Poplar Dock
Blackwall Basin
Blackwall Reach
The O2
North Greenwich Station
Bugsby's Reach
The David Beckham Academy
Tunnel Avenue
Edmund Halley Way
West Parkside
East Parkside
Millennium Way
John Harrison Wy
Thames Path
Silvertown Way
London City Airport Link
Dock Road
Royal Victoria Dock Watersports Centre
Crowne Plaza
N Woolwich Road
West Silvertown Station
Bell Lane
Stewart Street
Capstan Square
River Barge Close
New Union Cl
Amsterdam Rd
Mudchute City Farm
Mudchute Park
Millennium Prim Sch
Child La
W Parkside
Peartree Wy
Horn Link Wy
BUGSBY'S WAY
Greenwich Odeon
A2203
BLACKWALL LANE
Maritime Mus
Mauritius Road
Azof Street
East Greenwich Christ Church CE Prim Sch
Glenister Rd
Glenforth St
Fingal St
A206
WOOLWICH ROAD
Chevening Rd
Police Stn
Primary School
Westcombe Park
Humber Road
The Heart of Greenwich development
Trinity Hospital
GREENWICH
TRAFALGAR ROAD
University of Greenwich
Meridian Prim Sch
Old Royal Naval College
Cutty Sark Clipper Ship
Gypsy Moth IV
Greenwich Foot Tunnel
Trinity College of Music
Arches Leisure Cen
Maze Hill Station
Park Vista
Restell Close
Lasseter Place
Maze Hill
ROMNEY ROAD
Cutty Sark Station
National Maritime Museum
The Queen's House
Council Building
Greenwich Theatre & Art Gallery
The Fan Museum
Clinic
Police Stn
Flamsteed House Museum
Greenwich Park
Conduit House
Old Royal Observatory Greenwich
St Ursulas Convent School
John Roan Lwr Sch
John Roan School
Westcombe Park Road
Blackheath High Senior School
Invicta Prim School
Foyle Road
Coleraine Road
Beaconsfield Road
Mycenae Rd
Ruthin Road
Westcombe Hill
MANCHESTER ROAD
George Greens School
Island Gardens Station
0 ¼ mile
0 250 500 metres

BROCKWELL PARK & DULWICH PARK

This cycle ride links the two lovely parks of Brockwell and Dulwich, via some traffic-calmed roads.

Brockwell Park was once the estate of John Blades, a wealthy Ludgate Hill (in the City of London) glassmaker, who had the Georgian country house of Brockwell Hall built between 1811 and 1813 as the centrepiece of his park estate (the perimeter of today's park). However, since 1892 the park has been open to the public. It is a lovely green space, with lots of activities on offer, from miniature railways, BMX tracks, a children's playground and paddling pool, ponds, gardens, bowling greens, tennis courts, a community greenhouse and, of course, the Brockwell Park Lido, built back in 1937 but with facilities kept right up to date.

On the journey between the parks along the traffic-calmed roads, you pass very close to Herne Hill Velodrome, which makes a great little detour, if just to watch the riders going around.

Created in 1890, Dulwich Park started life as farmland, and many of the ancient boundary oaks are still alive today. Queen Mary was a regular visitor to the park, loving the American Garden, famous for its rhododendrons, which bloom in May. The park covers 72 acres and is packed with historic features, picnic spots, a lake, free tennis courts, a large children's playground, a cycle hire centre and an excellent cafe.

ROUTE INFORMATION

Start and Finish: Herne Hill entrance to Brockwell Park.
Distance: 5.5 miles (9km).
Grade: Easy.
Surface: Good cycle tracks in the parks, with roads elsewhere.
Hills: Dulwich Park is flat, while there are some small, gradual hills in Brockwell Park and on the roads between the parks.

YOUNG & INEXPERIENCED CYCLISTS

This route is perfect for young children and novices. There is a short section of road in between the two parks, some of which is on traffic-calmed roads.

REFRESHMENTS

- Brockwell Hall cafe, centre of Brockwell Park.
- Pavilion Cafe, centre of Dulwich Park.

THINGS TO SEE & DO

- Miniature railway, between the Lido and Herne Hill main gates in Brockwell Park:

A charity swim at Brockwell Park Lido

run by enthusiasts on a not-for-profit basis on Saturdays and Sundays from May to September (weather permitting) between 11am and 5pm.

- **BMX track, Brockwell Park:** a great track for the kids to play on; relocated from Brixton in 1990; www.brixtonbmxclub.com
- **Herne Hill Velodrome:** one of the best cycling tracks in the UK, designed for novices as well as experts; 450-m (495-yard) track, banking up to 30 degrees; www.hernehillvelodrome.com
- **Dulwich Riding School, Dulwich Common (A205):** hire a horse and ride around Dulwich Park, or even have a lesson; 020 8693 2944; www.dulwichridingschool.co.uk

TRAIN STATIONS

Herne Hill; West Dulwich; North Dulwich.

BIKE HIRE

- **London Recumbents, Dulwich Park:** huge variety of bicycles (not just recumbents) for adults and children; 020 8299 6636; www.londonrecumbents.com
- **Go Pedal!:** delivery to most areas of London; 07850 796320; www.gopedal.co.uk

FURTHER INFORMATION

- To view or print National Cycle Network routes, visit www.sustrans.org.uk
- Maps for this area are available to buy from www.sustransshop.co.uk
- **Transport for London (TfL):** contact for free map (no.10); 020 7222 1234; www.tfl.gov.uk
- **Brockwell Park:** www.brockwellpark.com
- **Dulwich Park:** www.dulwichparkfriends.org.uk
- **London Tourist Information:** 0870 156 6366; www.visitlondon.com

ROUTE DESCRIPTION

From inside the main entrance to Brockwell Park, by Herne Hill train station, bear right and cycle anticlockwise, past the toilets, miniature railway and Lido, and continue around the edge of the park, turning sharp left at the end of the football pitch, to meet a junction. The centre of the park is straight ahead (left) where you will find more toilets, the BMX track, bowling green

Dulwich Park cafe

and tennis courts. The route keeps right, past the playground and to the right of the ponds (the community greenhouse, walled garden, toilets and paddling pool are to the left). After bearing left, you will see Brockwell Hall on the left. A little further up, you exit the park to the right, through Rosendale Gate.

Go straight ahead on Rosendale Road, then left on Turney Road. At the crossroads, Herne Hill Velodrome is a short way to the left, while Dulwich Park is in the opposite direction. Go right at the roundabout at the end, on College Road, and second left into Dulwich Park.

You enter Dulwich park along Carriage Drive, with the cycle hire, car park, toilets and information on the left. The cycle route follows Carriage Drive around the perimeter of the park. There are shelters dotted here and there, and in the middle of the park you will find toilets, a big playground, a nature conservation area and an excellent pavilion cafe. There is also a pretty lake with a fun boardwalk path across it; a boat house should be constructed by summer 2010. You can even hire horses to ride from the local stables just outside Roseberry Gate.

Enjoying the shade of a Brockwell Park tree

NEARBY CYCLE ROUTES

National Route 21, along the Waterlink Way, runs southwards from Greenwich to South Norwood Country Park (see page 110).

The Commons Circular Route (see page 100), takes in Clapham, Wandsworth and Tooting Bec Commons.

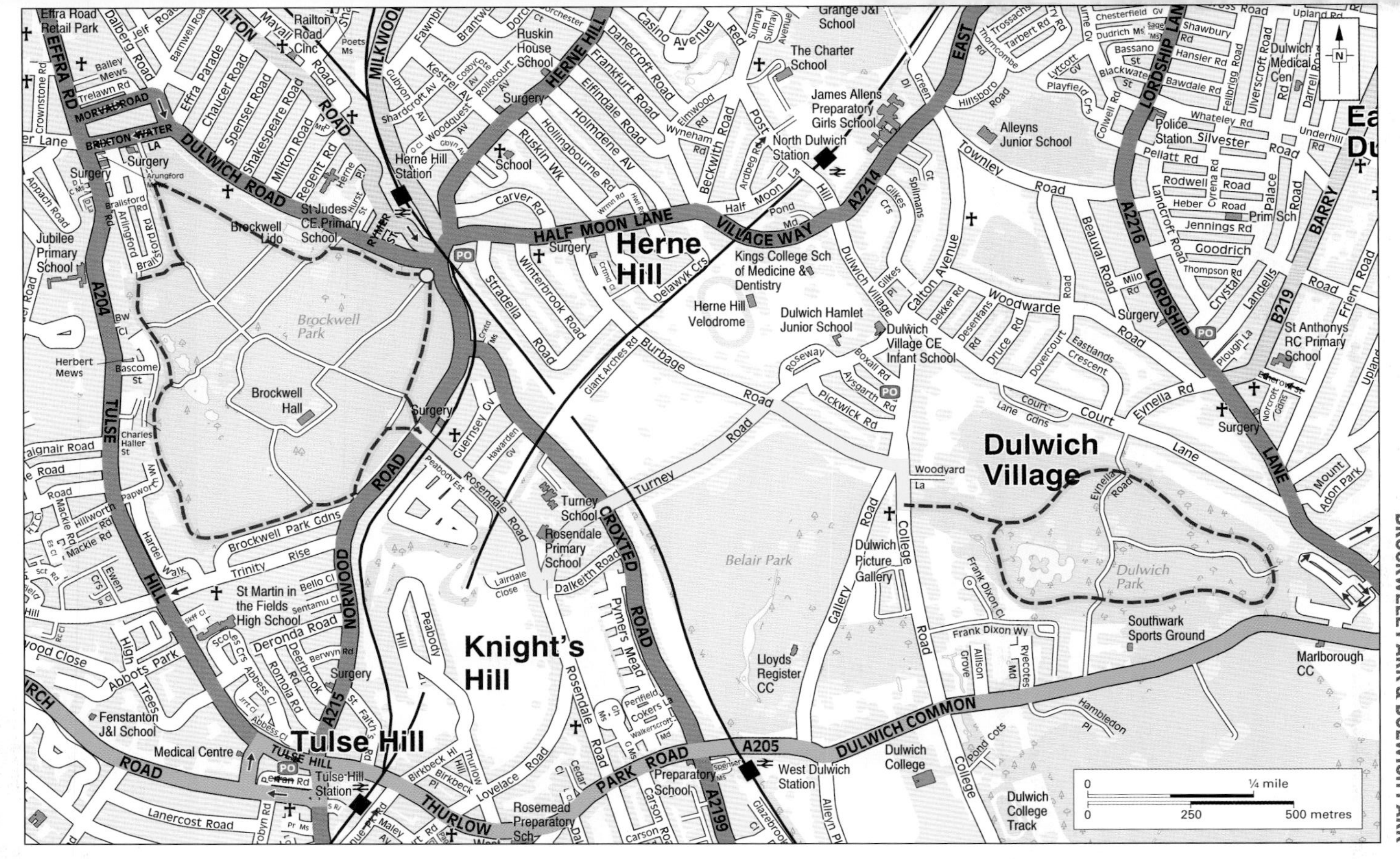
Dulwich Village
Herne Hill
Knight's Hill
Tulse Hill
Dulwich Park
Brockwell Park
Belair Park
Brockwell Hall
Brockwell Lido
Herne Hill Velodrome
Dulwich College
Dulwich Picture Gallery
Dulwich College Track
Southwark Sports Ground
Lloyds Register CC
Marlborough CC
Alleyns Junior School
James Allens Preparatory Girls School
The Charter School
Dulwich Hamlet Junior School
Dulwich Village CE Infant School
Kings College Sch of Medicine & Dentistry
Rosendale Primary School
Turney School
St Martin in the Fields High School
Ruskin House School
St Judes CE Primary School
Jubilee Primary School
Fenstanton J&I School
St Anthonys RC Primary School
Rosemead Preparatory Sch
Grange J&I School
Herne Hill Station
North Dulwich Station
West Dulwich Station
Tulse Hill Station
Police Station
Medical Centre
Effra Road Retail Park
LORDSHIP LANE
A2216
EAST
BARRY
B219
A2214
VILLAGE WAY
HALF MOON LANE
HERNE HILL
MILKWOOD
DULWICH ROAD
EFFRA RD
TULSE HILL
A204
NORWOOD ROAD
A215
CROXTED ROAD
A205
DULWICH COMMON
A2199
PARK ROAD
THURLOW
College Road
Court Lane
Gallery Road
Burbage Road
Turney Road
Rosendale Road
Townley Road
Woodwarde Road
Calton Avenue
Beauval Road
Eynella Rd
Dulwich Village
Hambledon Pl
Pond Cots
Alleyn Pk
Frankfurt Road
Danecroft Road
Elfindale Road
Holmdene Av
Hollingbourne Rd
Ruskin Wk
Winterbrook Road
Stradella Road
Milton Road
Shakespeare Road
Spenser Road
Chaucer Road
Effra Parade
Brockwell Park Gdns
Peabody Hill
Lovelace Road
Pymers Mead
Lanercost Road
Hardel Walk
High Trees
Abbots Park
Deronda Road
Trinity Rise
¼ mile
0
250
500 metres
N

NEXT STEPS...

We hope you have enjoyed the cycle rides in this book.

Sustrans developed the National Cycle Network to act as a catalyst for bringing cycling (and walking) back into our everyday lives. Between the 1950s and the mid 1970s cycling in the UK fell by 80%. Cycling now accounts for only about 2% of all journeys made in the UK, a fraction of what we used to achieve.

When you consider that nearly 6 in 10 car journeys are under 5 miles, it makes you wonder what the potential for increasing levels of cycling is? Evidence shows that, for local journeys under 5 miles, the majority of us could make 9 out of 10 journeys on foot, bike or public transport if there was more investment in making it possible to choose to leave the car behind.

And why not? We can all be more savvy when it comes to travel. One small step becomes one giant leap if we all start walking away from less healthy lifestyles and pedalling our way towards happier children and a low carbon world.

And that's where Sustrans comes in. Sustainable travel means carbon-reducing, energy efficient, calorie burning, money-saving travel. Here are a few things that we think make sense. If you agree, join us.

- Snail's pace – 20 mph or less on our streets where we live, go to school, shop and work – make it the norm, not just the four times a century when we get snow.
- Closer encounters – planning that focuses on good non-motorised access, so that we can reach more post offices, schools, shops, doctors and dentists without the car.
- People spaces – streets where kids can play hopscotch or football and be free-range, and where neighbours can meet and chat.
- Road revolution – build miles and miles of bike paths that don't evaporate when they meet a road.
- Find our feet – campaign for pedestrian-friendly city centres, or wide boulevards with regular pedestrian crossings and slow-moving traffic.
- Better buses – used by millions, under-invested by billions and, if affordable, reliable and pleasant to use, could make local car journeys redundant.
- More car clubs – a car club on every street corner and several for every new-build estate.
- Rewards for car-sharing – get four in a car and take more than half the cars off the road.
- Trains – more of them, more cheaply.
- Become a staycationer – and holiday at home. Mountains, beaches, culture, great beer, good food and a National Cycle Network that connects them all.

If we work towards these goals we have a chance of delivering our fair share of the 80% reduction in CO_2 by mid-century that we're now committed to by law, and some of the 100% reduction that many climate experts now consider essential.

ACKNOWLEDGEMENTS

Max Darkins would like to thank Nigel Brigham, Greg King, Simon Pratt, Tom Sharland, Matt Winfield and local Sustrans Rangers for their assistance with the writing of this guide.

The Automobile Association wishes to thank the following photographers and organisations for their assistance in the preparation of this book.

Abbreviations for the picture credits are as follows – (t) top; (b) bottom; (l) left; (r) right; (c) centre; (dps) double page spread; (AA) AA World Travel Library

Trade Cover: t River Thames, Houses of Parliament and Westminster Bridge at dusk, AA/C Sawyer; b Smiling girl, Jon Bewley/Sustrans

Special Sales Cover: t The London Eye and Hungerford Bridge at dusk, AA/C Sawyer; b Young couple cycling through a meadow, Digital Vision/Getty

3l AA/M Jourdan; 3r AA/S Montgomery; 4 Adam Hart-Davis; 5tl © TravelStockCollection - Homer Sykes/Alamy; 5tr AA/N Setchfield; 5c AA/M Jourdan; 6/7 AA/J Tims; 7tr AA/N Setchfield; 7tc © Matthew Mawson/Alamy; 7c AA/J Miller; 11tl Jon Bewley/Sustrans; 11tr Jon Bewley/Sustrans; 11c Jon Bewley/Sustrans; 11bc Andy Huntley/Sustrans; 11br Pru Comben/Sustrans; 13t Jon Bewley/Sustrans; 13c Nicola Jones/Sustrans; 13b Jon Bewley/Sustrans; 14/15 AA/J Tims; 16tl AA/J Tims; 16tr AA/J Tims; 16b AA/J Tims; 17 AA/S Montgomery; 20 © Bichelle Masrani/Alamy; 21 AA/R Strange; 23t AA/S & O Mathews; 23b Sustrans; 24 © amc/Alamy; 25 © Matthew Mawson/Alamy; 26/27 © Londonstills.com/Alamy; 30 AA/M Moody; 31 © Greg Balfour Evans/Alamy; 32t AA/N Setchfield; 32b © Greg Balfour Evans/Alamy; 36/37 AA/R Mort; 37t AA/N Setchfield; 38 Jon Bewley/Sustrans; 42 AA/M Trelawny; 43 AA/S Montgomery; 44t AA/R Turpin; 44b AA/N Setchfield; 48/49 AA/N Setchfield; 50/51 AA/M Moody; 50b AA/M Moody; 51 AA/K Paterson; 55 AA/L Hatts; 56 Sustrans; 60 © Garry Bowden/Alamy; 60/61 © Mike Booth/Alamy; 62/63 © Gordon Scammell/Alamy; 66/67 © Arcaid/Alamy; 68 © Gregory Wrona/Alamy; 72 AA/L Hatts; 73 AA/N Setchfield; 74 AA/N Setchfield; 77 © Londonstills.com/Alamy; 78t AA/M Trelawny; 78/79 © Greg Balfour Evans/Alamy; 79 Sustrans; 82 Sustrans; 83 © Bjanka Kadic/Alamy; 84/85 AA/N Setchfield; 88/89 © Neil Setchfield/Alamy; 89t John Grimshaw/Sustrans; 90t AA/N Setchfield; 90b John Grimshaw/Sustrans; 94 Andrew Sabin; 95t Jon Bewley/Sustrans; 95b Jon Bewley/Sustrans; 96 © The National Trust Photolibrary/Alamy; 100/101 © Frantzesco Kangaris/Alamy; 101 © Richard Donovan/Alamy; 102 © Gary Roebuck/Alamy; 106/107 AA/J Tims; 107 AA/N Setchfield; 110 Sustrans; 111t AA/N Setchfield; 111b AA/N Setchfield; 112t AA/N Setchfield; 112b AA/N Setchfield; 116 G L Jones/Sustrans; 117 AA/L Hatts; 118t AA; 118b AA/W Voysey; 122/123 © Jeffrey Blackler/Alamy; 124t © TravelStockCollection - Homer Sykes/Alamy; 124b Jon Bewley/Sustrans

Every effort has been made to trace the copyright holders, and we apologise in advance for any unintentional omissions or errors. We would be pleased to apply any corrections in the following edition of this publication.